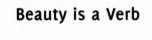

Beauty is a Verb

THE NEW POETRY OF DISABILITY

edited by

Jennifer Bartlett

Sheila Black

& Michael Northen

CINCO PUNTOS PRESS   EL PASO

Beauty is a Verb : The New Poetry of Disability
Copyright © 2011 by Jennifer Bartlett, Sheila Black and Michael Northen.

Printed in the United States.

First Edition
10 9 8 7 6 5 4 3 2 1

Library of Congress Cataloging-in-Publication Data

Beauty is a verb : the new poetry of disability / edited by Jennifer Bartlett, Sheila Black, and Michael Northen. -- 1st ed.
    p. cm.
 Summary: "Beauty is a Verb is the first of its kind: a high-quality anthology of poetry by American poets with physical disabilities. Poems and essays alike consider how poetry, coupled with the experience of disability, speaks to the poetics of each poet included. The collection explores first the precursors whose poems had a complex (and sometimes absent) relationship with disability, such as Vassar Miller, Larry Eigner and Josephine Miles. It continues with poets who have generated the Crip Poetics Movement, such as Petra Kuppers, Kenny Fries and Jim Ferris. Finally, the collection explores the work of poets who don't necessarily subscribe to the identity of 'crip-poetics' and have never before been published in this exact context. These poets include Bernadette Mayer, Rusty Morrison, Cynthia Hogue and C. S. Giscombe. The book crosses poetry movements—from narrative to language poetry—and speaks to and about a number of disabilities including cerebral palsy, deafness, blindness, multiple sclerosis and aphasia due to stroke, among others."— Provided by publisher.
 ISBN 978-1-935955-05-4 (pbk.)
 1. People with disabilities, Writings of, American. 2. American poetry—21st century. 3. American poetry—20th century. 4. People with disabilities—Poetry. I. Bartlett, Jennifer, 1969- II. Black, Sheila (Sheila Fiona) III. Northen, Michael, 1946- IV. Title.

PS591.D57B43 2011
811'.60809207—dc23

2011022269

Special thanks to Sue Austin, whose "Portal, 2008" graces the cover of *Beauty is a Verb*. Sue is currently working on a performance piece titled "Testing the Water" that will premier during the 2012 Olympic and Paralympic Games in London. Learn more about her work at http://www.trishwheatley.co.uk/suehome.html.

Book and cover design by the inimitable JB Bryan of La Alameda Press.

THIS BOOK IS DEDICATED TO
TOM ANDREWS, LARRY EIGNER, ROBERT FAGAN,
LAURA HERSHEY, JOSEPHINE MILES AND VASSAR MILLER,
WITHOUT WHOSE WORK THIS BOOK WOULD NOT BE POSSIBLE.

Jennifer Bartlett, Sheila Black and Michael Northen would like to thank our contributors. We would also like to thank Lee, Bobby and John Byrd, publishers extraordinaire for their belief in this project, and also Jessica Powers and everyone else at Cinco Puntos.

Jennifer Bartlett would like to thank for their direct help with suggestions, editing, daily feedback and/or childcare: Sheila Black, Michael Northen, Peter Littlefield, Morgan Ritter, David Weinberg, Nancy Wendel, Anne Foltz, Ava Capote, Michael Foley, Marie Stewart, John Stewart, James Yeary and Lisa Jarnot. In addition, for their constant support: Janet Rodney, Julia Hecomovich, Jeff Hoover, Sam Lohmann, Tara O'Connor, Rachel Peskin, Thomas Mitchell, Eric Chappelle, Barbara Beck, Deanna Ortiz, Anne Beyer, Tom Beyer, Maryrose Larkin, Royal Alvis, Brigit Nagel, Charles Bernstein, Susan Bee, Norma Cole, Ron Silliman and Edwin Torres. And the people without whom poetry would not be possible: Jim Stewart, Lee Bartlett, Emma Bartlett, Roxann Beck-Foley, Nathaniel Tarn, Andrea Baker, and as forever, Jeffrey.

Sheila Black wishes to thank her husband Duncan Hayse for his stellar proofreading skills and keen brain. Co-editors, Jen and Mike, without whom this project would have remained the ghost of an idea; dear friends: Karen Bucher, Cathy Carver, Michelle Granger, Melissa Kwasny, Michele Marcoux, Candice Morrow, Marnie Nixon, Bernadette Smyth, Megan Snedden, Stephanie Taylor, Carrie Tafoya, Michele Valverde and Connie Voisine for their unfailing good advice and support. Her children Annabelle, Eliza and Walker Hayse, who have helped me in every way they possibly could. Her parents Clay and Moira Black, and amazing sisters Samantha and Sarah, and last but not least, Lenore Parker, for all her wise counsel over many years, and the late Robert Fagan, for being such a wonderful poetic mentor.

Michael Northen is grateful for the support of his wife Lora and children Patrick, Maura, Melissa, Maya and Elijah. Special thanks to the Inglis House Poetry Workshop, especially Stuart Sanderson, Dana Hirsch, Yvette Green, Steve Parker and Denise March, without whom there would have been nothing to contribute to this book. He thanks his mother Elvera Northen and his brother Ed, for his continued belief in poetry. Finally, thanks to co-editors Sheila Black and Jennifer Bartlett for all their hard work, and to Jim Ferris for his encouragement and support.

CONTENTS

PREFACE, Jennifer Bartlett / 15

A SHORT HISTORY OF AMERICAN
DISABILITY POETRY, Michael Northen / 18

EARLY VOICES
Larry Eigner
MISSING LARRY: THE POETICS OF DISABILITY
IN LARRY EIGNER, Michael Davidson / 27
Six Poems / 33

Tom Andrews
from Codeine Diary / 37
The Hemophiliac's Motorcycle / 44

Vassar Miller
SWIMMING ON CONCRETE: THE POETRY
OF VASSAR MILLER, Jill Alexander Essbaum / 50
If I Had Wheels or Love / 52
Dramatic Monologue in the Speaker's Own Voice / 53
The Common Core / 54
Subterfuge / 55

Robert Fagan
Less / 56
Proem / 58
Stiege / 61

Josephine Miles
THE VOICE OF "REASON," Susan Schweik / 67
Doll / 81
Album / 82
Motive / 83
Intensives / 84
Payment / 85

THE DISABILITY POETICS MOVEMENT
Jim Ferris
KEEPING THE KNIVES SHARP / 89
Poet of Cripples / 94

Normal / 95
Poems with Disabilities / 96
From the Surgeons: Drs. Sofield, Louis, Hark, Alfini, Millar, Baehr,
Bevan-Thomas, Tsatsos, Ericson, and Bennan / 98
Lost Hyoid / 101

Kenny Fries
from STARING BACK: THE DISABILITY EXPERIENCE
FROM THE INSIDE OUT / 102
Excavation / 105
Body Language / 106
Beauty and Variations / 107

Petra Kuppers
THE SOUND OF THE BONES / 110
The Origin of My Wheelchair / 115
Crip Music / 116
from Spherical Song Cycle / 117

Daniel Simpson
LINE BREAKS THE WAY I SEE THEM / 120
School for the Blind / 123
Broken Reverie / 125
About Chester Kowalski I Don't Know Much / 127
A Few Things / 128

Laura Hershey
GETTING COMFORTABLE / 129
Working Together / 133
Telling / 134
Morning / 136
Thousand Island / 137

Jillian Weise
from THE DISABILITY RIGHTS MOVEMENT
AND THE LEGACY OF POETS WITH DISABILITIES / 138
The Amputee's Guide to Sex / 145
The Old Questions / 146
The Devotee / 147
The Body in Pain / 148

Kathi Wolfe
HELEN KELLER: OBSESSION AND MUSE / 151
On the Subway / 153

Ashes: Rome, 1946 / 154
She Loved Hot Dogs So Much / 155
The Sun is Warm: Nagasaki, 1948 / 156

John Lee Clark
TRANSLATING AND READING ASL POETRY / 157
Deaf Blind: Three Squared Cinquain / 160
Clamor / 161
Beach Baseball / 162
Long Goodbyes / 163

LYRICISM OF THE BODY
Alex Lemon
AND NOW I SEE / 167
Mosquito / 169
It Had Only Been Dead a Few Hours / 170
Other Good / 172
And No More May I Be / 173

Laurie Clements Lambeth
RESHAPING THE OUTLINE / 174
Hypoesthesia / 178
The Shaking / 179
Seizure, or Seduction of Persephone / 180
Dysaesthesia / 182

Brian Teare
LYING MEDITATION / 183
5 poems from The Empty Form Goes All the Way to Heaven / 186

Ona Gritz
A CONSCIOUS DECISION / 191
Hemiplegia / 193
No / 194
Prologue / 195
Because You Can't See My Photographs / 196
We Are Everywhere / 197

Stephen Kuusisto
DIGRESSIONS ON POETRY, PROSE AND A LINGONBERRY BUSH / 198
Letter to Borges from Houston, Texas / 200
Borges: They Are Knocking the Wind Out of Me in Iowa City / 201

Letter to Borges from Estonia / 202
Letter to Borges in His Parlor / 203
Only Bread, Only Light / 204

Sheila Black
WAITING TO BE DANGEROUS: DISABILITY
AND CONFESSIONALISM / 205
Playing Dead / 211
What You Mourn / 212
Reconstruction / 213
Objects Waiting to Be Dangerous / 215

Raymond Luczak
LISTENING SIDEWAYS TO THE BEAT OF A POEM / 217
Consonants / 222
Instructions to Hearing Persons Desiring a Deaf Man / 225
Ablutions of the Tongue / 226
Hummingbirds / 227

Anne Kaier
RIVER CREATURE / 228
Cosseted / 232
Accoutrements / 234
The Examining Table / 236

Hal Sirowitz
ZOMBIES ARE LOOSE / 238
A Step above Cows / 240
Legal Drugs / 241
A Famous Ball Player / 242
Avoiding Rigidity / 243

Lisa Gill
MAPPING CAESURA: THE ENCOMPASSING BODY / 244
from The Relenting: A Play of Sorts / 248
Wicker-Work: A Sestina for Zukofsky / 250
My Inquietude Constrained Briefly by Louise Bogan / 252
The Undering and Other Great Inhumanities on 3.6 Acres / 253

TOWARDS A NEW LANGUAGE OF EMBODIMENT
Norma Cole
WHY I AM NOT A TRANSLATOR — TAKE 2 / 257
Speech Production: Themes and Variations / 260

C.S. Giscombe
ON A LINE BY WILLIE MCTELL / 262
from Giscome Road (Northern Road, 2) / 267
from Prairie Style: Two Monster Poems / 271

Amber DiPietra
from MY NOTEBOOK HAS A RIGID SPINE OR
HOW TO OPERATE THE BODY IN WRITING / 272
bunny baby fast and slow / 275

Ellen McGrath Smith
"HEARING A PEAR": THE POETRY READING
ON A NEW FREQUENCY / 281
Afraid of the Rake / 286
The Magic Word Is *Partager* / 287
Spelling Down / 288
Theodore Enslin, Poet of Maine / 290

Denise Leto
OULIPO AT THE LAUNDROMAT / 291
Plaza Series. 1 / 294
The Lost Word Association / 296
26 Tries / 297
Crane of Angles / 298

Jennifer Bartlett
EXIT THROUGH THE GIFT SHOP / 299
5 poems from Autobiography / 301

Cynthia Hogue
THE CREATURE WITHIN: ON POETRY AND DIS/ABILITY / 306
Green surrounds the mind of summer / 309
In a Mute Season / 311
Radical Optimism / 312

Danielle Pafunda
MEAT LIFE / 313
In this Plate My Illness is Visible / 315
In this Plate My Illness is a Wire that Can Easily Cut Meat and Bone / 316
In this Plate I Receive My First Diagnosis / 317
In this Plate My Traumadome Has Come Unzippered / 319
In this Plate My Illness Splits Time / 320

Rusty Morrison
TO SATURATE THE MATTER OF THE PRESENT / 321
Ill-timed (24.1) & Ill-timed (24.2) / 327
Ill-timed (24.3) / 328
Ill-timed (24.4) / 332
Ill-timed (24.5) / 333

David Wolach
BODY MAPS AND DISTRACTION ZONES / 334
(muted domestic pornography) / 340
3. (corporeal self punishment) / 342
(forced feeding 1) / 344

Kara Dorris
BENIGN BONE TUMOR CITY / 346
Self-Portrait with Framing Effect / 348
Breton's Song of the Lark / 350
Fairytale: How Spring Comes to the Land of Snow and Icicles / (Dream Map) / 351
Wanting to Be a Girl / 352

Gretchen E. Henderson
POETICS/ "EXHIBITS" / 353
Exhibit "H" / 356
Exhibit "U" / 358

Bernadette Mayer
STATEMENT ON POETICS / 361
Sonnet Edmund Leites / 362
4th of July Demon Moped / 363
Chosca Mass Tinek / 364
EYJAFJALLAJOKULL / 365

Notes / 367
Contributors / 375
Acknowledgements / 381

Publisher's Note: Many of the contributors to *Beauty is a Verb* added citations and/or endnotes to their work. The endnotes, which included material that we felt was important to readers' understanding of the essays and poems can be found at the back of this book, beginning on page 367. A key to the parenthetical citations and a bibliography of additional resources are available as a free download at www.beautyisaverbbook.com and at www.cincopuntos.com.

Jennifer Bartlett

PREFACE

(for Reginald Shepard)

For me, the idea for *Beauty is a Verb* can be pinpointed to one single moment, December 10, 2005, the day Norma Cole read at the Bowery Poetry Club for the Segue Reading Series. A few years earlier, after a stroke, Cole lost and regained her ability to speak. Now, she used her temporary aphasia and slurred speech to compose a poem that noted a list of words she could no longer enunciate. The result of her reading this work was alternately hilarious and devastating. Cole laughed at the ridiculous, yet utterly wrenching, situation of a poet losing words, and the audience laughed with her. Yet, it wasn't as simple as that. Although the audience laughed, they were also visibly uncomfortable. From the sophistication of Cole's work and her genius as a person, one can guess that this was no accident. Can an entire anthology be sparked by one reading of one poet? I am sure crazier things have happened in this world we called poetry.

After, I began to consider a series of questions. What did it mean to have a disability poetics? What was the history of the movement? What about poets, much like myself, who have a disability, but do not align themselves with identity poetry or the disability poetics movement? How do they fit into such a context, if at all? Shortly after, I was invited by Sheila Black and Michael Northen to participate in a panel exploring many of these ideas at the 2009 Associated Writing Programs Conference in Denver. Over cocktails, the idea of our anthology, this anthology, was born.

While *Beauty is a Verb* includes many views of disability, we hope to consistently consider the social model of disability. It is for this reason that we primarily chose poets who have a visible disability. In this the poets' difficulty becomes twofold: a struggle with physical limitations (which, in themselves, can be a construction) coupled with society's critique of the non-normative body. We mean to explore not only what is means to have a genre called "Disability Poetics," but to look at poetry influenced by an alternate body and how this intersection forms a third language. Hence, we include not only poets who created and embrace the disability/crip poetics movement but also those who might resist such a classification and have never been considered in that exact context.

There are absences in the collection: we did not include poets writing about HIV/ AIDS or cancer. While these disabilities without a doubt fit into the social model, they could be arguably classified as illness. We also did not include alcoholism. As Michael Davidson notes, most poets could be looked at through a disability lens, even poets such as Robert Creeley, Allen Ginsberg and Robert Duncan—all of whom had vision problems of some variation. In addition, the collection tends to lean toward poets who are dedicated to publishing with independent presses: we did approach a few poets who publish with mainstream presses who declined to participate. Mainstream writers tend to reflect the predominant view of disability as tragedy. We wanted to avoid this norm not because it isn't valid, but because we are interested in investigating an alternative.

Beauty is a Verb is not, nor is it meant to be, a comprehensive collection. There are far too many wonderful American poets with disabilities, many of whom are noted in Northen's essay, to create such a book of a reasonable size. Rather, we mean to provide a selection that explores a range of poetic sensibilities. The three editors come together from very different backgrounds: Black, a poet and academic, is a long-time New Mexican working within the vein of narrative poetics. Northen, in addition to being a poet, is founder and editor of the disability poetics journal *Wordgathering* and a scholar of disability poetics. My own work and considerations embody an experimental lyricism informed by so-called Language Poetry. We hope the range in poetry here will reflect our range in knowledge and aesthetic.

Individual sections reflect this aesthetic range. The division is a mix of chronological and stylistic order. The "Early Voices," all of whom are deceased, are poets with disabilities writing in the mid-to-late twentieth century. These poets generally avoid having a narrative of disability as the forefront of their poetics. This, particularly in the case of Miles, was perhaps not only an aesthetic choice, but the result of writing in a time when disability was utterly shunned. Previous to the 1960s, the common attitude tended to be that in the rare case where a person with a disability was successful in any field that the disability was deemphasized as much as possible.

The second section—"The Disability Poetics Movement" or crip poetry—emphasizes embodiment, especially atypical embodiment and the alternative poetics generated from that perspective, which challenges stereotypes and insists on self-definition. Although these poets by no means want to be *defined* by their disability, they create a narrative that speaks to and celebrates identity, and politics are often the focus of their

JENNIFER BARTLETT

work. This section is not exclusively poets who align themselves with crip poetics. Jillian Weise, for example, strongly resists this label; yet her work also speaks to a celebratory narrative of the non-normative body.

The final two sections are more varied. Here are a number of poets who would be included in many different so-called schools if they aligned themselves at all. Many of these poets have not previously been explored through the lens of disability.

In "Lyricism of the Body" we gathered poets who, while still employing a narrative form to explore disability, do not necessarily make this the central focus of their work. Yet many of these poets are heavily informed by the lyric poem and often use this lyricism to celebrate the non-normative.

"Towards a New Language of Embodiment" includes poets whose work is informed by experimentation. Instead of narrative, disability is manifested directly through physical connection to the writing. Rather than explaining an individual story, bodily condition is manifested through the form. This is exemplified when Cole writes words that she cannot pronounce, and Wolach makes poetry under fabricated situations of physical stress.

While focusing on disability, *Beauty is a Verb* is made of poets who reflect on pressing issues of our cultural moment. These include the frangibility of the body, the intersection of body and machine (or body and technology), the commodification of the body, and other questions looming on our late-capitalist event horizon about the very nature and being of beauty and function. Part of what is so energizing about considering the current landscape of disability poetry is the degree to which thinking about disability enlists or engages viscerally many concerns animating other current poetry movements from the New Formalists to the Gurlesque. Much of human consideration of time and mortality hinges around the body—how it ages, changes, gains and loses capacities. Questions of how, why, whether this is in fact necessary, go to the deepest center of what it means to be human. We hope our efforts and the efforts of our contributors will begin to address such questions.

Michael Northen

A SHORT HISTORY OF
AMERICAN DISABILITY POETRY

In 1983, a brief article appeared in *Kaleidoscope* in which A. J. Baird, a scholar of medieval literature, condemned the current poetry written about disability as super-sentimental, self-pitying and eliciting superficial sympathy, a poetry that failed to rise to acceptable artistic standards and was deservedly ignored by mainstream literature. He put out a call for poetry about physical disability that was tough-minded and grounded in concrete, physical fact. The result was *Towards Solomon's Mountain*, published in 1986. While few of the writers in that volume went on to produce major collections, Baird's collection showed what disability poetry could be. It would not be an exaggeration to call the publication of *Towards Solomon's Mountain* the birth of disability poetry as a genre.

Of course, the writers in Baird's anthology were not the first American poets with disabilities to be published. Josephine Miles, Larry Eigner and Vassar Miller all had success with their writing, but had said little about their own bodies in their work. Because of this, Miles and Eigner, though known in literary circles, were overlooked by the first anthologies of disability writing.

Miles began writing in the 1930s when the public model for disability was Franklin D. Roosevelt, who hid his disability and projected an image of great capability. As a result of this climate, it was not until *Coming to Terms* in 1979—thirty-five years after the publication of her first book of poetry—that Miles directly refers to her own disability. At the beginning of that collection, she wrote ten autobiographical poems, among which several refer to her disability:

> This is a hard life you are having
> While you are young,
> My father said,
> As I scratched my casted knees with a paper knife.
> By laws of compensation
> Your old age should be grand.

The poetry of Larry Eigner, who is often associated with Charles Olson's Black Mountain school, was brought to prominence by Robert Creeley. Because of his cerebral palsy, Eigner did almost all of his writing from what he could observe from his own front porch. To an even greater extent than Miles, his poetry is devoid of reference to his own body, but the limitations under which he wrote affected the content of his work and the unique sense of space he developed in his writing.

The Independent Living Movement, initiated by Ed Roberts in the 1970s in Berkeley, did a great deal to spur on interest in disability and writing about disability. Individuals with disabilities began to see themselves as members of a larger group asserting their rights like African Americans and women. In the mid-1980s two important anthologies of disability writing were published that began to cull these individual writings. The first, *Despite This Flesh*, was edited by poet Vassar Miller—whose own writing career was roughly contemporary with Eigner's and who, until the publication of her own *If I Had Wheels or Love* in 1991, kept her own disability out of her poems. What Miller did do in *Despite This Flesh*, however, was to offer up a collection by writers with disabilities designed to provide materials that could be used by teachers of literature. The second anthology, *With Wings*, edited by Marsha Saxton and Florence Howe, was a much more political mix of disability poetry and prose. It became a seed book for many disability writings that followed. Neither of these books, as important as they were, advanced the manifesto for disability poetry to the extent that Baird's book did; it was not until the 1990s that single-author books of poetry—other than those by Deaf [1] writers—appeared that openly confronted the issues of disability.

The passage of the Americans with Disabilities Act in 1992 seems to have presaged a watershed moment for disability poetry. Of the over three hundred poems in Miller's lifelong collection, *If I Had Wings or Love*, published in 1991, only three poems mention disability and only one, "Dramatic Monologue in the Speaker's Own Voice," gives a direct expression of the impact of that experience upon her as an adult:

> I'm either a monster
> in search of a horror movie to be in,
> or else I'm a brain floating within a body
> whose sides I must gingerly touch while
> you glance discreetly away.

After the passage of the ADA, many outstanding books of poetry by writers with disabilities began to emerge: Karen Fiser, *Words Like Fate and Pain* (1992); Tom Andrews, *The Hemophiliac's Motorcycle* (1994); Floyd Skloot, *Music Appreciation* (1994); Kenny Fries, *Anesthesia* (1996); Dara McLaughlin, *A Map of This World* (1999), Stephen Kuusisto, *Only Bread, Only Light* (2000); and Jim Ferris, *The Hospital Poems* (2004). While there was great variety in these works, all writers agreed on two things—they eschewed sentimental poetry that made disability the object of pity or charity, and they rejected the image of the supercrip, the inspirational hero who overcomes insurmountable odds.

For two reasons, Kenny Fries may be the single most powerful representative of this group. First, his physical impairments are the greatest, and second, his physical impairments are the most observable. As a result, of all the writers in the above list, the body and the aesthetic of the body dominate his poetry the most. Interestingly *The Healing Notebooks*—which was originally published as a separate book in 1990 (i.e., before the ADA in 1992) and later resurfaced as the third section of *Anesthesia*—is the least graphic about his physical body. The poems deal more specifically with love, his feelings as a gay man and AIDS. Without prior knowledge, one would not know the nature of his disability or even that he had one. By contrast, the two later poems that he chose to put up front in *Anesthesia* hit one with a picture of disability immediately upon opening the cover. Such a move in this 1996 work points to an obvious shift in emphasis for Fries. In "Excavation" he says:

> Tonight, when I take off my shoes:
> three toes on each twisted foot.
>
> I touch the rough skin. The holes
> where the pins were. The scars.
>
> If I touch them long enough will I find
> those who never touched me? Or those
>
> who did? Freak, midget, three-toed
> bastard. Words I've always heard.
>
> Disabled, crippled, deformed. Words
> I was given.

Not only does Fries put his own body out in public view—something that Eigner and Miller, much less Alexander Pope, given the cultural milieu in which they lived, never could risk doing—he also questions the socially and culturally constructed nature of our concepts of beauty. Though Fries knows "No words unbend my bones. / Beauty is a two-faced god," he ends the poems with the assertion:

> So each night, naked on my bed, my body
> doesn't want repair, but longs for innocence. If
> innocent, despite the flaws I wear, I am beautiful.

In doing so, he rejects the moral blame for his situation, a blame that in the past was often attributed to those with disabilities. He is not asking to be fixed or made normal, thus rejecting the medical or rehabilitative model. He is asking instead for a redefinition of beauty and of the way that disability is perceived. He is at once an individual in his own particularities and part of a larger community asserting its right to self-definition.

Fries not only challenged social constructs of disability in his poetry, autobiography and personal essays, but also edited *Staring Back*, the first anthology of disability literature since *Toward's Solomon's Mountain* published in 1986 and the first to draw on the literary work of disability writers in the last decade of the twentieth century. Like Baird's work, *Staring Back* became a manifesto for disability literature and began to be widely used in college classrooms.

If Baird sounded the call for an honest, unsentimental poetry of disability and Kenny Fries showed how that call could be answered, Jim Ferris came up with the first book of disability poetry that could reasonably be called a best-seller: *The Hospital Poems*. Like Fries, Ferris puts the body, in particular his body, right at the center of his poetry. "Poet of Cripples," the leadoff poem in *The Hospital Poems*, is an anthem in Whitmanesque language that proclaims "let me be the poet of cripples." Just as Whitman focused on his own body, attempting to eradicate the boundaries between himself and others, Ferris says to the average person who looks askance at the disabled: "Look with care, look deep. / Know that you are a cripple too. I sing for cripples; I sing for you." By invoking Whitman in this opening poem, Ferris is able to align himself with the great American poet of the body and is able to plant the seeds for an aesthetic of disability. He is also able to center his poems within the context of the democratic spirit.

As the title suggests, Ferris focuses in on what the medical establishment and medicalization of the body does to a child who grows up in its throes. In doing this, Ferris recalls for the reader some of the models of disability, including the medical and charity models, both of which make objects of the disabled person. For all who try to make disability the subject of their gaze, he says:

> This world is not open to you—
> leave now, trespassers, you who seek to gaze
> on my humiliation.

Addressing the tendency to view the disabled as symbols, heroes who overcome adversity, he writes in the title poem of his second book, *The Facts of Life*:

> We are not signs,
> we do not live in spite of
> or because of facts,
> we live with them, around them, among

Of all the poets with disabilities, Ferris has perhaps worked the hardest to come up with a critical formulation of disability poetry. In his seminal essay "The Enjambed Body," Ferris provided the first attempt at a disability poetry aesthetic. Though the emphasis is on atypical embodiment, he also seeks to link his work to canonical literary figures like Whitman, Gerard Manley Hopkins and Emily Dickinson, whose famous definition of poetry declared that poetry should make your body feel unbearably cold and your head feel as though it will physically blow off.

In a 2007 article in *Wordgathering*, Ferris offered the following formulation:

> Disability poetry can be recognized by several characteristics: a challenge to stereotypes and an insistence on self-definition; foregrounding of the perspective of people with disabilities; an emphasis on embodiment, especially atypical embodiment; and alternative techniques and poetics.

Each of the poets with a disability who was able to get their writing into print during the 1990s and early years of the 2000s contributed a new perspective. Stephen Kuusisto's poetry was able to portray the perceptual imagery and daily experiences of a person who was functionally blind. Andrews' poetry captured the rhythms of a life with hemophilia. Fiser and Skloot wrote poetry that, in very different ways, examined the loss of memory that accompanied acquired disability. Patricia Wellingham-Jones' *Don't Turn Away* explored issues of disability in breast cancer.

MICHAEL NORTHEN

Almost thirty years after Baird threw down the gauntlet, disability poetry is starting to take shape as a genre. In addition to *Kaleidoscope*, magazines such as *Breath & Shadow* and the *Disability Studies Quarterly* regularly publish poetry by writers with disabilities, and in March 2007, *Wordgathering* appeared, dedicating itself primarily to the publication of disability poetry. For the past eight years, the Inglis House Poetry Workshop has held an annual disability poetry contest and published chapbooks of the winning poetry. In 2010, the Associated Writing Programs conference in Denver, and in 2011, the Modern Language Association conference in Los Angeles, offered panels on disability poetry. Petra Kuppers has gathered her writing on the teaching of disability poetry into *Disability Culture Poetry: Pleasure and Difference*, making it, if published, the first collection of essays to focus strictly on disability poetry. The wheels are in motion.

Literary critic Robert Scholes has noted that when new forms of literature emerge they are often looked at askance by those with a vested interest in maintaining the current boundaries. This is true even of poetry, the genre that one might expect to be the most open to innovation. Like disability itself, however, poetry is a mutable body. Thankfully, we are past the days when Franklin Roosevelt, a president of the United States, could not bring himself to be seen below the waist in public—the climate in which Miles' first books of poetry appeared. Reading a poem that confronts issues of physical disability directly, if not commonplace, is at least no longer surprising; yet identifying oneself as a writer of disability poetry or even admitting the legitimacy of a body of work that could be called disability poetry itself is still a bridge that many poets themselves are reluctant to cross.

As the fledgling field of disability poetry develops, it is inevitable that some who deserve credit will be forgotten. Due to the work of scholars like Michael Davidson and Susan Schweik, part of that credit has been recovered. In the field of disability studies, Davidson's work on Eigner and Schweik's on Miles have helped to reclaim the work of important writers omitted from those first anthologies of the 1980s. Other writers are not so fortunate. Dara McLaughlin's explosive *A Map of This World*, a poetic manifesto that explored the directions a disability poetry might take, is out of print and almost unobtainable. Poet/playwright Paul Kahn published a number of individual poems addressing the artistic, social and political concerns of being a writer with a disability, but never amassed enough to be published in a book. Whether the efforts of McLaughlin, Kahn and others like them who contributed to what they saw as a gap in the poetry they read in print would have been recognized if they had lived longer can only be a conjecture, but they too are there, if barely visible, in the history of disability poetry.

There is still a long way to go before disability poetry gets the attention that it deserves. While the poets above show the increased tendency of poets with disabilities to view physical disability as a social construction, it should not be thought that the saccharine and paternalistic poems about disability have ceased to be written. Just as the charity and medical models of disability still hold sway in the American mind at large, they also continue in poetry about disability. The poetry of Mattie Stepanik is a case in point. Much to the chagrin of Disability Studies activists and scholars, the poems of disability that the average bookstore browser is most likely to run into belong not to Fries, Ferris or Kuusisto, but to Mattie Stepanik and his ubiquitous *Heartsong* series. This is not the place to explore how a commercial culture cashed in on Stepanik's disability and death. Suffice to say that Stepanik has become the new literary Tiny Tim hoisted on the shoulders of the American public to reinforce the stereotypes of the disabled as objects of charity and/or courageous heroes and heroines. That Stepanik's books and those like them occupy the space that could offer the works of the poets discussed here demonstrates just how important it is to support the work of these writers. It also shows how equally important is the selection of disability poetry by teachers and the importance of introducing students to these poets by incorporating their work into the curriculum. No matter how much critical acclaim writers like Vassar Miller may receive among the disability community or poetic literati, until their poetry gets into the hands of students and thence into a more general public of intelligent readers, they are likely to be viewed as marginal.

The volume you hold in your hand, *Beauty is a Verb: The New Poetry of Disability,* is an important step in helping to transform disability poetry from marginalia into part of the American text. The time is right for it. By scanning this anthology, noting the writers included, copying a poem that especially strikes you or observing the way the writers dialogue with each other in their essays by reference to each other's work, you are already making your own contribution to this transformation.

Many fresh faces are coming onto the American disability poetry scene. Among those are writers like Ona Gritz, Paul Guest, Laurie Lambeth, Daniel Simpson, Linda Cronin, Anne Kaier, Marie Kane, Liz Whiteacre and Kathi Wolfe. Just as the Harlem Renaissance led to the development of African American literature and the 1960s to feminist literature, we are in a seminal period for the genre of disability literature. One day, perhaps, our children or grandchildren will look back at this decade, studying it in literature classes in the same way that we view the emergence of those other genres. It is an exciting time, and we have a chance to be in on the ground floor.

Michael Northen

EARLY VOICES

Michael Davidson

MISSING LARRY:
THE POETICS OF DISABILITY IN LARRY EIGNER

how to dance
sitting down
—CHARLES OLSON, "Tyrian Business"

My title refers to Larry Eigner, a significant figure in the New American Poetry, who is missing in a number of senses. On a personal level, I miss Larry—who died in February 1996—as a poet whose curiosity and attentiveness remain a model of poetic integrity. Although his movements were extremely restricted due to cerebral palsy contracted at birth, he was by no means "missing" from the poetry world, particularly after his move to Berkeley. Thanks to the efforts of Bob Grenier, Kathleen Frumkin and Jack Foley, Larry was present at many readings, talks and parties throughout the 1980s. Nor, as those who knew him can attest, was he a reticent presence at such events. He was a central influence in the emerging "language-writing" movement of the mid-1970s, publishing in their magazines (*L=A=N=G=U=A=G=E, Bezoar, This, Hills*) and participating in their talks and reading series. His emphasis on clear, direct presentation of moment-to-moment perceptions also linked him to the older Objectivists (George Oppen, Carl Rakosi, Charles Reznikoff and Louis Zukofsky) as well as to poets of his own generation living in the San Francisco Bay region such as Robert Duncan and Michael McClure.

A second dimension to my title refers to the Eigner missing from discussions of postwar poetry. Although he was centrally identified with the Black Mountain movement and corresponded with Olson, Creeley, Duncan, Corman and others, he is seldom mentioned in synoptic studies (including my own work) of that generation. What few critical accounts exist of his work come from poets. Robert Duncan, Denise Levertov, Clark Coolidge, Cid Corman, Charles Bernstein, Robert Hass, Ron Silliman and Barrett Watten have all written appreciations of his work, but he has had little response from the critics.[1] And although he was aligned with language writing later in his life, his name seldom appears in books or articles about that movement. Perhaps most surprisingly, given his centrality in the *New American Poetry*, he is seldom included in discussions of disability arts. With the exception of an appearance in Kenny Fries' anthology of disability writing, *Staring Back*, he is not included in major treatments of disability arts.

This brings me to the tertiary level of my title—the absence of cerebral palsy in discussions of Eigner's poetry. In what little critical treatment of his work exists, the fact of his physical condition is seldom mentioned. The lack of reference to cerebral palsy leads me to ask how one might theorize disability where least apparent: how to retrieve from recalcitrant silences markers of a neurological condition that mediated all aspects of Eigner's life.[2] In the process, we might discover ways of retrieving other social markers—of race, sexuality, class—where not immediately apparent. Eigner by no means adhered to New Critical warnings about the biographical fallacy—the idea that poems should finesse biographical or historical contexts through formal, rhetorical means. At the same time, he seldom foregrounded his mediated physical condition—his daily regimes of physical exercise, his limited mobility, his slurred speech—preferring to record real-time perception and observation. In order to retrieve disability from this lacuna we need to "crip" cultural forms, not simply to find disability references but to see the ways Eigner's work unseats normalizing discourses of embodiment. Cripping Larry Eigner allows us to read the body of his work in terms of his "different" body and to understand how the silences surrounding his poetry are, in some way, a dimension of—perhaps a refusal of—that embodiment.

In order to discuss Eigner's poetry in terms of disability we must first honor his own reticence on the subject. Throughout his memoirs, interviews and poetry, the subject of his cerebral palsy seldom appears. In his author's biography at the end of Donald Allen's anthology, *The New American Poetry*, Eigner describes himself as a "shut-in partly." Bob Grenier observes that "Larry's work does not *derive* from his palsy," but on the other hand, his poetry cannot help but be affected by it. In order to discover disability where it is not present, it is first necessary to find where it is—in Eigner's numerous prose writings, memoirs and stories. Consider the following passage from his 1969 memoir, "What a Time, Distance":

> Cigarette cigar signs stores mostly Variety groceries and how many things candy a little not much good might very well be a good deal everything smelled bread was designed with packaged loaf fresh and down the street daily paper words flashes and then sentence dateline dispatches...

MICHAEL DAVIDSON

Here, Eigner remembers childhood experiences in a variety store, the sights and smells of products and signage rendered in quick succession. One might imagine such passages divided into lines and splayed out over a page, but these memories are constantly mediated by conditions of restricted motion, regimes of physiotherapy and exercise, which frame his access to such "variety":

> Over the toilet rim in the bathroom at home into the bowl his weemer between large knuckles, cigarette shifted to mouth preparatory or in other of grandfather's hands. Coffee label. Good to the last drop. Waste not want not. To go as long as you could manage it. Bread is the staff of life, Grampa said many times buttering it at the beginning of dinner. Relax, try how get to fling ahead legs loosened quick as anything in being walked to different rooms the times he wasn't creeping to do it yourself as soon as possible, idea to make no trouble or spoil things but live when somebody agreed to a walk as he ought to have, sort of homework from the therapy exercising not to sit back need to start all over to come from behind. Thimble yarn darn stocking waterglass stretch wrongside patch, cocoon tobacco cellophane bullet wake finger ring.

A series of Joycean associations mark this passage—from peeing, with his grandfather's help, to a coffee label and its ad ("Good to the last drop"), to Depression-era adages about thrift ("Waste not want not") and health ("Bread is the staff of life"). These axioms rhyme with internalized parental imperatives regarding physical control ("Relax") and self-motivation ("do it yourself"), which for the young boy with motor impairment mark his distance from an able-bodied world. Those difficulties are rendered syntactically in the phrase "try how get to fling ahead legs loosened quick as anything," which may provide some verbal equivalent of the child's anxiety over muscular control.[3] Adult advice to "make no trouble or spoil things but live when somebody agree[s] to a walk," expresses a world of agency where everything from urinating to walking requires assistance.

This brief passage could serve as the "missing X" for many poems in which reference to physical limits has been evacuated, leaving only the "variety" of the variety store on the page. In his prose, Eigner merges sensuous associations with things seen and felt ("thimble yarn darn stocking...") with physical contexts of their apprehension. In his poetry, specific references to those contexts drop away, leaving acts of attention and cognition paramount. Those acts are deployed through three interrelated spaces:

the page on which he worked, the room in which he lived, the weather or landscape he saw from that room. I would like to look for Larry in these three frames.

Eigner's is decisively a poetry of the page, a field of intense activity produced entirely with his right index finger, the one digit over which he had some control. The page—specifically the 8 ½ by 11 inch typewriter page—is the measure of the poem, determining its lineation, length and typographic organization.[4] Although a few poems run on for several pages, often as not Eigner continues the poem as a second column on the same page.[5] Nor is the machine by which he produced those pages insignificant. Because Eigner needed to lean on the keys and peer closely at the sheet of paper, he could not use an electric typewriter and thus worked with a succession of Royal or Remington portables that permitted him a degree of flexibility in composition. The manual typewriter also allowed him to release the platen occasionally and adjust the spacing between words or lines, jamming letters or punctuation together or running one line onto the next. Eigner's careful spacing of letters and words, his indentations and double columns, could be seen as typographic idiosyncracy, a variation on Charles Olson's "field" poetics, but they are also cognitive maps of his internally distanced relation to space. In a video of Eigner's funeral made by Cloud House Productions, the filmmaker, Kush, returns to Eigner's house following the gravesite ceremony, and trains his camera on Eigner's typewriter for several minutes, a cenotaph for the poet's writerly remains.

The vantage from which he creates this page and watches the world is his room. The best description of his Swampscott room is in the author's biography at the back of *Windows/Walls/Yard/Ways*, which was probably written by Eigner, but utilizing a third person perspective. In it he describes:

> a 2-windowed bedroom (summer heat, winter cold, and snow, wind, springtime, Fall) overlooking backyard and porch with clothesreel in a closed-in while big enough neighborhood (sidestreet and 2 dead-end sidestreets, a path through woods, shortcut to the beach before the easterly one nearer the shore ended, after its joint with Eigner's street at the foot of the hill much steeper than the one going down from the town's main road.

When he moved to Berkeley, that room, as the PBS *United States of Poetry* documentary segment on him indicates, was crammed with pages, each filed in dated folders and placed in shelves at wheelchair height. Like Emily Dickinson, Eigner's

MICHAEL DAVIDSON

"endless/Room at the center" plays a significant role in determining the content of the poems. Until 1978 when he moved to California, Eigner spent most of his time in a porch at the front of his parents's home in Swampscott, Massachusetts, from which vantage he observed the birds, trees, passing cars, clouds, storms and sunlight that populate his verse, as in these two selections from *Things Stirring Together or Far Away*.

>   squirrels everywhere all
>   of
>   a
>   sudden (p.59)

>   what birds say comes in
>   all the windows
>
>   no end of wires through trees (p.36)

The haiku-like spareness of such lines suggests an Imagist emphasis on objects, but it becomes clear that Eigner's room is porous. He may hear birds through the windows, but he observes that they sit on the same wires that penetrate the house with news from elsewhere. What might appear as a limited perspective is instead figured by him as "inward performance," the active measurement of spaces and distances by an unusually sensuous, alert mind:

>   The midnight birds remind me of day
>   though they are
>   out in the night
>   beyond the curtain I can't see
>
>   Somehow bedrooms don't carry
>   tradition   I
>   and the boxed radio
>   is off. But what am I reading
>
>   inward performance

Has relevance. Allows me to hear
while something speaks. As for the bed
straightened by visible hands
only it is huge
when I feel   Down in darkness (*Selected Poems*, p.4)

Lying in bed at midnight, listening to birds outside, the poet feels like a radio, an instrument that although turned off continues to receive messages. The birds beyond his room, the tradition beyond the bedroom, "visible hands" that straighten the bed— these are forms of agency that seem "huge" and threatening. Yet against these "outward" forces, "inward performance" (of which the poem is a record) sustains his nocturnal reverie. The awkward phrase, "Somehow bedrooms don't carry / tradition" can be seen as a rueful recognition of the poet's confined position. In a world where individual talent is measured against a heroic tradition, one realized in domestic spaces like bedrooms may seem insignificant. Opposed to outward measures of cultural and social value rests the "inward" ability to imagine absent birds as present, night birds in day.

Once again, these examples do not address cerebral palsy directly; but they embody its effects on the poet as he registers the world from a stationary vantage. So attentive is Eigner to the processes of measuring thought and attention that the subject often dissolves into its acts of perception and cognition. This gives the work an oddly unstable feel as lines shift from one location to another, never pausing to conceptualize a scene but allowing, rather, the play of attentions to govern movement. What might be regarded as a form of impersonality turns out to be an immersion of the subject into his perceptual acts.

For Eigner in his closed-in porch, the issue of access is a problem and a way of being. For him, "travel and distance" *do* proportion themselves, relative to physical ability. The imperative to "be animate, and walk/turn, abruptly" can only be performed on the page; as a physical possibility, such imperatives must be measured in terms of "lines, broken curbs." One of the key provisions of the ADA was the erecting of curb cuts for wheelchair users, and although Eigner could not, in the late 1950s when the poem was written, imagine such accommodation, he is speaking of irregular surfaces within the poem as a prosodic principle, and in the world, as a physical set of limitations. That is, Eigner measures an objective world full of "lines" and "broken curbs" ("back to it," *Selected Poems*, p.4) as one which he must negotiate with difficulty.

MICHAEL DAVIDSON

Larry Eigner

if the earth were an eye
disembodied or not
there would still be frames

mist the road up
the hedges
bringing the sea to life

views
transparent
beside each other

this is all

the small
and the relative

the trees sharpening windows
taper to steady

the wind turns them
enhance the feel

the visible is the air

the hood the
glass
reflecting to the sky

sit on the hard surface
tug the small tree
the dog's sleeping under

times   it rains
and the sun shines

the far-away gets dim

the stars sleep in your dreams

AUGUST 12 65

there are all kinds of love   many kinds perhaps for each
object   don't think of yourself
there is always something else

the boats quiet in the sea
that have been to harbor ,   the skyline   coast

heavy white gulls
grade the bus windows

not to escape   father,   mother,   but get away from crowds

everywhere   fog in the distance

earth   water   come to the air
clouds say in the sunshine   to
have you   as if
by how much more than one

LARRY EIGNER

quiet thing   quiet thing

  walk

   in my eyes   death

  in the certain distance   how many

    go on

      I live not far away

     over the horizon

      still

JULY 21 69

The moon is cold

  a background by

 all hardward   more and more to

   go to a heavier place

    more miles

   in little pieces

     poor restless imagination

        bouyant motion awhile
       in stillness

the window opening

no, already opened

nothing but the wind up

the whole orchestra

risen

up   into the air

for dancing

after the storm   .

Tom Andrews

from Codeine Diary

On November 15, 1972—one week after Nixon was re-elected—I clapped my hands for fourteen hours and thirty-one minutes. I was listed in *The Guinness Book of World Records*. I was eleven years old.

My record was published on page 449 of the 1974 edition of the *Guinness Book*, landlocked between the listings for "Largest Circus" and "Club Swinging," in the chapter entitled "Human Achievements":

> Clapping. The duration record for continuous clapping is
> 14 hours 31 minutes by Thomas C. Andrews (b. April 30,
> 1961) at Charleston, West Virginia on November 15, 1972.
> He sustained an average of 120 claps per minute and an
> audibility range of at least 100 yards.

•

I would like to feel a stirring in my knee, calf, and ankle: a signal that the blood pooled there is being absorbed at last and the joints are opening again, like a fist or a jonquil.

•

I make $12,500 a year. I work as a copy editor for *Mathematical Reviews*, a bibliographic journal for mathematicians, physicists, statisticians, logicians, historians and philosophers of mathematics. When Joyce said he wrote for an ideal reader suffering from an ideal insomnia, he might well have had our subscribers in mind. At least they seem to be up all night, reading, assaying, scribbling after absolutes in a language the clipped densities of which rival, on a good night, any passage from *Finnegans Wake*.

•

I would like to feel a stirring.

•

Today is Thursday.

•

I'm writing this from my bed at the Universty of Michigan Hospital. It is 3 a.m. It is the half-dark of hospitals at night. I have had an accident. I have been in an accident.

From my window I can make out the iced-over Huron River and a tennis court covered with a taut white sheet of snow.

•

Philadelphia Enquirer November 28, 1972
Martin Bormann Reported Alive in South America
Champions' Routes to Glory
...And sometimes champions have highly developed imaginations
that help them in their quest for glory. Tom Andrews, only 11, of
Charleston, W.Va., applauded without interruption for 14 hours
31 minutes. His father, Ray, so attested in an affidavit he sent to *The
Guinness Book of World Records*.

The National Tattler January 28, 1973
Boy Breaks Hand-Clapping Record
He Probably Never Will Applaud Anyone!

Dear Tom,

It was certainly nice to read that you have broken the world's record in clapping. Keep your Dad busy getting that affidavit recorded.

We used to enjoy seeing how your Dad recorded you and John in your annual picture for Christmas. The last few years we had lost contact.

Congratulations again. Everyone is very proud of you.

Sincerely,

The Ripley Fishers

National Enquirer September 9, 1973

Director Who Made 'South Pacific' Reveals He Was Mentally Ill for 28 Years

Twins Engaged, Married and Have Babies on Same Day

Smothering Sneezes Can Harm You, Warns Doctor

11-Year-Old Boy Claps 94,520 times in 14 Hours 31 Minutes

Tom Andrews doesn't expect anybody to give him a hand for
breaking a world record. Especially after clapping for himself an
astounding 94,520 times!

"I just wanted to break a world record," grinned freckle-faced
Tom, who lives with his parents in Charleston, W.Va.

Norris McWhirter, co-compiler of the *Guinness Book,* told the *Enquirer*:
"We don't have many 11-year-olds in the *Guinness Book*. So this
is quite a remarkable feat."

Dear Tom,

Try to come out if you can, but if you can't that's o.k. I can play till
about 4:00 or 5:00. I hope you come out. Will you walk with me
today? Circle YES NO

I think you are the nicest boy over in Rolling Hills. I'm going to
try to get you something.

Love, Diane

P.S. Write back if you want to. Don't let anybody else see this except
Nan if you want to. Or Laura. I just showed Nan and Laura. Do you
mind? Circle YES NO

Answer questions and give back, please.

•

"That your scrapbook?" Ellen, the night nurse, asks.

When I mutter that, technically, it's my mother's, who brought it to the hospital
to cheer me up, Ellen glances at the *National Enquirer* headline and says, "You did that?
Clapped your hands?"

I nod.

"Lord!" she says. "Did you have a major bleed, or what?"

•

Two days after my brother died I learned to juggle apples.

As children John and I stared in wonder at jugglers, at the blurred orbits of their hovering knives or bowling pins, at their taunting nonchalance. Gravity flowed from their fingers. Two days after John died, in Charleston for the funeral, I traced on notebook paper the looping flight paths three objects must follow to remain aloft while being shuttled from hand to hand. I was staying at my great-aunt's apartment on Kanawha Boulevard. She kept a bowl of fresh fruit on a coffee table in the living room, where I found three apples of serviceable size and with them made an inelegant leap from theory to practice. I kept dropping the same apple. Once it fell against a corner of the coffee table: the yellow skin split and juice began to drip. I dropped it again. More juice. And again. The smell was terrific, sweet as just-washed hair. Eventually I could keep all three bruised, dripping apples weaving in midair, circulating. Gravity flowed from my fingers.

•

I have had an accident.

•

I have had an accident on the sidewalk. I watched my feet come out from under me on the iced concrete with a kind of anecdotal perspective. The bleeding inside the joints, the infusions of factor VIII, the weeks of immobility, the waiting for codeine, the inventions with which my mind would veer in the direction of solid ground—as my weight drilled into the twisting leg I saw the whole pantomime emerge with the clarity of blown glass.

•

Sunrise. The sky gray and pink.

•

My roommate, an elderly man with end-stage heart disease, was rolled in on a stretcher today. Oxygen tubes curl around his ears, line his cheek, enter his nostrils. His wife reads newspapers while he sleeps. They look uncannily alike: white-haired, slight, their salmon-colored faces stretched tightly across the facial bones. He's yet to be awake in this room.

•

When I told my hematologist that as a teenager I had raced motocross, that in fact in one race in Gallipolis, Ohio, I had gotten the holeshot and was bumped in the first turn and run over by twenty-some motorcycles, she said, "No. Not with your factor level. I'm sorry, but you wouldn't withstand the head injuries. You like the sound of yourself being dramatic."

•

The riffled sea of my sheets.

•

There is a mathematical process, useful to physicists and probability theorists, called the "self-avoiding random walk." Walter, one of MR's physics editors, once explained it to me as a succession of movements along a lattice of given dimensions, where the direction and length of each move is randomly determined, and where the walk does not return to a point already walked on. I almost wept with delight.

Walter looked confused. "You studied randomness in school?" he said, earnestly.

•

So many infusions of factor VIII...

As the concentrate filters into the IV drip, I feel the cold rise up through the upper arm, the shoulder, then branch off descending into the chest. I contain multitudes.

•

Heels clicking by in the hallway.

•

Later I learned that Walter would sometimes perform a kind of mime when he was drunk, a bodily interpretation of the self-avoiding random walk. Walter wore wire-rim glasses and a long, dazzlingly unkempt beard. He had close friends everywhere: Kyoto, Glasgow, Milan, Leningrad, Sao Paulo, Cape Town. I tried to imagine his self-avoidance.

Head crooked severely, eyes fixed, doll-like, in the opposite direction, feet turned alternately inward and outward, arms flailing somehow along trajectories his head, eyes, and feet did not intersect. I liked Walter. He refused to publish a review of any paper that referred to "cone-shaped objects" and their velocity, heat-seeking ability, etc.

•

In the hallway in the shunt-light
of the hallway
you wake
a nurse comes to show you
to your room
but can't find it
the entire wing is missing
you look outside
there in the gravel lot the sleet
pounding its fists
your white gown is walking home

•

Ellen takes the ice pack off my right calf and feels for a pulse at the ankle. She's been doing this every five minutes throughout the night to make sure the pressure of bleeding hasn't compressed and finally flattened the blood vessels. I'm a half hour or so into a dose of codeine: removing the ice pack doesn't make me cry out.

"It's still so hot," she says, meaning the skin around the calf. "You could fry an egg on it."

•

Glaring light. Shocking cold of the bedpan.

•

The President through the TV's drift and snow: "Things are even more like they are now than they've ever been."

TOM ANDREWS

•

Body positioning, weight distribution, throttle control.

Work with the bike. Don't fight it.

The sooner you shift your weight out of a corner, the sooner
you can accelerate. Don't lose time between braking and accelerating.

Use the bike's ability to control itself.

Preparing the bike—the gear ratios, the suspension, the jetting—
ahead of time will help your ability to concentrate on the race.

Concentration: don't let something stupid happen in the lulling
middle of a race.

Adapt to the track as it changes. Be on the lookout for alternative
lines.

Racing in the rain: controlled insanity. Get out front to avoid being
roosted with mud from the rear tires of other riders.

•

There are times, in the last minutes before I am allowed, or allow myself, more codeine,
when the pain inside the joints simplifies me utterly. I feel myself descending some
kind of evolutionary ladder until I become as crude and guileless as an amoeba. The
pain is not personal. I am incidental to it. It is like faith, the believer eclipsed by some-
thing immense...

The Hemophiliac's Motorcycle

For the sin against the HOLY GHOST is INGRATITUDE
—CHRISTOPHER SMART, *Jubilate Agno*

May the Lord Jesus Christ bless the hemophiliac's motorcycle,
     the smell of knobby tires,

Bel-Ray oil mixed with gasoline, new brake and clutch cables and
     handlebar grips,

the whole bike smothered in WD40 (to prevent rust, and to make
     the bike shine),

may He divine that the complex smell that simplified my life was
     performing the work of the spirit,

a window into the net of gems, linkages below and behind the given
     material world,

my little corner of the world's danger and sweet risk, a hemophiliac
     dicing on motocross tracks

in Pennsylvania and Ohio and West Virginia each Sunday from April
     through November,

the raceway names to my mind then a perfect sensual music, Hidden
     Hills, Rocky Fork, Mt. Morris, Salt Creek,

and the tracks themselves part of that music, the double jumps
     and off-camber turns, whoop-de-doos and fifth-gear downhills,

and me with my jersey proclaiming my awkward faith—"Powered
     By Christ," it said above a silk-screened picture of a rider in a
     radical cross-up,

TOM ANDREWS

the bike flying sideways off a jump like a ramp, the rider leaning his
whole body into a left-hand corner—

may He find His name glorified in such places and smells,

and in the people, Mike Bias, Charles Godby, Tracy Woods, David and
Tommy Hill, Bill Schultz—

their names and faces snowing down to me now as I look upward to
the past—

friends who taught me to look at the world luminously in front of
my eyes,

to find for myself the right rhythm of wildness and precision, when
to hold back and when to let go,

each of them with a style, a thumbprint, a way of tilting the bike this
way or that out of a berm shot, or braking heavily into a corner,

may He hear a listening to the sure song of His will in those years,

for they flooded me with gratitude that His informing breath was
breathed into me,

gratitude that His silence was the silence of all things, His presence
palpable everywhere in His absence,

gratitude that the sun flashed on the Kanawha River, making it
shimmer and wink,

gratitude that the river twisted like a wrist in its socket of
bottomland, its water part of our speech

as my brother and I drifted in inner tubes fishing the Great
White Carp,

gratitude that plump squirrels tight-walked telephone lines and
    trellises of honeysuckle vines

and swallows dove and banked through the limbs of sycamore trees,
    word-perfect and sun-stunned

in the middle of the afternoon, my infusion of factor VIII sucked in
    and my brother's dialysis sucked in and out—

both of us bewildered by the body's deep swells and currents and
    eerie backwaters,

our eyes widening at the white bursts on the mountain ash, at
    earthworms inching into oil-rainbowed roads—

gratitude that the oak tops on the high hills beyond the lawns
    fingered the denim sky

as cicadas drilled a shrill voice into the roadside sumac
    and peppergrass,

gratitude that after a rain catbirds crowded the damp air, bees
    spiraling from one exploding blossom to another,

gratitude that at night the star clusters were like nun buoys moored
    to a second sky, where God made room for us all,

may He adore each moment alive in the whirring world,

as now sitting up in this hospital bed brings a bright gladness for the
    human body, membrane of web and dew

I want to hymn and abide by, splendor of tissue, splendor of cartilage
    and bone,

TOM ANDREWS

splendor of the taillike spine's desire to stretch as it fills with blood

after a mundane backward plunge on an iced sidewalk in Ann Arbor

splendor of fibrinogen and cryoprecipitate, loosening the blood
   pooled in the stiffened joints

so I can sit up oh sit up in radiance, like speech after eight weeks
   of silence,

and listen for Him in the blood-rush and clairvoyance of the
   healing body,

in the sweet impersonal luck that keeps me now

from bleeding into the kidney or liver, or further into the spine,

listen for Him in the sound of my wife and my father weeping
   and rejoicing,

listen as my mother kneels down on the tiled floor like Christopher
   Smart

praying with strangers on a cobbled London street, kneels here in
   broad daylight

singing a "glorious hosanna from the den"

as nurses and orderlies and patients rolling their IV stands behind
   them like luggage

stall and stare into the room and smile finally and shuffle off, having
   heard God's great goodness lifted up

on my mother's tongue, each face transformed for a moment by
   ridicule

or sympathy before disappearing into the shunt-light of the hallway,

listen for Him in the snap and jerk of my roommate's curtain as he
    draws it open

to look and look at my singing mother and her silent choir

and to wink at me with an understanding that passeth peace, this
    kind, skeletal man

suffering from end-stage heart disease who loves science fiction
    and okra,

who on my first night here read aloud his grandson's bar mitzvah
    speech to me,

"...In my haftorah portion, the Lord takes Ezekiel to a valley full
    of bones,

the Lord commands him to prophesy over the bones so they will
    become people...,"

and solemnly recited the entire text of the candlelighting ceremony,

"I would like to light the first candle in memory of Grandma Ruth,
    for whom I was named,

I would like Grandma Dot and Grandpa Dan to come up and light
    the second candle,

I would like Aunt Mary Ann and my Albuquerque cousins Alanna
    and Susanna to come up and light the third candle...,"

his voice rising steadily through the vinegary smell and brutal hush
    in the room,

Tom Andrews

may the Lord hear our listening, His word like matchlight cupped to
   a cigarette

the instant before the intake of breath, like the smoke clouds pooled
   in the lit tobacco

before flooding the lungs and bloodstream, filtering into pith
   and marrow,

may He see Himself again in the hemophiliac's motorcycle

on a certain Sunday in 1975—Hidden Hills Raceway, Gallipolis, Ohio,

a first moto holeshot and wire-to-wire win, a miraculously benign
   sideswipe early on in the second moto

bending the handlebars and front brake lever before the possessed
   rocketing up through the pack

to finish third after passing Brian Kloser on his tricked-out
   Suzuki RM125

midair over the grandstand double jump—

may His absence arrive like that again here in this hygienic room,

not with the rush of a peaked power band and big air over the jumps

but with the strange intuitive calm of that race, a stillness
   somehow poised

in the body even as it pounded and blasted and held its line across
   the washboard track,

may His silence plague us like that again,

may He bless our listening and our homely tongues.

Jill Alexander Essbaum

SWIMMING ON CONCRETE:
THE POETRY OF VASSAR MILLER

I was introduced to Vassar Miller's poetry in college. The first day of college, in fact. The professor, herself a poet, handed out photocopies of poems that had to do with whatever it was we were getting ready to read. Alas, I no longer recall the poems themselves nor the context in which they were presented, but I do remember one important detail of my initial encounter with Vassar Miller's poetry: at some point during the discussion, my professor stood before the class and said, as an aside, *You've never been drunk until you've been drunk with Vassar Miller*. What a strange and wonderful fact! It was an earnest statement spoken honestly and (and this is important) in an absolutely reverent voice. I was eighteen and had never met a real poet before. I had also never been drunk, with or without a poet present (a deficit in my character that has since been amended). Still, my teacher's words of candor served to confirm something that I had fervently hoped was true: *That poets were purposed to drink life deeply and to share their intoxication with the world through their poems*. It was the first thing I ever learned at the university.

Vassar Miller spent her life in a wheelchair and died in 1998 at the age of seventy-four. Cerebral palsy made her body frail and her speech both intermittent and difficult to understand. A deeply committed Christian, Vassar Miller wrote at once with the soul of a mystical saint and the doubt of a skeptic, and she was never afraid nor ashamed of taking God to poetic task when she felt it a necessary action. In the same bold manner with which she wrote her religious poetry, Vassar Miller never shied away from addressing her disability, either. Her voice on the page is unflinching in its proclamations and insistent—almost urgent, possibly angry—in its assertions. As she writes in the poem "Dramatic Monologue in the Speaker's Own Voice":

> I'm either a monster
> in search of a horror movie to be in,
> or else I'm a brain floating within a body
> whose sides I must gingerly touch while you glance
> discreetly away

If poetry is anything at all it is the assimilation of experience into lines on the page. A Vassar Miller poem does not sentimentalize its own experience.

But what *is* the experience of a Vassar Miller poem? While her poems are often grave and dismal in their imagery, by their tone they are backlit with hope. It's easy enough to assign the origin of this optimism to Vassar's own Christian faith, but I think there's more to it than that (including, perhaps, her preoccupation with traditional form and the literal mechanics of resolution that occur, say, in a sonnet, but that is just a pet theory). Her poems are very compassionate, extraordinarily empathetic. When she writes of another's suffering, she speaks with the authority of one who knows full well what it means to live in physical agony. "Each man's sorrow is an absolute / Each man's pain is a norm," are the lines that begin her poem "The Common Core." There's an open and munificent heart at work in those lines and sympathy for the whole of humanity's broken condition.

Finally, though, what overwhelms me by her poems is their deep capacity for joy. You simply cannot read this woman's work—even her darker pieces—without being swept into the cloud of her witness to the possibility of bliss. On this point, her poems are resolute, unwavering:

> Spinning along the roadsides into dawn
> Feeling the flesh of lovers whom I'd lay
> I could make prayers or poems on and on."

There's nothing to do with those perfect lines but drink them in.

No, I never got drunk with Vassar Miller. But I've been drunk *on* her poems, many, many times. Go ye now and do likewise.

Vassar Miller

If I Had Wheels or Love

Chiefly for Joanne Avinger

I could make prayers or poems on and on,
Relax or labor all the summer day,
If I had wheels or love, I would be gone.

Spinning along the roadsides into dawn,
Feeling the flesh of lovers whom I'd lay
I could make prayers or poems on and on.

Whistling the hours by me as they drone,
Kissed on my breast and belly where I'd play
If I had wheels or love, I would be gone.

Over the next horizon toward the sun,
Deep in the shadows where I found the way
I could make prayers or poems on and on.

Along the country backroads flower-strewn,
Fondling your flanks, my dear, make clouds from clay
If I had wheels or love, I'd be gone.

Cool as the evening is and soft as fawn,
Warm as my fiddling fingers when they say
I could make prayers or poems on and on.
If I had wheels or love, I would be gone.

Dramatic Monologue in the
Speaker's Own Voice

I walk naked under my clothes like anyone else,

and I'm not a bomb to explode in your hands.

Of course, you are not (I would not accuse you of)

thinking of holding me down, but of holding me up.

Yet sometimes I'd love to be eased from the envelope of sleep,

stroked gently open (although it would take some doing—

on my part, that is). My lost virginity

would hurt me the way ghosts of their limbs

make amputees shriek, my womanhood

too seldom used. Have you ever viewed me this way?

No, none of you ever have. I'm either a monster

in search of a horror movie to be in,

or else I'm a brain floating within a body

whose sides I must gingerly touch while you glance

discreetly away. Sometimes when you hear it go—bump!

it gives you a nasty shock after which you insist I am glued

to my flesh like a fly in a paste pot. Maybe you think everyone is,

that, or a delicate lady in a dirty sty mincing on tiptoe.

I wish you'd learn better before we all totter

into our coffins where there's no straight way to lie crooked.

The Common Core

Each man's sorrow is an absolute
Each man's pain is a norm
No one can prove and no one refute.
Which is the blacker, coal or soot?
Which blows fiercer, gale or storm?
Each man's sorrow is an absolute.

No man's sickness has a synonym,
No man's disease has a double.
You weep for your love, I for my limbs—
Who mourns with reason? who over whims?
For, self-defined as a pebble,
No man's sickness has a synonym.

Gangrene is fire and cancer is burning.
Which one's deadlier? Toss
A coin to decide; past your discerning
Touch the heart's center, still and unturning,
That common core of the Cross;
You die of fire and I of burning.

Subterfuge

I remember my father, slight,
staggering in with his Underwood,
bearing it in his arms like an awkward bouquet

for his spastic child who sits down
on the floor, one knee on the frame
of the typewriter, and holding her wrist

with her right hand, in that precision known
to the crippled, peck at the keys
with a sparrow's preoccupation.

Falling by chance on rhyme, novel and curious bubble
blown with magic pipe, she tries them over and over,
spellbound by life's clashing in accord or against itself,

pretending pretense and playing at playing,
she does her childhood backward as children do,
her fun a delaying action against what she knows.

My father must lose her, his runaway on her treadmill
will lose the terrible favor that life has done him
as she toils at tomorrow, tensed at her makeshift toy.

Robert Fagan

Less

Less is more —Mies
Only when more is less —Wright
Which it always is —Diogenes

1.

Now that I'm deaf I'm listening to music. Until now I was too busy or too depressed and let the radio mumble on with cheery Vivaldi or soulful Tchaikovsky. Occasionally I would put on a CD, and sometimes a subtle little sound from Debussy would wake me up. Not any more. The high notes of Kiri Te Kanawa I mainly sense on her face on TV, as Strauss's Marschallin smiles at me.

It's all Cagean now. The truck that takes off on the street makes a great crescendo above Lulu's final shriek. And Sun Ra sounds as melodious as Glenn Miller. Above all I listen, transfixed, to rasping violin, viola, cello, knowing I'm hearing more than Beethoven did, and infinitely less. Still, since the less makes me strain for more, I'm beginning, maybe, to hear more.

2.

Now that I'm crippled I take long walks in the country. Until now I needed to move fast for exercise, and what I saw, heard, and smelled in the country could have been Central Park or even Broadway at rush hour. Life was a rush. One didn't stop to look at this tree, which is dying. I only noticed it because I fell over its dead branches and landed against its soft mossy trunk. It's like me, branches spread out on the ground, as my legs, arms and crutches are.

Falling is helpful for seeing the world. One has paused, as that hawk above me is pausing in the sky. One hears rustling sounds: branches and leaves moving, small animals scurrying. One smells the perfumes of blossoms or decaying things. The wind caresses. Once you've paused you'll never be the same again. You're not so...perpendicular, so apart. Then you can push yourself up along the trunk and continue your walk, moving at your own pace over the enormous earth.

3.

Now that my memory's gone I remember more. My mind wanders among so many scenes, so many more than actually happened. And they're set loose to recombine with scenes from other times, other places. And I know more people than I ever knew. Some of them I read or dreamed or wrote down. Others may have been real once, but are certainly more interesting now, as only their oddities or epiphanies remain. While those who could never be interesting are long forgotten. It takes a lot of forgetting to remember.

This is fortunate since all my trivial activities and half-hearted endeavors and absent-minded betrayals would make a vast nineteenth-century novel that would put any reader to sleep, including myself. Instead I don't doubt that everybody has been very nice and things turned out as they should have. So I have even forgotten what I have forgotten, and this is the greatest pleasure of all.

4.

Now that I'm impotent I make love a lot. It used to be that there were too many girls, women, wives, not exactly chasing after me, but beckoning or bending their little fingers around wine glasses or even around a button on my fly. Not that they weren't comforting and made me think at times that I was human. Still, I can barely remember a few faces.

This is all to the good since I'm concentrating nowadays on one face. Not my own, which is a bit of a *memento mori*, but this other face. And more than the face. In whatever state we're in of hurry or languor or unearthly awareness, there are simultaneous smiles at sudden absurdities, or quick nods of understanding, or just fingers absently touching, or murmured words lost in sleep, or even a lethargic cock gently flowing—so that one is constantly, never-endingly making love.

Proem

near the pond
I dance on four legs
without benefit of costume
hairy creature
     horny bald head
          one ear left
another sliced by surgeons
melanoma not madness

my unglassed eyes see
the pine forest as a steaming jungle
the sun melting
          the pond overflowing
while I gape from toothless mouth
that coughs in rhythm with the wind

my breastbone is still unbroken
holding fast to clogged heart
while shoulders keep me up on crutches
but shudder in pain
so I fall onto the tall grass
          and crawl to the water
accompanied by a small snake

     like the snake
my body would unjacket me
leaving behind striped skin
labyrinth of white scars
ancient lines and crevices
like the landscape of the moon

it might mean something
if those in the house
bird-watching with binoculars
would only read my body

but enough of an exhibition
now crawl into the pond
where cold water and sharp rocks
make my miniscule penis disappear
and allow me to be harmless child
or high-note castrato
or happy hermaphrodite
though my ass humps above water like a whale
                              trailing useless fin legs

splashing in rich green scum
arousing tiny fish
and transparent insects
through luxuriant strands of frogs' eggs
to touch pads and blossoms
and enticing reeds that reach out from the bottom
                              to embrace me

bonds that I may some day use
without Ophelia's glazed mind
but now can break free
          and round the pond
up to the red towel
cold wind forcing me
to hide in shirt and pants

and welcome
with shaved face
          and big smile
guests who hover over maps
planning excursions
to see the wonders of nature
out there somewhere

Stiege

1.

Do not be afraid. Just listen to my instructions.

The main thing is to remember not to walk straight. Instead you must bend one leg and then point the toes of the other into the void. Let your body sink forward. Unless you are unlucky, you will discover stone or steel or wood under you. And when you shift the enormous weight of your body (remember gravity!) from the redundant tail-like excrescence of your limp back leg to the firm column of your front leg, you will experience the dreadful and exhilarating knowledge of the vertiginous.

Perhaps you learned this as a child. First creeping up and down, as though each step was home, and the next step a strange land. Then, in an impetuous moment you began a lifelong habit of propelling yourself into space. As an adult you might be wise to reconsider this and take a more wary approach. I can give you some reasons why.

2.

it was the ruin of an abbey
                every abbey
        where every staircase
            is sheared in the air
                leading nowhere
            doors walled up
            nuns immured
            knees bared
            hell is here
                huis clos
            hold me
                close

the steps

were too steep

twisting up the tower

and twisting me

    away

from you

I said

   adieu

and the steps stopped

    one more

would have been air

 was sky

   I stepped

      out

there is no room

   in the air

search for a chamber

    chambre

where the top of the bed

   descends quietly

and crushes the lady

or the unicorn

  on the tapestry

     stirs

the wall opens

  steps lead up

    cold air

  touches

the skin

you cry out

yes, *oui*

sans merci

should I be

where I am

the guidebook said

take the steps up

it was in French

of course

I mistrusted the words

La-bas

Allez tout droit

a ghost beckoned

above the rampart

I saw below

    your hand

        waving

3.

Richard has left us in limbo. He did this by putting himself in limbo. We are paralyzed now, paralyzed by Richard, who lies paralyzed in the hospital. If he had died "naturally" or by "accident" or committed suicide, everything would be just fine. We would be free of him and we might even know more about life—that is to say death—which we can try to prepare for or be surprised by or perhaps even control by choosing the right moment.

Utterly sexually satiated, we drunkenly trooped out of the apartment of Richard's delectable new plaything that he'd stolen from one of us. As always, he was leading the way; obscenely lecturing on our magnificent animal natures. He reached the top of the stairs with us pushing hard behind him. Then suddenly he bent forward, raised his arms wide, and pronounced in birdlike twittering tones, "We can fly!"

Richard did fly. And we could not tell—as his beak and wings shot forward—if the whole thing was a dramatic exit from life that he had carefully planned, or a spontaneous gesture that was a miscalculation, or something more sinister. All we do know for sure is that we're still stuck with Richard.

4.
HBO is on
it doesn't matter
(don't move
in a narrow bed)
my sister
       fell off
             a ladder

another sister totters
MS doing its lazy work
she props herself carefully
in a narrow bed
and while the TV chatters
she plays dead

HBO is on
I turn it off
it doesn't matter
       the bed shakes
            like a ladder

5.

Wallace, the blood runs blue
towns are named for you
your family of senators.

Not Harvard, Choate, Sutton Place
but a tiny railroad flat
in an aromatic slum.

Your pride three rooms:
kitchen of strong food
and roaches everywhere.

Wallace, the blood runs
with alcohol, with pints of vodka
and gallons of cheap wine.

Living room full of kids for cock-
tails after you abandon the ancient
upright typewriter and the pages

that tell over and over
of your discovering the eternal youth
of a youth's enticing buttocks.

Paterfamilias, you wrote
of David and of Jonathan and Jamestown
and everything was gay, gay, gay.

The fops founded America
and the queens came to you
and you were mother too.

Falstaffean saint of sage advice
for every waif
you saved from suicide.

Wallace, the blood runs
down the rickety stairs
you take a tumble

backward, all lechery lost.
Was there someone with you
feral and beautiful?

6.

    The invention of stairs was a mistake. The Babylonians and Egyptians, who codified and glorified the invention, were also the inventors of civilization, another mistake. The lake-dwellers, who first created steps, at least lived on water.

Susan Schweik

THE VOICE OF "REASON"

Said, Pull her up a bit will you, Mac, I want to unload there.

Said, Pull her up my rear end, first come first served.

Said, give her the gun, Bud, he needs a taste of his own bumper.

Then the usher came out and got into the act:

Said, Pull her up, pull her up a bit, we need this space, sir.

Said, For God's sake, is this still a free country or what?

You go back and take care of Gary Cooper's horse

And leave me handle my own car.

Saw them unloading the lame old lady,

Ducked out under the wheel and gave her an elbow.

Said, All you needed to do was just explain;

Reason, Reason is my middle name.

Josephine Miles' widely anthologized poem, "Reason," appears in the *Norton Anthology of Modern Poetry* and elsewhere with a note citing her most widely quoted statement: "I like the idea of speech—not images, not ideals, not music, but people talking—as the material from which poetry is made." "Reason"'s focus on what Miles called "the spare and active interplay of talk" clearly appealed to academic editors of the postwar period (perhaps not surprisingly, since Miles was an academic herself, the first woman to be tenured in the English department at the University of California at Berkeley). The accompanying note in the *Norton* foregrounds Miles' talk-based poetics as the reason for "Reason": the poem's material is its method. And yet the footnote screens as much as it reveals. Its focus on "people talking" deflects attention from what, in this particular scene, they are talking about—the other material from which "Reason" is made.

What they are talking about is the question of whether a disabled woman can get access to a movie theater. Although nothing in "Reason" identifies Miles with her "lame old lady," and although she was by no means "old" at the time of the poem's first publication in 1955, this was indeed material of intensely personal significance for the author. Miles lived with rheumatoid arthritis from the age of two, mostly in a state of severe and visible physical disability. For years, unable to use a wheelchair, she employed personal care assistants to help her move from place to place. (During the Vietnam War years, when she actively involved herself in antiwar politics, she was left behind more than once when a gathering was teargassed and no one thought to help her leave the space.) When I first met her in our common workplace in 1984, at a reception for new faculty, she was carried into and across the room by a young aide.

In the image of Miles as described in the previous sentence, I recognize her as disabled, relying on what Lennard J. Davis has identified as one key modality through which disability is constructed: "The person with disabilities is...brought into a field of vision, and seen as a disabled person." So crucial is the gaze to the process of constituting disability in this formulation that Davis goes on to put the point even more forcefully: "Disability is a specular moment." "Reason" hinges on exactly such a specular moment. Interrupting its interplay of talk, the poem turns from saying to seeing: "Saw them unloading the lame old lady." Yet the return of idiom in "Reason"'s aphoristic final lines ("All you needed to do was just explain; / *Reason, Reason* is my middle name.") signals what I take to be the poem's subject: how disability is also a spoken moment, one made in discourse.[1]

In this essay, I wish to gloss "Reason" differently, substituting for the usual footnote about the idea of speech another set of ideas from new work in disability studies. I wish to place "Reason" not only within the history of American poetry, but also within the history of American constructions of disability, following Miles in showing what the one has to do with the other. I also wish to reclaim Miles for disability studies. This last project matters not because the field needs to find exemplary literary ancestors (although disability studies on the whole still lacks the sort of basic archival groundwork that necessarily preceded, and indeed therefore made possible, the post-Foucauldian critique of "reclamation" that has occurred in feminist and queer studies). It matters because disability studies needs to understand its histories. And literary disability studies can benefit from a look at a writer whose professional role gave her a heightened consciousness of language-making and a particularly sharp set of tools for expressing a set of social ambivalences about disability that were by no means hers alone. The very aspect of Miles' work that most aligns her with recent "social model" theories of disability—her focus on discourse—may paradoxically have prevented some readers today from recognizing in her poems a significant body of writing on disability. Miles' apparently affable and conciliatory rhetoric, her seeming poetics of cheerful overcoming, concealed a keener form of social comment.

Susan Schweik

"The [politicized] anger I am talking about," writes Albert Robillard, "does not arise within a general social order, but within the social order achieved through just this talk...and with *just* what these [social] members make of the talk...the perception of disabled bodies is...an interactional category." In a variety of ways, Miles' poetry of "just this talk," I will argue, anticipates aspects of later social models of disability.[2] This does not mean that Miles' poems reveal her to be a premature disability rights activist in the guise of a modern poet, but that when we read her early poems within their own historical context we can find both a critique of and a swerve from the standard discourses of disability in her day. In a sense, too, we can read in her poems signs of the conditions for the emergence of a new contemporary social group—but only if that group is understood in both broad and complex terms. If Miles' poems of the 1940s and 1950s seem to capture a version of the "language of the disabled" before there was a disabled community imagining itself as such, this may in part be because—as the recently rediscovered 1942 disability memoir, Katharine Butler Hathaway's *The Little Locksmith*, has also helped show some historical sources present discourses of disability that prove, upon critical examination, to be braver, subtler and more ingenious than standard narratives of the development of contemporary disability consciousness can generally account for.

Two things complicate—perhaps even seem to contravene—my invocation of an activist, social model of disability as a tool for reading Miles. The first is Miles' own public resistance to being identified, later in her life, with the broadbased disability rights movement—or indeed, from her youth on, with the category of "disabled" at all. The second is the striking absence of Miles' writing from the scholarly work on disability and literature that has been inspired and organized by social model theory.

Miles consistently refused to define herself in terms of her "medical condition"; she never represented herself in later years as part of any particular identity politics or collective struggle around disability issues. In a late-1970s interview, she commented breezily on a library that was inaccessible to her: "They didn't build it personally for me, that's all." Often, she described her impairments as productive limitations, invoking Robert Frost's description of free verse as playing tennis with the net down: "One of the great problems in living now is that people have such a multitude of choices to face, and in an existential world making choices is everything. It's when choices are limited that it's easy to make intelligent decisions, and my choices were always very limited." (Larney 1993: p.82). In 1979, though she did go on to stress the importance in her own life of her struggle for economic self-determination, she presented the Independent Living Movement, which had originated in part on her own campus, as largely irrelevant to her concerns: "Independence today, especially in relation to disablement, means physical independence or personal independence. It's very curious, but neither of these crossed my mind very much." (Larney 1993: p.81)

Quotations like this pose a problem for anyone attempting to enlist Miles in a contemporary poetics of disability presence.[3] The biographical archives by and large offer few inroads for critics looking for the "ragged edge" of a subversive disability consciousness, and plenty of opportunity to pinpoint examples of internalized oppression. I am uninterested in this tack for many reasons (beginning with—but only beginning with—my sense that as a nondisabled reader I do better to examine my own relation to disability oppression than to criticize anyone else's).[4] The problem in reading Miles and disability is in part a theoretical one; that is, it requires a calling into question both of Miles and of disability as organic and self-evident concepts. We might read Miles' refusals to identify with disability or with a disability rights politics in the context, for instance, of Henri-Jacques Stiker's (1999: p.134) stringent critique of the category of "disability" itself in the twentieth century:

> The "thing" has been designated, defined, framed. Now it has to be scrutinized, pinpointed, dealt with. People with "it" make up a marked group, a social entity...The disabled, henceforth of all kinds, are established as a category to be reintegrated and thus to be rehabilitated. Paradoxically, they are designated in order to be made to disappear, they are spoken in order to be silenced.

And equally, or perhaps even more important, the problem of reading Miles and disability is a historical one, a task supported by new work in disability historiography.

Growing up in an era in which public policy consolidated a model of disability as "incapacity because of medical pathology" (Longmore and Goldberger 2000: p.1-2), Miles consistently presented herself as both agreeable and capable. She came of age in the 1930s, a period in which the most obvious part given to her, the delegitimated role of "cripple," was countered or altered only by the ideology of rehabilitation modeled by that indomitable overcomer Franklin Delano Roosevelt.[5] It is no surprise that she adopted a posture of "continuous, cheerful striving" (p.12). Poems like Miles' "Reason" enact a certain kind of contract with the reader: a poetics of affability, its liberal mode strikingly

SUSAN SCHWEIK

at odds with the more militant stance enacted and demanded by later movements for disability rights.[6]

Recent collections of disability writing have had no use for Miles, finding their precursors in less deferential forebears. Kenny Fries' 1997 anthology *Staring Back: The Disability Experience from the Inside Out*, for instance, incorporates not a poem by Miles— or other possible representatives of her generation like Flannery O'Conner or Vassar Miller—but an invocation, from the play *P.H.*reaks: The Hidden History of People with Disabilities*, of the militant activism of the League of the Physically Handicapped. (The LPH was a group of organizers in the 1930s who occupied New York's Emergency Relief Bureau in protest of the Works Progress Administration's exclusion of handicapped people from access to federal jobs.) *Toward Solomon's Mountain: The Experience of Disability in Poetry* (Baird and Workman 1986) includes Miller, but not Miles; Miller's own anthology, *Despite This Flesh* (1985), has no poems by Miles in it. Nor do the anthologies specifically focus on disabled women's writing. This last omission especially troubles me, both because Miles' life was partly shaped by how—in Eli Clare's (1999: pp.123, 137) resonant phrases—"gender reaches into disability ...disability snarls into gender," and because Miles' poems admit a wide variety of feminist readings. "Reason," for instance, is composed entirely of men's talk, dime-novel and Western-movie talk, hard-boiled detective talk, but also, first and foremost, *car* talk. Within this talk, cars as well as (disabled and old) women are gendered feminine: "Pull her up a bit." Surely, as Paul Friedrich (1991: p.52) has noted, these are working-class men, and class as well as gender dynamics are part of the culture of "Reason" (as Friedrich notes, this is an exchange between "a chauffeur, a trucker [*sic*] and a valet"); but what I want to emphasize here for a moment is not the class markings of this dialect, nor its Americanness, but its masculinity. At the hub of the poem is the metonymy of "her"; both woman and car, the "her" is a machine, to be parked, pushed and unloaded.[7] If, as Julia Kristeva writes in her review of Stiker's *A History of Disability*, people with disabilities are to be seen as "ourselves—not as machines," the men of "Reason" do not know this, especially where the woman is concerned. The joke of the poem—whether we read it as laughing at the men's world or with it—lies in part, then, in the way that the playful pastiche of guy talk toys with Cartesian models of (woman's) body-as-machine. "Reason" seems to allude to the classical age in other ways as well, and perhaps to participate in something approaching, or congenial to, a postmodern feminist orientation. The poem concludes with a scene of cockeyed masculine chivalry toward a patronized "lady." Whether that chivalry is meaningless is a question the poem raises, but does not overtly answer. It is certainly possible to read "Reason" as a gentle, wry exemplum in the tradition of feminist work described by Susan Bordo (1995: p.41): "Feminist philosophers have frequently challenged dominant conceptions of rationality, morality, and politics through reevaluations of those 'female' qualities—spontaneity, practical knowledge, empathy—forbidden (or deemed irrelevant) to the 'man of reason.'" "Female qualities," of course, were often forbidden or deemed irrelevant to Josephine Miles by the ableist construction of gender in her culture.[8] One oral historian quotes Miles as saying that "some years ago a Dean of Women told her, 'The very fact that you are a woman sets the cause [of women] back fifty years because you don't pose the same problems another woman would'" (Teiser and Harroun 1980: p.318). In another version of the same story, Miles describes the dean as saying, "You offer a substitute rather than role modeling. You're more of a mascot; you're an exception, so you don't threaten people" (Marie and Offen 1978: p.26). "It was a cruel remark," the oral historian continues, "and more cruel because half true" (Teiser and Harroun 1980: p.318). I encountered an even more extreme, but hardly unusual, version of this attitude myself in 1985, when I included Miles' poetry on the syllabus of a graduate course at Berkeley on modern women poets. One of my colleagues, who had worked with Miles closely for many years, said to me simply, "But Jo Miles was not a woman."

Miles reacted to this oppression publicly in a variety of ways. She spoke about her feelings of having been betrayed and excluded by nondisabled women: "I not only didn't have women role models, I don't think women were very helpful to me at all. They were rather obstructive. I can't explain it..." (Marie and Offen 1978: p.2). She allied herself with the Women's Caucus in her English department in the 1970s, telling interviewers, "I realize that sometimes for sheer justice's sake a category has to get some recognition... You know, nobody philosophically believes in special treatment of categories...but what if a category has not been treated even up to par? So this is a philosophical issue which hit me pretty great, and there's still plenty of people fighting it" (p.22). At the same time, she portrayed herself as resistant to all categorization and underscored in particular her complex relation to gender. She wrote a remarkable play during the 1950s, *House and Home*, in which gender and domesticity become so stylized, so alterable, so artificial and performative, that perhaps only now, with Judith Butler as a guide, can we begin to understand it as a very queer text, one whose mocking of heteronormativities might be said to have something to do with Miles' departures from 1950s norms of domestic

SUSAN SCHWEIK

femininity.[9] But Miles followed up her strongest statement of gender trouble—"I just don't feel the sense of the significance of the woman's category *for me*"—by dancing away from disability as an explanatory tool, and displacing it through reference to generational difference and professional ethos: "I haven't had the whole child-family experience. But I think this is part of the past, in that professors in the old days didn't, so that wasn't so strange either" (Teiser and Harroun 1980: p.36). Always the hint of, and then the backing off from, the "strangeness" of disability.

Academic studies that focus on Miles' poetry or on biographical sketches of the author have tended to follow her lead, either downplaying the significance of Miles' rheumatoid arthritis or framing her within a narrative portraying her as triumphantly transcending (or pragmatically avoiding) her physical condition.[10] Miles is commonly said to have addressed her own experience of arthritis only late in life, in the directly autobiographical sequence of poems that makes up the beginning of her 1979 volume *Coming to Terms*. In these late poems, the best known of which is "Doll," Miles wrote her own version of autopathography, contributing to a historical moment in which autobiographical narratives of illness or disability were coming into their own. By the late 1970s, disability was becoming increasingly destigmatized, a trend that made books like *Coming to Terms* possible and that autopathographies like "Doll" sought to advance. This certainly accounts for some of the appeal of Miles' late disability poems. There is another reason, too, for the preponderance of critical focus on *Coming to Terms*. "Doll" and its surrounding poems return to the scene of the childhood onset of Miles' arthritis. "Doll"'s subtle and spectacular disability effects—its exploration, through the figure of the doll, of the *corps morcelé*; its seemingly matter-of-fact but skittish and unsettled uses of the story of recovery; its depiction of a coming into identity embedded within a matrix of social relations—are worth exploring in detail, and are beyond the scope of this essay. What I want to emphasize here is another factor at work in the critical fixation on these late poems as the sole examples of writing disability in Miles' oeuvre: the poems play out the "before-and-after" scenario identified by Yvonne Lynch as a dominant disability narrative. Lynch (1997: p.127) points out that representations of disability in film and television commonly focus on the transition from "unimpairment" to impairment, a form that works to secure the identification of a nondisabled audience. "Why is there such a concentration on that transition?" she asks. "It isn't the only dramatic thing that ever happens in a disabled person's life."

Long before *Coming to Terms*, in fact, Miles' poems came to terms of disability, though not easily legible terms, since they neither employed the before-and-after plot nor utilized the autobiographical imperative that made her late poems popular. These earlier poems have not been recognized—at least not publicly—as poems about disability. In 1935, the same year that the League of the Physically Handicapped sat in at the Emergency Relief Bureau, for instance, Miles achieved her first major publication, a set of lyrics in the famous anthology *Trial Balances*. The group of poems concluded with "Physiologus," a poem that ostensibly contrasts—and finally conjoins—curable afflictions of the body and irremediable suffering in the mind:

> When the mind is dark with the multiple shadow of facts,
> There is no heat of the sun can warm the mind.
> The facts lie streaked like the trunks of trees at evening,
> Without the evening hope that they may find
> Absorbent night and blind.
> Howsoever sunset and summer bring rest
> To the rheumatic by change, and howsoever
> Sulphur's good medicine, this can have no cure—
> This weight of knowledge dark on the brain is never
> To be burnt out like fever,
> But slowly, with speech to tell the way and ease it,
> Will sink into the blood, and warm, and slowly
> Move in the veins, and murmur, and come at length
> To the tongue's tip and the finger's tip most lowly,
> And will belong to the body wholly. (Miles 1983: p.7)

Employing the 1930s discourse of rest and rehabilitation (perhaps at FDR's Warm Springs, or in Palm Springs, where Miles was sent to recover as a child), "Physiologus" opposes to this therapeutic theme one narrative of remedy only, that which comes "at length / To the tongue's tip and the finger's tip."[11] The poem offers a kind of counterdiagnosis of *rheum*, or stream, in which the dark, unconscious "fact" of a congealed rheum thaws into written or spoken language.

We can read here vestiges of Miles' own experience of unpredictable flareups and remissions, and of early-twentieth-century systems of physical rehabilitation—and

SUSAN SCHWEIK

perhaps, also, in the poem's initial stark distinction between the cured rheumatic body and the incorrigible mind, traces of another history of disability in Miles' life. In the 1920s during her teen years, according to Miles, her father fought a bitter legal struggle against his insurance companies for his right to compensation for the dangerously high blood pressure that had forced him to retire. When brought to court, the case hinged on a contested definition: whether hypertension was to be understood as a *disabling condition*. Eventually, Miles' father won his case; he died within the year, when Miles was eighteen, of a massive stroke. According to her testimony, Miles' adolescence occurred, therefore, in the context of a life-and-death economic and legal struggle, close to home, over what constituted *disability*.[12] "Physiologus" may be read as a poem in which that which is visible and can abate (some flare-ups of arthritis, for instance) is set up against that which is invisible and cannot (a father's high blood pressure, but also the strong pressures of memory, worry, grief, trauma), and both are finally collapsed, as distinctions between normal well-being and abnormal malady blur, into the single mode of resolution the poem accepts as possible—the talking or writing cure.

This poem complicates a model of Josephine Miles as cheery prevailer. Miles' public stance in 1935 may have generally resembled that of the liberal polio survivors working in high-level positions in FDR's administration, whose view of disability Paul K. Longmore and David Goldberger (2000: pp.46-47) characterize as "a private tragedy most appropriately dealt with by sympathetic public support of individuals' striving." But "Physiologus" suggests she also had something in common with the far more radical organizers of the League of the Physically Handicapped: a critique of the basic opposition that underlies the framing of the category "physically handicapped"— the binary distinction between "normal and disabled" (or between "sick" and "well" or "incurable" and "cured") that operates not just as "a description of a group ...[but] as a signifier for relations of power" (Baynton 1997: p.82).

Throughout her career as a poet, Miles consistently countered sentimental, charitable, medical and heroic narratives of disability. She did this in a variety of ways. Her earliest poems employ diffused, submerged and refracted images of the body; her poems of the Vietnam War years extend to a broad concern with the body politic and body politics.[13] But these poems still write disability. To look for its traces in Josephine Miles' poetry is not to reduce her or her work to (one aspect of) the corporeal; it is to recognize how the poems *in*corporate—involve, re-cognize, work out of, work into—the totality of Miles' experience: social, physical and emotional.[14]

Take, for instance, the poem "Care" (Miles 1960: p.126), which winds around the double meaning of its title: *care* as (giving) aid, as (feeling) distress. Addressing an unnamed "you," the poem contrasts this "you / That makes me worsen" to "Most that I know" who "make me better than I am, / Freer and more intent, / Glad and more indolent." I had read this poem indifferently many times over many years before the obvious occurred to me: it explores not so much general forces of sociability as the specific dynamics of personal assistance service, the relationship between "attendant" and "client."

For a long time, this subject was simply illegible to me. We have no literary history of the "poetry of attendance," no named genre within which to place this lyric interaction, however intensely charged with feeling the dynamic might be. Collections of love poems, for instance, do not generally include examples of erotic or affectionate poems addressed by disabled clients to paid personal care assistants or vice versa. Miles' poem to a bad attendant takes the relationship seriously.[15] In a move with implications not just for attendant-client relations but for interactions in general between disabled and nondisabled people, "Care" reassigns and complicates *lack*, transferring lack off the body of the disabled speaker and onto the inadequate and projecting attendant: "Or do I learn your lack, / Not mine, and give it back, / As mine, the empty lack as mine / That makes me worsen?" By its end, the poem takes the phrase put into the mouths of disabled people thought to be in need of care—"Help me! / Help me"—and alters it, both by making the question of whether to say it the subject of the lyric speaker's meditation and by changing its conditions: the speaker considers herself at risk not physically but spiritually, threatened by the hate and disdain she feels for her clueless aide. Miles is commonly understood as a poet of the everyday. The poem "Care," a meditation on the effects of being improperly assisted, is one of many in which Miles' "quotidian" incorporates the daily life of disability.

"Care" may be the most moderate hate poem ever written. Its affability is marked both at the beginning of the poem, with the assertion that most caregivers do far better than the one addressed, and throughout, in its staging as a meditation on the state of hate rather than as an expression of rage itself. Here is a poet who seems, in the words of an influential review of her work by Denis Donahue (1975: p.442), to have no ax to grind.[16] But in Miles' poems, affability goes hand in hand with avowal, not denial, of the intricate set of social relations that constitutes "disability."[17]

Susan Schweik

Though rarely articulating them in the form of complaint, these poems do express grievances: against the negligent and hostile assistant, for instance, or the clinician or social worker, or—to return to "Reason"—against the man who blocks access in the parking lot. They may be *contained* grievances, compressed into poems like the grievances in Miles' 1966 poem of the same name: "I keep one or two and press them in a book, / And when I show them to you they have crumbled / To powder on the page." But, as that poem concludes: "The stems of grievance put down their heavy roots / And by the end of summer crack the pavement" (Miles 1983: p.156). There is—as the poem itself makes clear—anger in "Reason" (and in reason). Think, for instance, of the way the man's final giving of an elbow to the "lame old lady" suggests not only chivalry, but also shoving, "elbowing aside"; think, too, of the charged use, twice, of the harsh word "unload." Enough pavement-cracking ammunition lies behind the wisecracking in that "unload" to justify the speculation that Emily Dickinson's (1955: no. 754) "My Life had stood—a Loaded Gun" may be an intertext for this poem, which is tense with the dynamics of being loaded and unloaded, of being animate with anger but dependent on another to move one about.

But Miles' emphasis on interchange, "the idea of speech," shifts the scene of grievance away from the "plight" or tension of the disabled individual and toward the "cracking" of the public, the civic, the social. Disability theorist and photographer David Hevey lists progressive stages of disability representation; the last two most-advanced levels are as follows:

> The sixth move, then, is to travel off the body...The seventh move would be to record the interface between the person and their space or non-space...between impairment and disablement: the wheel of the wheelchair against the first step of stairs; the gawking of schoolchildren; the lean-over of patronizing men and women; and so on. Such a narrative would record the clash, the paradox, the struggle between the person with the impairment and his or her disabling environment. (Hevey 1992: p.31)[18]

"Reason" travels off the body in just this sense. Miles is not alone in this strategy; other disabled poets of the 1940s, 1950s and 1960s explored verbal forms of traveling off the body that may be read as precursors to the more direct activism of poets such as Cheryl Marie Wade or Mark O'Brien. Take, for example, the views through window frames that occur so frequently in the poems of another Bay Area writer, Larry Eigner—texts that also uneasily invoke poetic tradition's usual mode of "traveling off," lyric transcendence. Like Eigner's work, Miles' poetry both complicates and accentuates a social model of disability by making it clear that what that poetry travels into, and what it travels in, is (accessible and inaccessible) language. "Reason" does this in two ways. One may be read as a form of social comment on how people talk about, and hear each other talk about, disability; the other refers to nothing but poetry itself. First, the social comment. In her public statements on the pleasures of "Reason," Miles followed her stress on "the idea of speech" with this statement: "The accents of a limited and maybe slightly misplaced pride interest me. Good, strong, true pride we need more of, and the oblique accents of it at least sound out the right direction" (Larney 1993: p.57). This genial, comic view of "Reason"'s blocking, blustering character, the man who refuses to move his car and then says "all you needed to do was just explain," offers only the mildest of critiques; the "accents of his pride" are "limited," "maybe slightly misplaced." But the focus—however gentle —on his limits, on his misplacement, still strongly revises prior models of the politics of narcissism in scenes of disability.

As Lennard Davis notes in his important essay "Bending over Backwards," people with disabilities "are often seen as narcissists, particularly by psychoanalysts" and by judges in ADA (Americans with Disabilities Act) court cases. "By definition," writes Davis (2000: p.197), "a concern for one's disability is seen as self-concern rather than a societal concern." Or, in Miles' own words: "I can never quite say why I don't hit it off with people. I think part of it is that they just fear that I'm going to ask favors" (Teiser and Harroun 1980: p.43). Davis tracks this association between narcissism and disability by turning to a well-known psychoanalytical reading of one of the most powerful representations of disability in poetry: Freud's discussion of the opening soliloquy in Shakespeare's *Richard III*. Richard explains to the audience that he is "determined to prove a villain" since, because of his deformities, he cannot "prove a lover." In Freud's analysis, Richard's real message (one with which the audience identifies, even as it projects it onto "deformed" Others) is: "Nature has done me a grievous wrong in denying me the beauty of form which wins human love. Life owes me reparation for this, and I will see that I get it. I have a right to be an exception, to disregard the scruples by which others let themselves be held back. I may do wrong myself, since wrong has been done to me" (Freud 1989: p.593).

SUSAN SCHWEIK

In "Reason" and other colloquial poems, Miles devises a vigorous alternative to this particular tradition, one in which colloquy replaces soliloquy. The poem deflects identification, or at any rate renders it elastic and provisional. In "Reason" and elsewhere, Miles develops a (counter)narcissistic poetic that challenges a dominant equation of disability with aggrieved self-absorption, not by evacuating narcissism, but by revealing and reveling in it—as the basis of *all* (un)reasonable spoken interaction, and as a force that both generates and is tempered by conversation.

This is conversation *in poems*, and this leads me to my second, and final, point. I want to return to Miles' "idea of speech" as "the material from which poetry is made." To read "Reason," we must finally return to the poem's claim to make something of "the spare and active interplay of talk"; we must take poetic talking seriously, as a mode in dialogue with, but not identical to, other forms of discourse. "All you needed to do was just explain," says the man who has been hogging the spot with the best access to the theater, as he ducks out from under the wheel to offer his elbow to the "lame old lady." "Reason" offers no overt comment on this late attempt to replace selfishness and rudeness with patronizing courtesy: this is a comic resolution, one that mediates as much as it mocks. The poem itself will not explain. Its dialogism exemplifies civility, and in the process, if it skirts the political and emotional risks of open judgment and complaint, it also declines the endless task of "just explaining" that people with disabilities are forced to do, over and over again. To the debate over reasonable accommodation at the curb, it offers not the argumentative voice of reason, but the voice of "reason"—misplaced and re-placed, citational, deflected.

Nowhere is this deflection clearer than in the poem's final line: *"Reason, Reason is my middle name."* There are two pleasures here. One is the ridiculousness of the man's claim, the send-up of a long tradition of appeals to so-called reason (and the funniness of the assertion, in crime-novel style, of the "middle name," which simultaneously claims rationality as inherent and places it in a secondary position).[19] This line, and the whole poem, wittily capture in redoubled form what F. Davis (1961: p.123) calls "the familiar signs of discomfort and stickiness [in encounters between disabled and nondisabled people]...the artificial levity, the compulsive loquaciousness." The second pleasure is a lyric pleasure: the rhythmic repetition and italicizing of the word "Reason," which mark the poem's conclusion not with the effect of the overheard, but with the effect of writing and refrain—of poetry calling attention to itself.

I close by invoking these pleasures, mindful of Simi Linton's (1998: p.112) forceful point that:

> the capacity to engage in pleasurable activity—experiences sought for their own sake, for the stimulation and enjoyment they provide—is assumed to be out of reach of the disabled. This notion is fed by deterministic arguments that accord tremendous weight to disability, in effect saying that it eclipses pleasure, joy, and to an extent, creativity...The humanities and the arts can benefit from an analysis of who in society is believed to be entitled to pleasure and who is thought to have the capacity to provide pleasure.

Focusing on the pleasures of Miles' poetry, I hope I have shown how those pleasures incorporate, and help us to grasp, "disability." "Writers are needed," Linton continues, "who can demonstrate that success in terms of disability is more than a personal triumph over physical adversity; it is a life that consciously reckons with the social forces that oppress and control." In her own time and in her own way, Josephine Miles provided such a reckoning.

SUSAN SCHWEIK

Josephine Miles

Doll

Though the willows bent down to shelter us where we played
House in the sandy acres, though our dolls,
Especially Lillian, weathered all the action,
I kept getting so much earlier home to rest
That medical consultation led to cast
From head to toe. It was a surprise for my parents
And so for me also, and I railed
Flat out in the back seat on the long trip home
In which three tires blew on our trusty Mitchell.
Home, in a slight roughhouse of my brothers,
It turned out Lillian had been knocked to the floor and broken
Across the face. Good, said my mother
In her John Deweyan constructive way,
Now you and Lillian can be mended together.
We made a special trip to the doll hospital
To pick her up. But, they can't fix her after all, my father said,
You'll just have to tend her with her broken cheek.
I was very willing. We opened the box, and she lay
In shards mixed among tissue paper. Only her eyes
Set loose on a metal stick so they would open
And close, opened and closed, and I grew seasick.

Album

This is a hard life you are having
While you are young,
My father said,
As I scratched my casted knees with a paper knife.
By laws of compensation
Your old age should be grand.

Not grand, but of a terrible
Compensation, to perceive
Past the energy of survival
In its sadness
The hard life of the young.

Motive

A window in the shadowed room where I lay
Opened on a dark brick wall
And high beyond, the sooty block
Of buildings stood in rain.

Heat in bones under blankets burned
With aspirin. Keeping me warm,
What else? Grandfather shrugged.
Stepgrandmother reheated the hot milk.

Later she brought also a small box
Which turned out to be filled with six small bottles.
Of perfumes, assorted, six colors,
Oho! There is something to life!

Intensives

Loving intensives of Intensive Care
Bear down on your given name,
Margaret, attend, attend now
Margaret, they call you to live intensely
At the moment of your medication.

What if for a while they call you Frances?
Enjoy this intensive
Error, it frees you,
You can float in Frances,
Sip Frances liquids.

What I wait for is the intensive moment
When you flip, turn over, look around.
Well, hello, Dolly, back where
Hello, Dolly,
Where you belong.

Payment

The time sticks, the crazy anesthetic

Bloodless brain and open throat,

Wild weak angry coming home,

The ambulance orderly listing at each intersection

Fatal accidents he had seen there,

What parts severed, what held by a thread.

Under the sycamores, past my mother cracked by the gate,

My stretcher carried all the falling leaves,

Until I found my checkbook under me

And wrote the slipshod check.

Weak, wild, a saccharine

Taste in every food, and saccharine

In every voice I asked help of.

Slowly his help, the sharp egoist's,

Slowly avoiding the favors of his colleagues,

Slowly turns to pillow, footsole, diet,

These smaller makeshifts in their saltier tones.

My barbed-wire heart

I turn on when I turn

Keeps count the compromises of his role, deepening

As skill concedes to sense.

THE DISABILITY POETICS MOVEMENT

Jim Ferris

KEEPING THE KNIVES SHARP

In November 2010 the Library of Congress announced that Lucia Perillo was to receive the Rebekah Johnson Bobbitt National Prize for Poetry for her book *Inseminating the Elephant*. The prize is awarded "for the most distinguished book of poetry published in the preceding two years," according to the news release.

"In her 30s," the release reports, "Perillo was diagnosed with multiple sclerosis. She has written about her illness with humor and honesty ever since, but her poetry is not totally defined by it."

Not totally defined by it. Not totally. Not...totally.

My hips are aching quite a bit this weekend...perhaps because of the impending storm front, the first great snowfall of the season...or perhaps just because I am alive with used hips. I love to ask *why*, even though I suspect sometimes I may sound like a three-year-old. I am not always persuaded by the answers—especially the ones *I* provide—often not persuaded that there even *are* answers. If I were, I might ask why my left hip aches right now, even though it has no nerves, even though it is no longer bone and sinew but rather a machine, an elegant architecture of titanium and high-test plastic. Does it ache to remind me of the hip that was, to claim its rightful place as my hip?

Dame Evelyn Glennie is renowned as an amazing percussionist, the first full-time solo percussionist in classical music, all the more amazing because she has been profoundly deaf since the age of twelve. Glennie might be described as the epitome of the "overcoming overachiever": she started losing her hearing at age eight, but with the help of her percussion teacher Ron Forbes she spent hours upon hours schooling herself to feel sound vibrations with other parts of her body. "I would stand with my hands against the classroom wall while Ron played notes on the timpani (timpani produce a lot of vibrations)," she wrote in "The Hearing Essay." "Eventually I managed to distinguish the rough pitch of notes by associating where on my body I felt the sound with the sense of perfect pitch I had before losing my hearing. The low sounds I feel mainly in my legs and feet and high sounds might be particular places on my face, neck, and chest."

Symmetry is a fundamental principle of human endeavor: we see it, and we seek it, all around us: in nature, in our bodies, but also in the things we humans make. In mathematics, chemistry, physics and biology; in engineering and technology; in art and architecture—symmetry is something that resonates in us, it is the order that we impose on a sometimes unruly universe, it is the predictability that we may at times burn to disrupt.

But what would it mean to have a different starting point, a different foundation, a different center...or to have no center? What would it mean to live in a world that understood asymmetry as a prime characteristic? To live in a world sensitized by a crip aesthetic?

"I see the body as a huge ear," Glennie said. She has seemed rather put out at all the attention that her deafness has attracted. "Deafness does not mean that you can't hear, only that there is something wrong with the ears. Even someone who is totally deaf can still hear/feel sounds."

Hearing is still fundamental to Glennie's musicianship. What she has developed is a way to hear differently, a way to experience and make sense of sound that privileges other parts of the body more than her ears.

Finding ways to do things differently is a hallmark of living with disability—and a hallmark of disability culture.

Bodies are not absolute. As an artist, as a disabled person, as one who believes in the possibility of social as well as personal change, I resist any attempts to make our bodies determinative, to keep disabled people in their places, to force our bodily facts to be destiny. Every body has limits, to be sure. But what we can accomplish within those limits must not be constrained by the limits in the thinking of the nondisabled people—and even the disabled people—around us.

But my disabled body surely informs my consciousness; I am not a disabled mind that happened to land on a disabled flower for a moment. Neuroscience shows not only that body and mind are inseparable but that bodily differences affect brain development and how brains work. For example, studies suggest that the brains of left-handed people work differently than those of righties—not that one is better or worse, but that different brain regions are used to accomplish the same tasks. Comparable differences appear between deaf and hearing people and between blind and sighted people. Disability changes things, not only social conditions but physical circumstances. If the

JIM FERRIS

working of the mind/brain is changed by differences in handedness, it is a reasonable extrapolation that the different embodiments that come with physical as well as mental disabilities will also change how the mind/brain works. And whether disability influences one's being-in-the-world through nature, nurture, or, inevitably, both—disability does affect how one experiences and responds to the world we find ourselves in. And so it cannot help but have an impact on the artistic production of people so marked.

In "Disability Essay," Dame Evelyn cautions against disabled people forming community, fearing that such community will reinforce a sense of separateness from the larger society. But she also expresses concern that "impaired communities" will lead disabled people to think of themselves as inferior to nondisabled people, to accept the stigma that is thrust upon them by the normalized world.

But for many disabled people, including poets, musicians and other artists, connection with other people with disabilities can be affirming, empowering and generative. The rugged individualist is a trope that is hard to sustain in contemporary life, harder still for disabled people. Disability culture, which values interdependence over the illusion of independence, privileges not a uniform perspective but the validity and value of a wide range of ways of moving through the world—and the varied perspectives those different experiences engender.

When I first wrote about what I called "crip poetry," I was seeking not only to describe things I was seeing among a small number of poets, but also things I wanted to see, particularly a flowering of a poetry that did not make so big a deal of the differences called *disability* but did not take them for granted either. A poetry that grew out of disability culture, that didn't have to be "about disability" all the time but didn't shy away from it either, that was based in what I was beginning to understand as "crip poetics," a poetics that valorizes the wide range of ways of being in and responding to the world, that claims space for alternative, non-normative experience, language, thought and feeling.

Are we there yet? Hardly. The larger world of American poetry pays little attention to disabled poets so far, with a few exceptions, not unlike how the larger world of American culture pays modest attention at best to contemporary poetry. And it is worth noting that the disabled poets who seem to get the most attention often write about their disability while asserting that disability does not define them—a rhetorical tack that fits squarely into the "overcoming overachiever" disability stereotype so reassuring to the nondisabled population. Disability identity and disability culture are seen to threaten well-established systems for understanding and valuation, so perhaps it is best just to stick with the same tired tropes and schemes.

There is rich irony here, dammit and thank God. Audience is essential to artistic expression. Audience completes the circuit. But if we pay too much attention to chasing audience, we will be scurrying this way and that, forever changing direction to chase the fickle and fleeting flicker of mainstream attention and approbation. Then we lose the value of the marginalized: the perspective to see what we see, perceive what we perceive, to bring language together with thought and feeling in order to make something that may never be highly valued in the hurly-burly of the sacred marketplace (apostasy!) but is important, challenging, real. If producing bestsellers were most important to us, we likely wouldn't have chosen poetry as a literary genre, we likely wouldn't have responded when poetry chose us.

"My job is all about listening," Dame Evelyn Glennie told the TED Conference in February 2003. "My aim really is to teach the world to listen...It sounds quite simple but actually it's quite a big, big job."

So what is a future for crip poetry? I'm not sure what the present for it is, let alone a future. For me the idea of crip poetry provides a description, a way for me to think about some of what I seek to do, an invitation to community. Poetic community is always to a great extent imagined (to draw upon Benedict Anderson's concept of the nation as *imagined community*): poets trace their connections, their influences, their ancestry, across time and space, across manifesto and school, across national and continental boundaries, even across language. Building a usable past is always a constructive process—like the famous M.C. Escher image of two hands drawing each other into existence, the past shapes us even as we find and construct the past. Who poets look to in past and present, who we seek to engage in conversation may be as telling as anything. I want to be in conversation, with Yeats and Hopkins, Shakespeare and Pope, Auden and Roethke, Larry Eigner and Vassar Miller, Jo Miles and Gwendolyn Brooks and so many others now gone. (Ask me tomorrow and the list might be entirely different.) But I also want to engage my fellow crips, my brother and sister poets, and our contemporaries in the larger culture and the larger world. Ambitious? You bet. Because I still think that poetry can change the world. Though those changes may seem impossibly small—a phrase here, a feeling there, an idea that may eventually find fertile ground—though they may be subtle, I've got some changes I'd like to see. I hope that's one future for crip poetry.

My hip is feeling better right now. I know it's there, but tonight it is not grinding away at wit and goodwill as it sometimes does, and for that I am grateful. In an interview recently I was asked if artists today have responsibilities to those who come after us. I said something about doing our best work, about setting the bar as high as we can. But what I wish I'd said is what I hope: to keep the knives sharp and the guitar tuned, to leave the door open, not to drink up all the liquor or breathe up all the air. After that...

Poet of Cripples

Let me be a poet of cripples,
of hollow men and boys groping
to be whole, of girls limping toward
womanhood and women reaching back,
all slipping and falling toward the cavern
we carry within, our hidden void,
a place for each to become full, whole,
room of our own, space to grow in ways
unimaginable to the straight
and the narrow, the small and similar,
the poor, normal ones who do not know
their poverty. Look with care, look deep.
Know that you are a cripple too.
I sing for cripples; I sing for you.

Normal

Across Oak Park Avenue
is a city park, lush
and busy, where men play softball all

evening, too far away
to watch, their dim voices
drifting across the green. Their cars line

the streets as far
as I can see. Sammy and I,
Robert and I, Hoffmann and I call out

the makes and models
as the cars pass. *Dodge Dart.*
Chevy Nova. We are seldom wrong—*Corvair,*

Pontiac GTO—we who drive
wheelchairs and banana carts—
Mustang, VW, Rambler American—who have not yet

rounded second—
'57 Chevy! My dad had one of those—
who watch out windows a world so soft—*T-bird*—

so fair—*Corvette*—
so normal—*Ford Fairlane*—
a world going on, going by, going home.

Poems with Disabilities

I'm sorry—this space is reserved
for poems with disabilities. I know
it's one of the best spaces in the book,
but the Poems with Disabilities Act
requires us to make all reasonable
accommodations for poems that aren't
normal. There is a nice space just
a few pages over—in fact (don't
tell anyone) I think it's better
than this one, I myself prefer it.
Actually I don't see any of those
poems right now myself, but you never know
when one might show up, so we have to keep
this space open. You can't always tell
just from looking at them either. Sometimes
they'll look just like a regular poem
when they roll in...you're reading along
and suddenly everything
changes, the world tilts
a little, angle of vision
jumps, your entrails aren't
where you left them. You
remember your aunt died
of cancer at just your age
and maybe yesterday's twinge means
something after all. Your sloppy,
fragile heart beats
a little faster

JIM FERRIS

and then you know.

You just know:

the poem

is right

where it

belongs.

From the Surgeons: Drs. Sofield, Louis, Hark, Alfini, Millar, Baehr, Bevan-Thomas, Tsatsos, Ericson, and Bennan

6-10-60. History. This child is the second of three
children—the other two are perfectly normal. He was the product
of a normal pregnancy and delivery. At birth it was noted
that the left lower extremity was shorter than the right. The child
had a fragmentation and rodding of the left femur
for stimulation of bone growth. Prior to that procedure a 2″ discrepancy
existed. This procedure was repeated in 1957 and again in 1958. Prior
to the procedure in 1958 a 2″ discrepancy was again noted. The child's
early development was normal. He has, of course, been periodically set back
in his physical progress because of the surgical procedures.

6-10-60. Physical Examination. Head: There is nothing
abnormal about the head. Left lower extremity: There appears
to be only a very moderate degree of atrophy in the left thigh, but
this is explainable on the basis of his surgical procedures.
Gait is moderately abnormal but caused only
by the leg length discrepancy.

7-28-61. History. He began sitting at six months of age, walked
at one year, and began talking at about one year of age. There have been
some periods of regression following the early surgical procedures. The boy
is attending school and is apparently well adjusted.

7-28-61. Physical Examination. Examination reveals a slight
compensatory scoliosis. This is corrected by equalization of leg lengths.
This boy walks with a left short leg limp. He is able to run without difficulty,
and can hop on his right foot, but he is unable to hop on his left foot.
When performing the duck waddle his left leg leads the right.

JIM FERRIS

12-7-62. Neurological Examination. Deep tendon reflexes
are physiological. There is a slight diminution of the left knee jerk
as contrasted with that on the right. No sensory loss nor pathologic reflexes.

8-28-63. Progress Notes. The mother relates that the boy has been
stumbling more and more in recent weeks. His quadriceps are
quite weak, probably from the multiple surgical procedures
done on this thigh. Quadriceps are rather bound down at the knee.
The leg length discrepancy is 3″ and it is very difficult
to have a satisfactory shoe lift on this dimension. A long leg brace
was ordered with knee locks and with a 2″ pylon extension.

11-8-63. Progress Notes. This boy has received his long leg brace
with the caliper extension today. The brace is satisfactory,
except for the fact that the ankle joint is rigid and
he has a great deal of difficulty getting his trousers on and off
and needs to split the seams.

8-14-64. Progress Notes. This child who is almost 10 years of age
is wearing a long leg brace with a stilt on it, but the mother says
that he objects to this and apparently is undergoing considerable
emotional disturbance. The mother has noticed this since his return
from the hospital at which time he had a repeat fragmentation and rodding.

4-7-67. Physical Examination. Lower extremities: Circumference:
There is obvious atrophy of the left thigh: This cannot
be accurately compared with the right because of the shortness
of the extremity and the dislocation of the patella.

6-6-69. History. The child is in the ninth grade and does fair
and goes to a regular school.

10-30-70. Progress Notes. Final Discharge. The patient is essentially

unchanged since last visit. His leg lengths measured to the heel

on the right measures 101 and 86 on the left from the anterior superior

iliac spine. He has occasional episodes of pain. He is still

wearing the long leg brace with the high lift below

and there was no indication on the mother's part that she plans

on having anything done in the near future.

Lost Hyoid

Two hundred bones in the human body,
they wait for me to die so they can tell
their stories uninterrupted—I wait
for different reasons, surround each bone
with my ignorance, phalanges, metacarpals,
spongy hollows in surprising places,
it's the joints that give the trouble, the twist,
the shout, worn away, worn out-
side in, I knew a woman, lovely in her bones,
I jousted with the emperor of bones,
he always wins, talus, fibula, tibia,
calcium and phosphorus are his elements,
and time weeps for no hand, radius, ulna,
humerus—insert joke here—the smallest bone
is the stapes, the stirrup which rides across
your ear—hear? But the lost hyoid connects—
roll this over your tongue—to no other bone.

Kenny Fries

from STARING BACK:
THE DISABILITY EXPERIENCE FROM THE INSIDE OUT

*We've been shadow spirits lost between our nondisabled (for most of us) upbringing
and our disability lessons in life.* —CAROL GILL, Ph.D.

Throughout history, people with disabilities have been stared at, defined by the gaze and the needs of the nondisabled world. Many times, those who live with disabilities have been isolated in institutions, experimented upon, exterminated. We who live with disabilities have been silenced by those who did not want to hear what we have to say. We have also been silenced by our own fear, the fear that if we told our stories people would say: "See, it isn't worth it. You would be better off dead."

Over two decades ago, when I first began searching for the words with which to begin speaking about my own experience living with a congenital physical disability, a disability I was born with for no known scientific reason, a disability with no medical name except for the generic "congenital deformities of the lower extremities"—one way of saying I was missing bones in both legs. In the summer of 1989, I took the initial steps of finding the language, unearthing the images, shaping the forms with which I could express an experience I had never read about before, so that my experience as a person with a disability could become meaningful to others.

What I remember most about that summer is wanting to throw all those drafts away, not thinking them poems. Not having a role model whose steps I could follow, unsure of my own identity as both a writer and a person who lives with a disability, I felt like one of those "shadow spirits" Carol Gill writes about, unable to meld successfully on the page the nondisabled world I lived in with my experience of being disabled in that world.

I also felt afraid. I felt a fear that Anne Finger was writing about at almost the same time in *Past Due: A Story of Disability, Pregnancy, and Birth.* In *Past Due,* Finger recounts her experience at a feminist conference when she talked about her inhumane treatment as a child in the hospital because of complications from polio. After Finger publicly shared her story, a colleague said: "If you had been my child, I would have killed you before I let that happen. I would have killed myself, too." Finger reacted:

My heart stops. She is telling me I should not be alive. It is my old fear come true. That if you talk about the pain, people will say, "See it isn't worth it. You would be better off dead."

If this was a friend's response to Finger's experience, how would my friends, not to mention those who did not know me, react to what I had to say? And, after knowing what I had gone through, how could they believe there was so much more to living with my disability than pain?

A lot has happened since I first began to write about my experiences living with a disability. In 1990, the process—which began in 1968 with the Architectural Barriers Act and sections 504 and P.L. 94-162 of the Rehabilitation Act of 1973—culminated in the passage of the Americans with Disabilities Act, called the most far-reaching civil rights legislation since the Civil Rights Act of 1964. As historian Paul K. Longmore points out, with the ADA's passage, even as the "quest for civil rights, for equal access and equal opportunity, for inclusion" continues, we have moved on to a second phase, which he defines as "a quest for collective identity" in which "the task is to explore or to create a disability culture":

> Beyond proclamations of pride, deaf and disabled people have been uncovering or formulating sets of alternative values derived from within the deaf and disabled experience...They declare they prize not self-sufficiency, but self-determination, not independence but interdependence, not functional separateness but personal connection, not physical autonomy but human community.

As we move away from viewing disability within the confines of the moral and medical models, we are moving toward a social definition of disability. As social scientist Victor Finkelstein so concisely states, whereas in the medical model the "focus of attention is firmly on the physically impaired individual," now it shifts to where "the focus is the nature of society which disables physically impaired people."

That the disability experience is not solely rooted in bodily impairment is evidenced by how the definition of disability changes from society to society. What is considered a disability in some societies, for example club—or flat—feet is not considered a disability in others. And what was considered a disability in our culture years ago would no longer be considered a disability today. Consider poor eyesight before eyeglasses, for example. In a preliterate, agrarian society, visual acuity, the need to read print or traffic signs, was not necessary or could be compensated for.

Viewed from this perspective, it is clear that it is the barriers, both physical and attitudinal, that need to be changed, not the impairments or the bodies with which we live. I have asked numerous disabled persons what causes them more difficulty, the disability itself or the discriminatory barriers put in their way. The answer is overwhelmingly the latter.

The experiences of those with disabilities prove that there are countless different ways of moving through the world. But old models die hard. Literature, which reflects the richness of the different ways we conceptualize how we live within the world and the ways the world lives within us, thankfully does not, and should not, conform to the dictates of current political or social discourse.

What differentiates the oppression and discrimination of the disabled from other traditionally marginalized groups is that in one quick instant—a slip in the bathtub, a virus-borne disease—anyone can join us, the disabled (currently estimated at 54 million in the United States). In fact, at some time in our lives, each and every one of us, sooner or later, will be, whether for short term or long, in some way disabled. Because of this, those of us who live with disabilities are viewed with a fear, though irrational, that is perhaps too easy to understand. (And if there's one thing those of us who live with disabilities understand, it is change.) Ultimately, those of us who live with disabilities are too often treated as unwelcome reminders of the mortality that is the fate of us all.

Over the years, I learned that I was not alone in my struggle to give voice to the disability experience, an experience that throughout history has been marginalized or co-opted, if not ignored. It is my hope that my work is just one step in an ongoing effort to bring the lives of those of us who live with disabilities closer to the center, where a truer understanding of the richness of our lives can be forged.

Excavation

Tonight, when I take off my shoes:
three toes on each twisted foot.

I touch the rough skin. The holes
where the pins were. The scars.

If I touch them long enough will I find
those who never touched me? Or those

who did? *Freak, midget, three-toed
bastard*. Words I've always heard.

Disabled, crippled, deformed. Words
I was given. But tonight I go back

farther, want more, tear deeper into
my skin. Peeling it back I reveal

the bones at birth I wasn't given—
the place where no one speaks a word.

Body Language

What is a scar if not the memory of a once open wound?
You press your finger between my toes, slide

the soap up the side of my leg, until you reach
the scar with the two holes, where the pins were

inserted twenty years ago. Leaning back, I
remember how I pulled the pin from my leg, how

in a waist-high cast, I dragged myself
from my room to show my parents what I had done.

Your hand on my scar brings me back to the tub
and I want to ask you: What do you feel

when you touch me there? I want you to ask me:
What are you feeling now? But we do not speak.

You drop the soap in the water and I continue
washing, alone. Do you know my father would

bathe my feet, as you do, as if it was the most
natural thing. But up to now, I have allowed

only two pair of hands to touch me there,
to be the salve for what still feels like an open wound.

The skin has healed but the scars grow deeper—
When you touch them what do they tell you about my life?

KENNY FRIES

Beauty and Variations

1.

What is it like to be so beautiful? I dip
my hands inside you, come up with—*what*?

Beauty, at birth applied, does not transfer
to my hands. But every night, your hands

touch my scars, raise my twisted limbs to
graze against your lips. Lips that never

form the words—*you are beautiful*—transform
my deformed bones into—*what?*—if not beauty.

Can only one of us be beautiful? Is this your
plan? Are your sculpted thighs more powerful

driving into mine? Your hands find their way
inside me, scrape against my heart. Look

at your hands. Pieces of my skin trail from
your fingers. What do you make of this?

Your hands that know my scars, that lift me to your
lips, now drip my blood. Can blood be beautiful?

2.

I want to break your bones. Make them so
they look like mine. Force you to walk on

twisted legs. Then, will your lips still beg
for mine? Or will that disturb the balance

of our desire? Even as it inspires, your body
terrifies. And once again I find your hands

inside me. Why do you touch my scars? You
can't make them beautiful any more than I can

tear your skin apart. Beneath my scars,
between my twisted bones, hides my heart.

Why don't you let me leave my mark? With no
flaws on your skin—how can I find your heart?

3.
How much beauty can a person bear? Your smooth
skin is no relief from the danger of your eyes.

My hands would leave you scarred. Knead the muscles
of your thighs. I want to tear your skin, reach

inside you—your secrets tightly held. Breathe
deep. Release them. Let them fall into my palms.

My secrets are on my skin. Could this be why
each night I let you deep inside? Is that

where my beauty lies? Your eyes, without secrets,
would be two scars. I want to seal your eyes,

they know my every flaw. Your smooth skin, love's
wounds ignore. My skin won't mend, is callused, raw.

4.
Who can mend my bones? At night, your hands press
into my skin. My feet against your chest, you mold

my twisted bones. What attracts you to my legs? Not
sex. What brings your fingers to my scars is beyond

desire. Why do you persist? Why do you touch me
as if my skin were yours? Seal your lips. No kiss

can heal these wounds. No words unbend my bones.
Beauty is a two-faced god. As your fingers soothe

my scars, they scrape against my heart. Was this
birth's plan—to tie desire to my pain, to stain

love's touch with blood? If my skin won't heal, how
can I escape? My scars are in the shape of my love.

5.
How else can I quench this thirst? My lips
travel down your spine, drink the smoothness

of your skin. I am searching for the core:
What is beautiful? Who decides? Can the laws

of nature be defied? Your body tells me: come
close. But beauty distances even as it draws

me near. What does my body want from yours?
My twisted legs around your neck. You bend

me back. Even though you can't give the bones
at birth I wasn't given, I let you deep inside.

You give me—*what?* Peeling back my skin, you
expose my missing bones. And my heart, long

before you came, just as broken. I don't know who
to blame. So each night, naked on the bed, my body

doesn't want repair, but longs for innocence. If
innocent, despite the flaws I wear, I am beautiful.

Petra Kuppers

THE SOUND OF THE BONES

S ince I was a little girl, I have been fascinated with Greek mythology, sung in verse. That world explained my world to me. In these stories, there were always so many people I could feel myself into, try out different characters one at a time. Of course, I would not just be limping Eurydice, her foot bitten by a snake, now on wobbly feet trying to escape the world of the shades, only to be betrayed by her lover's glance—I would be searching Orpheus, too, using his sweet words to extricate his beloved out of Hades, only to lose her again. And I would also be Agave, the queenly leader of the Bacchae, those wild women who eventually rip the singer apart in their drunken, ecstatic revels, or, even, Bacchus or Dionysius himself, laughing at the young king who tries to defy a god who has set the king's people on fire with wine and love. Transformation, transgression, cruelty and sex: these were the Greeks I devoured from early on.

And although I would have to reach far, far back to find actual memories to support my observation, as I grew older I felt sure that this fascination had an origin in my own bodily being, in the difference I finally pronounced and outed as *disabled* many years later. I have found on Mount Olympus my land, my people. People who limped, fell down where they stood with inexplicable pain, people who were daily visited by tortures, and yet lived, and were defiant, not meek. I found the Sirens—women with body parts made of brass, called disfigured and yet singing beautifully. I found my avenger fantasy, Medusa, the woman who could kill with one look—who could turn to stone any boy who'd come to laugh at her.

Greek myths, and Greek themes—I still find them, and they find me, in the pages of disability poetry. Sometimes, they seem obscured by a political will that denounces them for their meaning, their hold over disabled cultural lives. But they are names of old stories, and powerful, as feminists know when they long to hear Medusa's laugh: they are not easily contained, not framed and done away with. Just like tricksters and other figures of many other traditions, they infiltrate, and their longings leave their mark deep in my bones.

In the summer of 2006, during a disability culture graduate seminar at the Institute for Medical Humanities in Galveston, Texas, we held a crip poetry banquet. We had just spent an afternoon watching and discussing poetry in non-written formats, such as Shelley Barry's film/video *Trilogy*, which shows us that "scars need to be crowned, too," stitched and loved and clad in beads, and a video of Peter Cook and Kenny Lerner's Deaf performance poetry where hands give birth to words and worlds in wide swooping gesture. That evening, we went low-tech over crab meat and shrimp in the private room of a restaurant. Dionysian wine prepared us for the task: a reading of crip poetry.

That evening of the poetry banquet, around the table, my students and I discussed a word that vexes me and thrills me, *cripple*, and how it echoes so differently to disabled and non-disabled audiences—an issue often on the table in our shared time, and one that provides much exciting material for discussion. The language skills of my bones, as well as those of others in our class community who identify as disabled, read a halting step meter differently than those of someone who strides out straight and full, and we found often that members of crip culture are attuned to the small shifts of pain breath, or fluttering fingers, or a furrow building between the eyes.

In *Angel of Healing*, Welsh poet laureate Gwyneth Lewis gives voice to an old *ars poetica*. Her angel, another mythological figure of poetry, speaks: "Every disease is a work of art / if you play it rightly."

She teases out the implications: "By this he meant: whatever the form / Imposed by arthritis, or by the gout / Your job's to compose yourself around about / Its formal restrictions, and make that sing, / Even to death /..."

And yes, the poet's body as the source of a poem's breath shapes the specific alignment of contour ridges and experiences that make sound. Her own sound lilts strongly on my tongue, a tongue that got used to and familiar to English sounds in the bilingual valleys of Wales. Lewis' Welsh-English tones are still so much closer to home to me than American poetry. But while I share that kinship with her, crip culture offers me another land and language. To go beyond the individual form, tensely just on the limit, self and non-self, communicating-just-about: that is the trajectory of poetic force. To give a poem a home in the country called disabled, as American poet Neil Marcus does in "Disabled Country," means to stake out a claim that goes beyond one's individual body:

> If there was a country called disabled,
> I would be from there.
> I live disabled culture, eat disabled food,
> make disabled love, cry disabled tears,
> climb disabled mountains and tell disabled stories.

To claim disability as an identity, rather than a shape for an individual body, means struggle, submission, elation, comradeship and a location. The form around which a body of work composes itself is no longer the tension between the abstraction of language and the specificity of one's individual bodily being. Instead, a third can enter: a way of knowing, a structure of feeling, of being in community that does not subsume the individual, but can provide a different baseline, one in which *the disease* or *difference* has a different register, and where some things can be left unsaid, implicit, homely—a shared myth. Marcus ends his poem:

> In my life's journey
> I am making myself
> At home in my country

To make oneself at home: to find stories, fit old ones to new landscapes, invent traditions, give birth to language. Publishing in the U.K. mental health system survivor journal *Poetry Express*, Wilma Kenny writes in her poem "Odyssey," "Like a reptile / I clung to a tree of normality," and again, it is myth that gives shape to a disabled country that can hardly be spoken, and only painfully heard, as Odysseus, lashed to the mast after stopping up his sailors' ears, listens to the songs of the sirens. Scavenging on ancient wanderings can provide the building materials for shape-shifting habitations. Here, chameleons can find tenuous purchase, a clasping of vowels and consonants that offer a hold, shape and heft that sustains.

That land, disabled country, has many shapes, forces and myths—and the Greek myths are some of the building stones, some of the books, that those who claim disabled country can use. They can build contradictory homes, with different keys for different people, make people think of their limbs and their senses, their breath, as they enter this world.

One of the citizens of disabled country is Philip Dowd, an Australian poet. In his poem "New/Unnamed," he rides on a different river, catches a different wave, finds and lives a different breath. He also acknowledges access issues in disability culture poetry: an asterisk opens up meaning and explanation, asking me to bring different sensibilities to poetry appreciation, to look beyond a poem's shape on a page. I read and honor this gesture as a commentary on the histories of exclusion that crip culture people have faced in education and beyond:

PETRA KUPPERS

Cerebral palsy moves as in tides
Sometimes high, sometimes low,
And I must follow.

Tidally something cosmic
Moves through me
The comic
The forge
Haphaestus.*

My body changes
Patterns
Become
Shifting
Desert like
The sand and time.

Born again
With each muscular contraction,
The excitement
The challenge
The new me.
begins

* Greek god of fire and Volcanism was the artisan of the gods and perceived disabled.

This poem opens me onto a land of contradiction, of watery dryness, tidal burn. Here is a desert forge, a dry basin that is old and new. The lines are short, condensing as they go, to the "begins"—open-ended, a new sentence, pushing forward. An "I" appears belated, entering the land of the poem after the conditions of being, those tides—beholden to some other star, or moon, or something that exerts its force. What could be elegiac, long-flowing—an acknowledgment of a control elsewhere, a surrender in romantic verse—is precise, specific, condensing downwards into individual words: "Haphaestus" and "begins." To read this poem, I gasp, quickly, as the lines chop across my breath, making me weigh the length of each syllable, the cost of the word. The intake and outflow of breath are audible to me as I read, again and again, following the punctuations into pauses. Again, a different bodily being presses against my ear, onto my tongue, into my windpipe. I sing a new rhythm into my bones, and enjoy the ride.

Is Dowd singing himself into being, like Whitman did, willing connection—or is he sung? Who sings, and how do Haphaestus' anvil and hammer strike sparks out of movement? The forge is at the heart here: the heat of creation, of coming into being. Hephaestus is the maker-god, the anvil-god, the one who makes nice playthings (like the first woman, Pandora) for the other inmates of Olympus. He is the craftsman of the gods, who can create out of nothing: Poesis. Vulcan in his Roman guise, this god remembers the material of his body. He doesn't just hasten away, unthinking—for he limps, and better thinks through where he's going. His foot is an undefined mass, yet-to-be-shapen (like Byron's, the devil, the fallen angels)—always a draw with the poets. He is also Venus' husband, horned a few times, but game for a laugh about it, it seems.

I can hear that hammer coming down, hammering matter into fiery shape, in each breath drilling the lines of the poem, the "New/Unnamed," that can be made by the god of cripples. The weight of the hammer, "each muscular contraction:" Words are heavy, and create a new beginning. The "I" of the poem is wrenched between forces of astral bodies, god-bodies, but can withstand the heat, and spreads itself out, like "sand and time" across a new land, a new body, a new breath. What "I" this "begins" will point to, mould and sing, is not fixed yet.

Would a non-crip culture reader read differently? Would the first two words of this poem, "cerebral palsy," paralyze the reading, would the chopped breath become the in-take of the breath of fear, or worse, of pity? I do not know, since I live by the bylaws and rules of my land, disabled country, even if I rally against them from time to time. I like my insider status, even if it gives me no more insight into Dowd than my German passport gives me into another citizen there. Tourists are always despised, and there's fun to be had in the crip culture game, where I can suspend the attack of *palsy*, *paralysed*, *cripple* and *limp*, and riff around their wordy sound.

Poetry, and this skillful rearrangement of words and myths into new countries to live in, can add much to crip culture, measure its width and depth, turn our faces away for moments, at least, from the sub-cultural paradigm that requires us to bravely grin as we grope towards pride. Poetry offers a respite, a site of contradiction, a land uncharted: here be dragons.

PETRA KUPPERS

The Origin of My Wheelchair

It had foremothers, yes,
cradles an ancient history
drenched in veteran's blood, snakebite,
sepsis and the chlorophyll-rich juices of the healer.
But when I touch the steel wheel, I feel
that it grew as a silver plant
in a waterless waste, drew from a deep clear well,
a shoot pushed hard through the crust,
thrust past caked clay and grey rock.
With the effort of metal and bone,
the plant grasped the air, no resistance
pressed fast moving cells,
it arched up, spiraled back onto itself,
completed a circle that pushes far out,
forward, on and on:
my body, propelled by evergreen forces,
touches fire and earth, forge and flow,
my finger tight on the rim.
I know what I wish for:
below not only clouded blood,
clay clod, and the deep worm's coil,
below runs the clear, clean water.

Crip Music

A beat behind, sycophant, you
Sisyphus, roll and run,
Sybil whistle in the dark
the shoe steps the rhythm
behind, behind, you
with the crutch cane stick beat
the cripple who ripples across
the street with the wheel on the rack
rackle and giggle the cripple
till the music stops.
We step out
and then, and then,
the sound,
melody of cane,
melody of crutch,
melody of wheel,
and the tap of the stick,
the tick of ventilators,
dilate, pulse,
push breath through the street,
roll forward and on.

PETRA KUPPERS

from Spherical Song Cycle

Mercury

Colors are stardust. Minerals cooled with the core.
Iron is red, copper blue, and sulfur yellow.
Let's live in a Steiner house,
edges round
no angles
saturated in color
glazed, in complex patterns, jeweled walls to code my life
Is it my purple phase?

Nervous system, nervously wriggling just next to my skin, so hungry for the
Vitamin D, which is how I think of sunlight, of course: it's good for me, right
now, in moderation. I will monitor.

Blue.
Or orange. In the bathroom
Koyaanisqatsi "a state of life that calls for another way of living"
Builders are so expensive these days.
It's the recession,
a regression,
a doom for the exploitation of the earth:
mined out, leaching,
red and white scars where the soil shifts.

Lemon yellow:
lemon so much less jaundiced,
jealous,
gelb, can you imagine that being good for you?
But the sour, and astringent, pulling it together, all together now, it's the
nesting idea: we live in insecure times.

Let's live in a Steiner house,
One here and one there, and no edges.
Organically, I fall all over myself to get to the sun
I hide in the cellar
my head pounds.
Eyes fall out.
Eyes grow hollow.
The back of the neck far away from the forehead that screams pinched from
above and pulled and
the bed offers not enough black.
Paint the world black behind your eyelids.
Blackness creeping over the world.

Paint black the room and the city and this strip of land and the snow and the
river and the whole of the US and the earth and the round marble in space
and space, and space itself, and the spaces between space
and then there is black to be painted
and space is black.

•

Aria — Mezzo

Invagination implies a confusion about the side you are on.
Which team do you play for
and what about the organs?
The heart
is more or less in the middle
you know, and you only hear it louder
on one side because there is more
for it to resonate with, the lungs
wrapped lobular
around the action-packed muscle
in its sac.

PETRA KUPPERS

metabolic acts lose direction
stuff gets shuttled aside into wastelands
I have to make the best of it.
Trash art, found object sculptures
exquisite corpse
never mind the old crystal image
feel it now,

this translucent sacrificial dagger sawing away at the membrane.
inflammatory responses attack the pollutant

help wouldn't hurt so much

let me speak with my liver

Daniel Simpson

LINE BREAKS THE WAY I SEE THEM

For several years, I apprenticed in writing poetry with Molly Peacock. Since Molly lives in Toronto, and I live near Philadelphia, I e-mailed her my work about a week prior to each phone conference so she could have time to look it over and prepare her response. When the lesson rolled around, I would call her on a speakerphone and tape our hour-long conversation. This proved to be an immensely useful process for me, since I didn't have to distract myself with taking notes during our "back and forth" about the poems; I could take those notes and make revisions later.

What impressed me most about my initial talks with Molly was the kind of questions she asked me before she critiqued a single word of mine: "How did you come to write poetry? With whom have you studied? What poets have most influenced you, and how? How has your poetry changed since you started? How would you describe the poetry you are writing now?"

When we turned to the poetry itself for the first time, Molly observed: "I notice that in many of the poems you sent me, you seem to make an effort to keep lines of nearly equal length. Is that intentional?"

"Yes," I said.

"Tell me your thinking behind it," she said, "because I find it a little puzzling."

I explained that Gregory Djanikian, my mentor and instructor at the University of Pennsylvania, found that even lines created a pleasing appearance on the page, and so, knowing how much I admired and resonated with his work, I took his suggestions about visual shaping of the poem into my own aesthetics.

"But that's exactly what leads me to wonder why you would care about the visual appearance," Molly rejoined. "Having lines of relatively the same length can make a poem look beautiful on the page, but that's a painterly thing to do. Why do you care how it looks on the page? You're blind, and that seems like a particularly sighted concern. Besides that, you're a musician. Wouldn't it make more sense in the context of your life to treat the poem and its line breaks more like a musical score than a painting?"

I had to admit this made some sense. As we talked more about it, I remembered how I always had to guess where the line breaks should come in this "even up" approach.

Perhaps I wouldn't have had to guess so much if I had been using the unabbreviated form of Braille, known as Grade 1 Braille, where there is a one-for-one correspondence between print and Braille letters. I, however, like most Braille users, write Grade 2 Braille, the standard for books and all forms of communication, which is replete with abbreviations for frequently encountered combinations of letters. Thus, two lines that look even in Grade 2 Braille will not necessarily come out that way in print, once all of the contractions have been expanded.

"For now, at least for your next couple of poems," Molly said, "why not try this? Don't worry about making the poem look pretty on the page. Just listen to your natural cadence and let the line breaks act as indicators in a musical score as to where you want the performers to breathe or to place more emphasis. And if one line sticks way out like a big shirt billowing on a clothesline, and the next line hangs like a limp little sock next to it, so be it. What do you care?"

I was intrigued. Besides, I generally take the attitude that if a mentor has agreed to devote time and attention to my development as a writer, I owe it to him or her to try his/her recommendations at least once.

Stuck without an idea for my next poem, I pondered Molly's suggestion that week... and then it came to me: use the billowing shirt and limp sock as opening images in a poem, and let the lines containing those images reflect them in length. This is where it took me:

Man Story

His rage hung in the house like a shirt billowing on a clothesline,
her silence
like a sock
beside it.

Decades ago, unmarried,
reading upstairs, sneaking off with Sally,
or flying model airplanes after school,
his dreams, like giant streamers or sky-writing, stretched out far behind him,
accompanying him everywhere.
"We've heard this story a million times before," you say.
"It's nothing new, so why do you go on about it so?"

Because it's nothing new,
and some like him came back from two world wars
and everything was supposed to be put behind them like the dead family dog
but then more came back from Korea and Vietnam,
the Gulf,
changed
utterly
to sit in multiplex movie theaters watching
as their great-grandfathers or men just like them made sure
someone else's wife and children got a life raft off the sinking ship—
to hack and spit in poorly-ventilated refineries
with sophisticated shower drains
that trapped the precious platinum residue
which washed off them like water-color paints.

The conscious choice to look at line length in this way somehow liberated my unconscious mind and my slightly more conscious "formal poetic" mind to collaborate in a new way. My unconscious mind took an echo from Yeats' "Easter, 1916," and turned it into the two shortest lines in the poem: "changed" and "utterly." Only later, when my conscious mind looked back on these two one-word lines did it imbue them with something symbolic; their brevity came to represent the abruptness of the change that war wreaks on someone's life. (One moment, you can walk; the next, you can't. One moment you feel relatively innocent; the next, you are a killer.) What I call my "slightly more conscious formal poetic mind," being a half-step behind the unconscious mind, realized, after the fact, that since I was allowing myself to play with lines of extremely varying lengths, I could consciously choose to make form follow content in a line like "his dreams, like giant streamers or sky-writing, stretched out far behind him."

In the poems I've written since "Man Story," principles of cadence and musical scoring guide my line breaks, but more moderately. I haven't felt the need to write another poem with such acute attention to "billowing shirt" and "limp sock" lines. At the same time, I have never again concerned myself with a painterly evenness of lines.

DANIEL SIMPSON

School for the Blind

Chair,
bed,
dresser.
New world
scaled down
small as the
cream-soft palms
of the four-year-old
left tonight
at the boarding school
in an open dorm,
(aisle nearest the lockers,
second bed down)
suitcase from home,
touch bed-spread
his hands pried
from his mother's skirt.

Best thing, she said:
braille and new playmates,
still home for the weekends.
Then they drove off.
Kathy and Connie
got to watch Lassie.

Down he lies.
Down he lies.

But tomorrow morning,
his shoelaces tied,

he will decide
to make new friends,
learn every language,
study the birds
to know how to sing,
read every book,
plot his escape,
and fly from the playground
on airplane swings.

Broken Reverie

I am not going to write a political poem,
but in my neighborhood, a truck is in reverse.
It has been backing up for a long time.
It beeps incessantly.
It has ruined my reverie.

When they were rebuilding the train station,
trucks backed up all night long.
Some people wrote the newspaper.
Get rid of those beepers, they said.

It's not good to write political poems.
They are so obvious.
That's why, any minute now,
I'm going to get back to my imagination.

But my blind friend made a simple decision one day—
simple as, shall I wear the knit dress
or wool pants to work?
She was just going to buy a sandwich;
she would leave her dog in the office
and take her white cane.

The truck had no beeper.
It was hard to know
in all that city noise
whether to stand still
or keep moving.

Soon I will be able
to stop writing polemics

and start writing poetry.
People want something fresh.
They don't need me
to repeat the obvious.

About Chester Kowalski I Don't Know Much

One morning, while we waited in line to see
the school nurse, he showed me how to fool a friend
through the power of suggestion.
Smacking his fist with his hand,
he pretended to crack an egg on top of my head,
then let his fingers drift like yolk down my hair.
I don't know where he learned it.
Perhaps a bigger, cooler, sighted brother,
who didn't have to go to boarding school,
duped the week before in front of girls,
had tried it out that weekend
when Chester had come home.
Or maybe it was his father who, like mine,
would show him the Full Nelson or a nest
some hornets built out back behind the shed.

I never asked him what his father did,
or what kinds of cookies his mother made for Christmas,
or his middle name,
but at night we breathed
the same fetid air of the open dorm
with thirty other eight- to ten-year-olds,
boys with healthy, shallow lungs who had played full tilt,
then said their prayers by rote—
"Now I lamey downda sleep."

I didn't know how much I didn't know
about him until they said he'd drowned
in the swimming pool. I walked past his empty bed,
heard them pack up his things,
and felt my breath against my hands.

A Few Things

I don't know how they keep you on a cross

when they first start the hammering.

I don't know how they make chocolate.

I don't know which parts of a tuna they put in a can

and what they do with the rest.

I don't know what I'll do with the rest of my life.

I don't know any more who sat

behind Bobby Sabol in fourth grade,

but Allen Hawk's dad worked for the phone company.

I don't know why we tell so many sad stories.

I don't know what the Skinheads next door talk about

or what the cockatiel lady likes for lunch.

I've heard that birds resolve disputes through singing contests.

I don't know what a rainbow looks like,

or that my life would be better if I could see one.

I don't know why I'm writing all of this down.

I know all the vegetables in V-8 juice.

There are at least a dozen ways to say "snow" in Inuit.

I know vulnerability is related to hope,

but I can't say how.

I don't know who killed the grooms in Duncan's room.

I don't know at what point you should retire a working dog.

They have three rollercoasters at Knoble's Grove.

My mother belly-laughed when we got splashed on The Flume.

Or maybe it's four. I can't remember now.

I don't know why some people give up and others don't.

Laura Hershey

GETTING COMFORTABLE

I just spent the past twenty minutes getting comfortable. "Move the head pillow down and a little to the right," I told Ruth, my attendant. "Push my shoulders up and to the right...a little more. Now push the pillow down again. Straighten out my hips please."

What I really wanted to do was write. First, though, I had to get comfortable. "Now could you pull my right knee to the left. More." It will be a while before another attendant comes—which is a good thing, offering promise of some quiet time, with just my partner Robin, without my having to instruct, advise, respond or wonder whether an aide is hearing and/or seeing the private words I dictate to my computer. But that precious time undisturbed is also time unaided. "Shift my hips a little more to the right. Then pull my feet down. Also, can you move my hands up a little." For a while at least, my body will have to stay in whatever position Ruth leaves it.

"Move my shoulders up and to the right," I said. "Hmm. Okay, now pull my hips down just a little...Now shoulders up again. No, straight up."

This went on for a while.

"My back still doesn't feel quite right," I said. "I think we need to start over. Sorry." I said "Sorry" even though Ruth had shown no sign of annoyance. "Could you lower the head of the bed. Take out the pillow for now...Okay, now, pull me up straighter by my arms, pretty far up...even further. Now scoot my hips to the right again. All right, let's raise the head of the bed again...There, stop. No, maybe a little higher. Good. Now will you put the pillow back under my head. Move it down and to the right. Pull my chin up, up and a little to the left. Now pull it straight up. And pull my right knee to the left."

I stopped to assess my position. "All right?" Ruth asked. "You comfortable?"

"Yeah," I answered. "So could you set up my lap table and my computer?"

"You sure?"

"*Yes*," I said, a little impatiently. I was anxious to write.

For a long time, and still sometimes, I have hidden the part of my life that involved the services of another woman's strong hands, arms, legs, back. I saw no literary potential in scenes like the one above. They were merely background music to my story, I thought, not the story itself. My simple, seemingly straightforward, first-person sentences conceal the truth of the help I need in order to carry out my daily actions. I say, "I went to the bookstore and looked through a dozen books and finally bought this book of poetry by Adrienne Rich"—(*not*, "Carmen drove me to the bookstore, and held a dozen books up for me to look at, turned the pages for me, put all of them back onto the shelf except for one by Adrienne Rich. Then Carmen got my wallet out of my purse for me and handed my credit card to the cashier, who rang up the sale."). My grammar gave no ground to the idea of dependency, for that's what I've heard it called in fundraising appeals and theoretical discussion. Instead, I spoke of my actions the way I feel them, as self-determined events filling my days. To people my scenes with a supporting cast might conjure me, the main actor, as a tragic figure, as a body with need but no will.

Readers, I feared, may not be able to read such a writer, may not relax enough to follow me on the paths I choose to chart. A reader must trust her writer, even if that means meeting only the physical writer, a floating intellect. So I deleted the dance of *turn, shift, lift, pull, push*.

Why now, then? Why reveal the tedious process involved in getting comfortable? Why not just forget about all that, and *write*?

"Just a minute," I say to Ruth. "Before you go, I need my knees straightened out. And pull my elbows outward and up a little bit. Also, could you scratch between my eyebrows...Good, thanks."

Why write about this? Why divulge the esoteric secrets of this craft of getting comfortable?

I could, and usually do, write without telling what it takes to get ready to write. I could disembody my writing, let my words *stand* alone, *march* across the page, a straight line of characters on paper, of ideas soaring through the ether. Text without context, at least without the physical context of its creation. A pretext of text, sexy or sexless. Text extracted from existence, text that excludes distress. I could write mind-over-matter text. Text expressing the best of the story; text repressing the rest of the story. (Or is it the other way around?)

Now my joints rest in comfortable positions. Each tissue-inch holds its proper share of weight and pressure. I'm breathing easily, my head well supported and turned to just the right angle, my back straight as it's going to get. Ruth is gone; Robin is in the next room. I sit in a silent space that awaits my words.

Laura Hershey

Now that I'm comfortable, I can start making choices. Do I start the story *here*, with my focused concentration and blank screen? Or do I start the story *there*, with the concentrated effort needed to assemble a body capable of thinking and writing? Do I write as disembodied mind, or discombobulated body?

I could try to write in the voice of a body easily arranged, a body requiring only a thoughtless stretch of limb or a self-controlled fidget to achieve comfort. Since that simple, graceful body is not my own, that would be the same as writing without a body.

If I leave behind my body to write, what (how) does the reader read? Can a reader read a mind without having a body to read?

On the other hand, when I write from, of, about a discombobulated body, how (what) does the reader read? Can a reader read a mind while worrying about a body?

And what about the writer? If I write about my body, will I disappear into the shadow of the taller, stronger, more mobile body of the woman working on my body? Will her quick, easy movements draw the reader's attention away from my main points? As I highlight my attendants' contribution to the plot, do I make myself irrelevant?

That sometimes happens in real life. A store clerk will listen to my question, and then turn to face my attendant, replying, "The elevator is at the back. You can take her this way, through the magazine section—there's plenty of room for the wheelchair— and then turn right and go all the way back." Some strangers must see my attendants as keepers, as wardens wholly responsible for me, serving alternately as nurse, as guardian, as conduit to the world of the normal.

If these strangers knew about the extent to which I depend on these helpers for the smallest maneuver, for relief from discomfort, and for readying myself for any productive activity, would this not deepen their sense of my utter helplessness?

So why should I be the one to script that stereotype? Why describe the bodily ministrations performed by other people for my benefit? Why not concentrate on my own heroic journeys?

This *is* my journey, from chaos to order. I locate the stress points and iron them out, shuttling like a diplomat among my brain, my voice, my attendant and my body. My quest carries me to far shores, elbow to toe, neck to tailbone. I do battle with inertia and pressure. No: I negotiate a dynamic peace.

This is also my narrative: I envision an aesthetic of comfort, the parts of my body that *do* function—eyes and windpipe, tongue and imagination, nerves and ears and judgment—working together to optimum effect. I begin to tell that story, assembling sentences, then rearranging them. My discombobulated body the conflict, my attendant the instrument of resolution. Who is the protagonist? Perhaps we both are. A narrative not linear, but circular.

The process of getting comfortable demands a certain style, both explicatory and poetic: *You see, this is the way I want it. This is what I mean. Not quite that far. Left, not right. Pull a little further. Push again.* A careful calculation of timing, tune and tempo. This is my language: explication, correction, repetition.

This is my poetry: an incantation for rain, or for a new era of peace, or for the comfort to write. Poetry aims for the thing itself, not just to name the thing. Poetry draws a straight line connecting the desire, the request, the fulfillment. Poetry *is* power of words to effect change, to move people—in this case, to move me, the author. Literally.

I've decided that I needn't leave my disabled body behind in order to fool and comfort my reader. Instead I'll violate what Nancy Mairs, that chronicler of her own discombobulated body, calls "the conventions of polite silence," in order to write, as she puts it, "as plainly and truthfully as the squirms and wriggles of the human psyche will permit" (p.xi).

One day, one reader, or perhaps many readers, will be reading this after—or while—going through a similar process of request, instruction, adjustment, to get comfortable. Such a reader may peer into the page and see herself reflected, at last. This reader may weep with relief, or may snort with relieved impatience—*What took you so long?* For this reader was way ahead of me, always already knowing that there is no authentic thought that is not born in the thinker's body's cells, nerves, secretions, in its kinetic and/or sensate experience.

No real journey can happen without a foot on some piece of ground (or a bottom in some seat) and the wind's kiss on skin. There is no philosophy in the absence of a sweating fear; no humor without hiccups; no love without blood in a beating heart.

So get yourself comfortable, and let's begin.

LAURA HERSHEY

Working Together

Her job: brisk bristle circle on teeth
My job: sneer
open wide

Her job: apply soap
loofah
hot spray
My job: how hot
say stop

Her job: heft my flesh
point a to point b
My job: remind her of our
respective spines and limbs

Her job: what no one thinks of doing
except for self or child
My job: make her forget
help her remember
tell her she can

Telling

What you risk telling your story:
You will bore them.
Your voice will break, your ink will
spill and stain your coat.
No one will understand, their eyes
become fences.
You will park yourself forever
on the outside, your differentness once
and for all revealed, dangerous,
the names you give to yourself
will become epithets.
Your happiness will be called
bravery, denial.
Your sadness will justify their pity.
Your fear will magnify their fears.
Everything you say will prove something about
their god, or their economic system.
Your feelings, that change day
to day, kaleidoscopic,
will freeze in place,
brand you forever,
justify anything they decide to do
with you.
Those with power can afford
to tell their story
or not.
Those without power
risk everything to tell their story
and must.

LAURA HERSHEY

Someone, somewhere
will hear your story and decide to fight,
to live and refuse compromise.
Someone else will tell
her own story,
risking everything.

Morning

I count on key click
crack swish front door open
bump close
footsteps
my eyes tight
against daylight
but awake
waiting

I count on whining grinder roar
crush beans
hiss perk roast scent
tickle thirst

Those sounds those smells
signal she has arrived
again
to roll me
realign my hips
wipe deep sleep drool
from my lips
wash blur
from my eyes

Or
I wait
back stiff
throat dry
eyes open
speculate
traffic sick kid hangover
whether she's not coming
or only late

Thousand Island

I wheel through the line, get my ticket punched—
a perk of dorm living, lunch
or dinner ready on schedule, cold or heated,
with no planning or shopping needed.
And the salad bar: carrots, cottage cheese,
lettuce, sprouts, bacon bits. All these
held together with orangeish, ketchup-sweet,
thick Thousand Island dressing. I greet
an acquaintance or two, then make
for an exit, go down a hall, take
a booth in the snack bar, face the wall,
read my history book, while
my aide feeds me my creamy
salad, small flattened bites, easy
to swallow. Later, in library or dorm, I'll be more
social, but that's not what meals are for.
For four years, I eat mostly apart, often silent,
making myself, at least a thousand times, an island.

Jillian Weise

from THE DISABILITY RIGHTS MOVEMENT AND THE LEGACY OF POETS WITH DISABILITIES

I. BEGINNINGS

N o one seems to like people with disabilities," writes David Pfeiffer in an essay titled "The Disability Movement: Ubiquitous but Unknown." Pfeiffer considers why such distaste continues to be prevalent today:

> Disability is seen as a personal tragedy, a disgrace to the family, and/or a
> punishment from God. People with disabilities are to be pitied and they
> are regarded as a burden to society, to the family, and to themselves...
> These attitudes are due to the fact that people with disabilities are diag-
> nosed. They are viewed as having a deficit named in that diagnosis. Un-
> like members of other social movements they are not allowed to
> self-identify.

Given these perceptions of disability and the lack of self-definition associated with disability, it is easy to understand why poets with disabilities might be reticent about self-identifying. Here's a personal example. I was at the book fair of the Associated Writing Programs Conference in Austin, Texas, standing beside Jim Ferris, who wrote *The Hospital Poems*, when a woman approached, and without any introduction, asked, "Are you a crip poet?" I didn't know what to say. I know what a crip is, and I know what a poet is, but I'd never heard the term "crip poet" before. I answered yes because it seemed like that was the answer she wanted, and it also seemed like to answer no might get me in some hot water, perhaps an argument on whether my poems were crippled enough, or whether I was, and these are not typically things I discuss upon meeting someone. I don't know what would've happened if I had answered, "No, I'm not a crip poet." I answered yes, and then she gave me a big hug and it seemed I had just been initiated into something without knowing what it was.

II. The Terms "Crip Poet" and "Poet with a Disability"

My reservations about the term "crip poet" are similar to my reservations about the terms "disabled poet" or even the politically correct term "poet with a disability." What does any of it mean? Ferris published an essay on defining "crip poetry" in the June 2007 issue of *Wordgathering*, an online journal of poetics. In the essay titled "Crip Poetry, Or How I Learned to Love the Limp," Ferris writes, "Crip poetry centers the experience of disabled people; it shows disabled people taking control of the gaze and articulating the terms under which we are viewed." Ferris cites characteristics of "crip poetry," which include "a challenge to stereotypes and an insistence on self-definition; a foregrounding of perspectives of people with disabilities; an emphasis on embodiment, especially atypical embodiment; and alternative techniques and poetics."

While it's encouraging to begin to have acknowledgment of poets with disabilities, I find it also discouraging that these first efforts are essentializing, seeking to brand a common disabled experience, and define the work according to a grid, rather than simply opening the field for disabled poets to enter the conversation on their own terms. For the purposes of this essay, I will dispense with Ferris' definition. Instead, I define "poet with a disability" as exactly that, a poet who has a disability.

III. Poet of the Disability Rights Movement

When I began researching this essay, I was hoping to find a poet affiliated with the Disability Rights Movement. The movement reached its apex in 1977 when the disabled and their advocates took over the fourth floor of the San Francisco Federal Building for three-and-a-half weeks. During this protest, people with disabilities and their advocates received support from the American Legion, the Black Panthers, the National Association for the Advancement of Colored People and the National Organization for Women, among others. The protest resulted in the ratification of Section 504 of the Rehabilitation Act, which prohibits any federally funded program from discriminating against persons with a "qualified handicap." Section 504 paved the way for the Americans with Disabilities Act of 1990. The Disability Rights Movement has been called "the last inclusion." I expected to find someone who wrote poems in tandem with the movement, and who appeared at sit-ins and demonstrations, since poets are commonly known for their famous acts of solidarity: Ginsberg walked into the Stonewall Inn and shouted, "Gay Power! Isn't that great!" After the assassination of Malcolm X, Amiri Baraka packed his bags on the Lower East Side and moved to Harlem and the Black Arts Movement was born. Adrienne Rich refused to accept the National Book Award individually, and instead banded together with Alice Walker and Audre Lorde to accept it on behalf of all silenced women. These examples show two main things that the Disability Rights Movement lacks: 1) poets whose work reflects the time and culture of their movement and 2) a sense of community.

Since the Disability Rights Movement has no such spokesperson, I'd like to consider Josephine Miles as a foremother to the movement. Miles is a poet with a disability whose life and work have been instrumental in my understanding of what it means to be a poet and a woman and a disabled person and a teacher and an activist. "I felt sort of on the sidelines," Miles says in an interview conducted by Ruth Teiser and Catherine Harmon and published as "Teaching Poet: An Oral Autobiography."

IV. JOSEPHINE MILES

Miles was the first woman to receive tenure (1947) in an English Department. She taught at the University of California, Berkeley, where she founded the *Berkeley Poetry Review*. She produced thirty-three books of poetry and literary criticism. In books such as *The Vocabulary of Poetry: Three Studies* (1946) and *The Continuity of Poetic Language* (1951), she traced the usage of words as they appeared in poems, and created charts to report which words were in vogue, out of vogue, or recurring.

Mobility was always an issue for Miles, who used canes, walkers and wheelchairs, though she did not address it directly in her poems until her final collection, titled *Coming to Terms*. She lived at the height of activism in Berkeley in the 1960s and 1970s, but she did not align with any one faction. When questioned about "women's lib," Miles said that "They [the feminists] didn't ask me to be a part of this because, as I say, I think women always take the attitude toward me that if they'd lean on me, I'd fall over."

In an earlier section of the interview, Miles describes the layout of her high school and how it contributed to her development as a poet:

> The high school was divided by floors. The science and the languages were on
> the second floor. I had to climb up one flight of stairs. English and history were
> on the third floor, which was really very hard for me to get to. I could climb

stairs then, with help, but it was awfully hard. So I postponed as much of English as possible and did a lot of languages and sciences—whatever I could on the second floor. I remember writing a poem at the end of my junior year which was called "To Dr. Edwards, On Going to the Third Floor."

After high school, Miles encountered resistance when she wanted to attend UCLA. The dean of women advised against it.

The dean said...I'd have to ask too many favors, and she thought it was right that I should go to a small college where I could be protected. So I was weeping heavily as I went out the gate. The cop had let me in, and so this cop—I guess he was waving us on, and then he sort of stopped and said, "What's wrong? Why are you crying?" I said, "Because the dean of women wouldn't let me come here because I'd ask too many favors." He said, "What favors do you have to ask?" The ones that were on my mind, of course, were very trivial. It was just a matter of registering. I said, "I'd have to stand in line to get registered, and I'd have to get permission to drive on campus." He said, "You get somebody to stand in line for you, and I'll let you drive on campus."

Miles' experiences predate the Disability Rights Movement. And while that movement brought changes to public policy, issues of access are not entirely resolved. Likewise, the attitude that the disabled "ask too many favors" remains prevalent. Perhaps the greatest achievement in 2008 toward access for the disabled happened in June when an appeals court ruled that the government must issue paper currency with Braille.

I'd like to reference a poem of Miles from her final collection, *Coming to Terms*. Prior to this collection, Miles' work engaged the quotidian details of life in such poems as "Market Report on Cotton Gray Goods" and "Apartment" and "Shade." She seems like the granddaughter of Wordsworth by including fragments from everyday speech in her poems. In *Coming to Terms*, Miles presents her disability along with her usual touchstones of everyday life.

Before

Earlier, what I remember: a small
Flame of arthritis in the midst of fields

In the Euclidian Sunday mustard fields
And the mud fields of the potted palm,
In Jackie's airy room,
And at the fire station
All the brass
And all of us
Feeding the gulls.
A fresh salt breeze and foam
Around a plaster leg.

Away from the chloroform intern, joy
Of the long journey when I ran
Free of the plaster, and got back
Down those long hills, spent out.
Where had I been, oh tell me.
And where
Under those vast sunny
Apricot trees in the front yard?
Go tell Aunt Rhodie the old gray goose is dead.

What I like about this poem is its frank interrogation of Miles' childhood experience of disability: frank in its beginning, "what I remember" and interrogative in that line, "Where had I been, oh tell me."

V. Louise Glück

For comparison's sake, I'd like to take a look at a poem by Louise Glück who uses similar subject material. Unlike Miles, however, Glück is not disabled. She puts on a disabled persona. The poem is from her 1969 collection *Firstborn*. Here is how *Kirkus* describes the subject material of *Firstborn*: "She [Glück] deals in wastelands... the lost lives of cripples... the hopeless and loveless."

The Cripple in the Subway

For awhile I thought I had gotten
Used to it (the leg) and hardly heard
That down-hard, down-hard
Upon wood, cement, etc. of the iron
Trappings and I'd tell myself the memories
Would also disappear, tick-
ing jump-ropes and the bike, the bike
That flew beneath my sister, froze
Light, bent back its
Stinging in a flash of red chrome brighter
Than my brace or brighter
Than the morning whirling past this pit
Flamed with rush horror and their thin
Boots flashing on and on, all that easy kidskin.

While I'm not going to linger on these two poems and the different ways they ad-dress disability, I'd like to note the different ways the poets use the word "tell." Miles writes, "Where had I been, oh tell me," engaging with the reader, while at the same time not completely disclosing; and without a question mark, the line reads as if Miles expects no answer. Glück writes, "I'd tell myself the memories / would also disappear" in a self-reflexive tone, turned in rather than out. Her imagination of this disabled experi-ence is much more explicit and objectifying.

VI. AUTHENTIC AND INAUTHENTIC REPRESENTATIONS OF DISABILITY

I wonder what we think of these two poems? Certainly Glück isn't alone in personify-ing disability (Bidart's *Book of the Body* gives us plenty of examples as well). Why do able poets write from this perspective? Before I began seeking poems written from a disabled perspective, I found plenty of poems written on the subject of disability, and in persona, from an able perspective. I can hardly pick up a journal or collection of poetry without coming across blindness or deafness or madness as metaphor. I used to count the number of "phantom limbs" that cropped up in poems; the phantom limb is typically a metaphor for the loss of a loved one. This has always struck me as funny because my phantom limb is ticklish rather than painful.

When I had a colleague read this essay, she commented that one of her writing teachers actually used the term "phantom limb" as a way to describe the writing process. It was the same writing teacher who was African American and protested the use, any use, of the word "dark" as a negative.

In an essay titled "Feminist Disability Studies," Rosemarie Garland-Thomson notes the "major aim of all of my work in both literary and feminist studies is to show that the always overdetermined metaphoric uses of disability efface and distort the lived experience of people with disabilities, evacuating the political significance of our lives and mitigating the influence of disability culture."

VII. The Future

More and more people are self-identifying as disabled. With the explosion of the blog, disabled people have a new medium in which to exchange ideas and act towards social change. Temple University's blog touts itself as "cool stuff in the world of geography, disability studies, and educational leadership." I find this tagline particularly intriguing for three reasons—1) disability has only recently been considered "cool," 2) the use of "geography" advances the disabled as a mobile and far-spread group and 3) the mention of "leadership" acknowledges the disabled in a role of power rather than victimhood. I'd like to see more studies, within the field of poetry, that consider the long history of disability and literature. But first, I'd like for us all to know the poets with disabilities of the twentieth and twenty-first centuries. Until we know who we are—who wants to be included and who does not—how can we further integrate disability studies in the field of poetry?

JILLIAN WEISE

The Amputee's Guide to Sex

I. REMOVAL OF PROSTHETIC

Wait for partner to exit room, or initiate their exit by requesting a favor. For example, "Could you check the front door? I can't remember if I locked it." Wait for shadows to stand still, then quick, under the covers, remove the prosthetic. Let it slip beneath the bed, under clothes, behind a door.

II. FOREPLAY

To create an uninhibited environment for your partner, track their hands like game pieces on a board. For leg amputees, keep arms on upper body. For arm amputees, keep arms on lower body. Engage with like limbs. Keep half-limbs out of reach. Your goal is to achieve a false harmony with their body.

III. SEX

Mobility is key. If they see the half-limb then they become inhibited, nervous. They think: "Will it hurt like this? Would she tell me if it did?" Mobility shows confidence. Think for two people. Know where your limbs are at all times; know where your partner's limbs are at all times.

The Old Questions

When I asked you to turn off the lights,
you said, *Will you show me your leg first?*

I heard Rachmaninov through the wall,
a couple making love without prerequisites.

Do you sleep with it on? I forgot
there would be this conversation.

Do you bathe with it on?
I need to rehearse answers to these questions.

Will you take it off in front of me?
I once stepped into a peep show in New Orleans.

Over the door, signs read: Hands off our girls.
Is it all right if I touch it?

I am thinking of a hot bath, a book.
The couple on the other side of the wall laughs.

She has found the backs of his knees.

The Devotee

This man, short, balding, in his forties,
approached me at a reading & asked if
I would sign his book. His hands shook.

I thought he had some kind of condition.
Three days later, he sent this email:
"I was at your reading in Louisville.

I loved the way you limped to the stage.
Do you know you're beautiful? Do you
feel beautiful during sex? What's it like?

I bought your book, which is about,
you know, this topic. I deserve a reply."
I looked out the window for the birds

& the deer other poets are always seeing.
I want to be another poet, I thought.
I want to be any other poet but me.

The Body in Pain

For a long while I was with you & faithful
as I was to the black hair dye on aisle eight,
as good at covering-up.

For a long while I gave you to the stage
in exchange for Aunt March in *Little Women*,
Laura Wingfield in *The Glass Menagerie*.
It felt entirely like an act, but wasn't.
The curved back of the spinster, the clunky leg.
I read the lines like hell I read them loud
and clear I read them well.

•

This is the spine)
A closing parenthetical.
What did my body mean to say as an aside?

•

All states of being have referential content:

ashamed of
belief in
devotion to
gratitude for
hunger for
longing for
love for
relief from
pity for
struggle for
thirst for
tired of

except pain.

A friend calls, her brother shot himself
in Tennessee. She says,
I need to talk to you
because you & he
both are were
disabled.

•

Now it is Saturday night & I am writing
another letter to Lucy Grealy, who I will never meet.

Dear Lucy,

You do not know me. It feels wrong
for me to know about the heroin, the bags
of mail you kept, the bolt in your face.

For what it is worth, I have a bolt in my hip,
a hook along my spine. I don't want to talk
about any of this. Tell me: what was your last

good thing? Can we stay there?

•

The boy, nineteen, in his car driving through
Tennessee, left a note taped to the rearview mirror:
I am always in pain.

•

Elaine Scarry writes that pain is simultaneously
a thing that cannot be confirmed & cannot be denied.

In me, a shooting like a flash like a planet like a fire.
In you, a question mark.
The boy & I both with a bird in our lungs.

Ribs press in, constrict. The medical
dictionary describes it as *crab-like ribs*.

Even they resort to figurative language.
The boy's sister on the phone asks,
Are you also in pain? How does it feel?

She means to say, Tell me why this happened.

•

For a long while I was with you & faithful.
I did not mind, you shooting, you itching
as if you did not know we lost that foot.

Someone would have played lover to her brother
& meant it. This happens all the time:
When mine said, I am getting used to
your body, it sent me batty, bawling, bastard,
how could he love this husk? Then I flipped
that switch. I no more notice the twitch
of a lover's eye because it is *my* lover & *his* eye.

•

Descartes was always partial to cross-eyed women,
because the object of his first love had such a defect.

This doesn't explain
the boy the gun the car the drive the mountains
the woman the drug the skin the face the floor

•

Dear Lucy,

I am angry with you. Which was it?
Did you abdicate to beauty or pain?
Say pain. It is easier for me to understand.

JILLIAN WEISE

Kathi Wolfe

HELEN KELLER: OBSESSION AND MUSE

G rowing up with low vision, I wanted nothing to do with Helen Keller. Keller, I knew from *The Miracle Worker* and public service ads on TV, was an "inspiration"—a saint. I was an ordinary kid, who never did her math homework, never cleaned her room and didn't, even if I could have, want to be saintly. There was no way that I would ever want to or be able to hang out with Helen. She was Wally and the gang; I was the Beaver.

The Miracle Worker, the Academy Award-winning film, glued "inspirational" images of Helen Keller and her story into the public consciousness. Based on William Gibson's play of the same name, *The Miracle Worker* is Hollywood's version of how twenty-one-year-old Annie Sullivan, herself visually impaired, taught the meaning of language to seven-year-old Helen Keller, who became deaf and blind at age eighteen months. The film ends with the iconic image of Keller, her hand under the water pump, saying "Wa! Wa!"

The other image of Helen Keller that is widely known is that of Keller as a saintly, (presumably) sexless, elderly women, urging people to help blind people in public service ads. I remember seeing these ads when I was a child. Keller (who lived from 1880 to 1968) appeared quite old then.

Because I didn't want to be lumped in with the "inspirational" icon, the tantrum throwing child or the saintly, sexless elderly woman, I kept my distance from Helen Keller.

Not that this was easy. For as Kim E. Nielsen notes in *The Radical Lives of Helen Keller*, Keller is the most famous person with a disability in history, and how people perceive Keller impacts how they perceive all people with disabilities. I had my own experiences with *that*. Once when I was a teenager, my grandmother came into my bedroom. "No one will marry you," she told me, "but you can be another Helen Keller."

Years later, I was at a gay bar in New York. "I love Helen Keller!" a woman exclaimed to me, "but what are you doing in a place like this?" The implication of her question was that Helen Keller did many good works, but that people like Helen, like me, wouldn't or shouldn't be looking for romance or sex.

I became interested—then obsessed with Keller—when I was a graduate student at Yale. Looking at books in the library, someone pointed out a book to me called *Helen Keller: Her Socialist Years.* That got my attention.

I learned that Keller graduated from Radcliffe College in 1904, at a time when few women—or that many men—let alone disabled women went to college. Keller, I discovered, was an early feminist, an author and vaudeville star. While she did not have a drinking problem, she enjoyed a drink (especially scotch).

In 1916, Keller and Peter Fagan planned to get married; but Keller's family nixed their plans. Keller loved dogs, Japan, hot dogs, and at age seventy-four, danced with Martha Graham and her dance troupe. Keller was one of the earliest supporters of the NAACP and, without pity or condescension, she comforted wounded soldiers after World War II. She read and wrote in Braille, knew several languages (English, French, Greek, German—among others) and communicated by finger spelling or reading lips.

Over the years, like many others (especially, blind and visually impaired women), I've had a "love-hate" relationship with Helen Keller. Frequently, I've tried to run away from Keller's all too encompassing presence. For a considerable time, I resisted focusing my work as a poet on this disability icon, whose saintly *Miracle Worker* aura is still so entwined with our cultural stereotyping of people with disabilities. As a poet whose sensibility is steeped in disability culture, I wished to create new characters unsullied by "inspiration" or ableism. Yet Keller, like a dog scratching at the door to be let out, kept pulling me toward her. Whether I liked it or not, she insisted on becoming my muse. "Let my spirit live! Give me an inner life in your poems!" She insisted, "You know I was a complex, three-dimensional person, not a one-dimensional saint! Build an *ars poetica* from that." Gradually, I stopped resisting and listened.

KATHI WOLFE

4 poems from HELEN TAKES THE STAGE: THE HELEN KELLER POEMS

On the Subway

A man with breath like sour milk
spits into my ear with the aim
of a pool shark sinking
the ball in the corner pocket.

A baby crawls into my lap,
wrinkles the dress
I'd picked as if I were a diva
debuting at the Met.

I'm stuck to my seat
a stamp on an envelope.
Ash perfumes the air
of this underground fashion show.

Yet here there is more breathing room
than in all of Central Park,
I'm richer than J. P. Morgan
with his hoard of gold.
Here, I'm not on a pedestal,
just a dame on the Broadway Local.

Ashes: Rome, 1946

Soot bombards my hair.
Soldiers, blinded in battle,
tell rough-edged jokes to hide
their tears. If only I could
conjure spells. I caress their faces.

My hands smolder. The Braille
dots smell like acrid socks.
Your home in Connecticut
is gone. It went up in smoke,
everything lost except
the silver, a friend writes.
The dining room chairs,
Japanese vases,
the dog's water dish,
my manuscripts
turned to ashes.

I wipe sweat off foreheads
of wounded vets, brush dust
from my wrinkled dress, and write
in the beginning was the word,
the potion against self-pity.

Kathi Wolfe

She Loved Hot Dogs So Much

Inhaling their sweat, licking their salt,
was like kissing Peter on the night train

as if only their tangy passion mattered,
before her teacher's protestations,

her mother's remonstrations,
her brother's gun-waving,

against her deaf-blind,
mouth-watering love

ended their ride to what she'd
always wanted, not fame or fortune,

but the salted happily-ever-after,
where kisses taste like mustard,

embraces char on the grill, and love,
like onions, makes the eyes water.

The Sun is Warm: Nagasaki, 1948

Standing with Mr. Nagai, a scientist,
in the corpse of the medical college,
I feel the bomb-blasted walls. Jagged
pipes, twisted girders, timbers, flakes
of smoked flesh cover this graveyard
that once trained healers. Twenty-four
teachers scorched, doctors decapitated,
patients incinerated. And they say
America won the War? I do not want
peace that passes understanding; I want
understanding that brings peace. Mr. Nagai,
I touch your singed, nearly skinless face.
I don't have much time left, you say,
but I am well, for the sun is warm.

KATHI WOLFE

John Lee Clark

TRANSLATING AND READING ASL POETRY

I. ASL TO ENGLISH

Some American Sign Language (ASL) poets remain skeptical of translation. After all, some do not know English well, let alone English poetry. The most beautiful English poem in the world may mean nothing. It can be hard for some to imagine how it is possible for all of those stupid fancy words to convey what they sign. Also, many of the pioneering ASL poets taught ASL and linguistics for a living and were engaged in academic battles against mainstream linguists who were not yet convinced of ASL's status as an actual language. So they may have felt protective of their ASL poems, preferring that one know ASL first before having any access to their work.

Now that ASL is widely recognized as a legitimate language, some ASL poets are growing more practical about their work and agreeing to have it voiced, glossed or translated. I am slowly working on getting more poets to allow me or others to translate their work. It may take five more years before we have a full-length collection of translations of ASL poetry.

I think the way I approach translation is the same way most translators do: crumple the original poem into a tiny wad, chew it for a while, spit it out, unwrap it, try to pat it down as flat and neat as possible. Because ASL grammar is quite different though, the process may be more like translating between English and Chinese than between two Romance languages. ASL's basic grammatical structure is topic-comment. Sometimes this means short, contained passages are object-subject-verb. Instead of "That's a beautiful blue car" it is essential in ASL to start with the topic, which is the car, and then comment on it: CAR THERE BLUE THAT WOW BEAUTIFUL.

The "there" is important for placing the car somewhere in the visual-spatial signing space. The next time the car is referred to, it will appear in the same "place" as would things and characters in movies. If the hero looks to the left of the screen and the heroine in the other direction, they stay that way throughout the scene if not the whole movie. This gives the viewer a sense of the space within the movie. We do the same in ASL. If I am recounting a conversation I had with my six-year-old son, I would look down to the right as if talking to my son, and when I quote my son, I'd be looking up to the left to reflect how he looked up to me during that conversation. In my recounting, I create a short film in which I play both myself and my son. The challenge in translating this is to create equally clear and consistent switches between people and things, what they are like or doing. Fortunately, there are nifty tricks in English that accomplish all these things, though not in a literally cinematic way.

When translating from English to ASL, I often have to start with something later in the original poem because it offers the best point of entry, that is, the topic. Otherwise, the descriptions would mean nothing in ASL. The thunderstorm, the winds, the crashing sea would mean nothing without first knowing there's a house on a cliff. In English, it may be all right to hold the house until later, but not in ASL. If the English depends too much on the house being held back, it is possible that the ASL version wouldn't be a good poem. That can happen. Sometimes, it's not worth it. But if the English poem has other sources of power, it shouldn't be a problem to start with the house and make up for the radical rearrangement somewhere else.

II. ENGLISH TO ASL

Some of my poems in English I have not bothered translating. It COULD be done, but the best possible result in ASL wouldn't be worth performing to a Deaf audience. The best translations come from poems that lend themselves readily to sets of similar handshapes or a visual space that has a pattern in it that distinguishes it as ASL poetry. For example, my poem "Long Goodbyes" plays with the idea of time and is about Deaf people talking around the table in the kitchen, which is the most important place in Deaf culture. When Deaf friends come, they stay forever around the table, chatting for hours and hours before anyone stands up to go. When everyone stands up, it will take hours yet before they actually leave. The sign for "hour" is the hour hand going around the face of an imaginary clock, and the table is round too, and the Deaf people, whether they are sitting or standing, stay in a constant circle. So a pattern emerges for the ASL version in which the circle as a shape plays a prominent role. This influences how I choose to sign other things, all toward the circular motion of signing hands and the passing of time.

Are the versions completely different? No. But that one is on paper and the other signed would give the illusion that they are. But if someone translated my ASL version back into English, the skeleton should be there, maybe some meat. But the skin and hair and the clothes would probably be different. For example, I doubt that the line "light

JOHN LEE CLARK

to light bright in the night" would reappear because this is more of an English flourish that disappears in the ASL version. In its stead is an ASL flourish in which the two hands signing the flashing of light segues into an innovative doubled sign for "night" that happens to be circular in shape. As different as the two flourishes are, they don't alter the skeleton at all. They're just flourishes.

III. ASL Poetry Readings

For Deaf poets, giving a reading presents a peculiar mixture of problems. Aesthetically, there is the question of how to read their poems in public. Although some can speak, many don't feel comfortable using their nasal, broken speech in public. Others, like me, do not speak at all. Signing, then, is a strong preference. However, as I've mentioned, translating written poems into ASL doesn't guarantee that they will be good ASL poems. A Deaf poet is not necessarily an ASL poet. Many are not even native signers and would feel equally awkward signing poems in public. If they can only sign pidgin versions that would not be very pleasing to Deaf audience members and if the hearing audience members are listening to an interpreter reading the written poems while they gape at the signing Deaf poet, what's the artistic point of the reading?

Still, I am sure that Deaf poets would be able to resolve such aesthetic issues if they had more opportunities. They could, for example, enlist the help of an ASL poet in producing rich, full translations and be coached in the art of sign performance. But there's a practical problem that has long limited Deaf poets' opportunities to do readings: interpreting costs. This same issue also means there are very few literary events that are accessible to Deaf people. In most parts of the country, interpreting services start at $120, which covers the first two hours and is required even if you only need one hour or fifteen minutes. So it's automatically $120, and sixty dollars per hour after the first two hours. This effectively excludes bookstores, for the costs would blow away any sales. The great bulk of other readings are hosted by small organizations with little or no money. This leaves the larger organizations and colleges, which could handle the costs, in theory if not in practice.

It's no wonder only two Deaf poets in my anthology have given more than one reading. A few, myself included, have given just one. The rest have never had the privilege.

Deaf Blind: Three Squared Cinquain

BARBARA WALTERS IS IN AWE

of a deaf-blind man
who cooks without burning himself!
Helen Keller is to blame.
Can't I pick my nose
without it being a miracle?

AM I A NOBODY, TOO?

I am sorry to disappoint,
but I am. But nobody
would let me be one,
not even when I catch
a bus stinking of Nobodies.

ONE AFTERNOON, I FOUND MYSELF

walking with my cane dragging
behind me but still knowing
the way. There was nothing
to see. Everything saw me
first and stayed in place.

JOHN LEE CLARK

Clamor

All things living and dead cry out to me
when I touch them. The dog, gasping for air,
is drowning in ecstasy, its neck shouting
Dig in, dig in. Slam me, slam me,
demands one door while another asks to remain
open. In bed afterwards she asks me
how did I know just where and how
to caress her. I can be too eager to listen:
The scar here on my thumb is a gift
from a cracked bowl that begged to be broken.

Beach Baseball

Even when I fold my white cane in half
to double my chances, my batting average is a joke.
I am much better at knowing which smooth stones
the ocean wants back from the shore.
But when there is a metallic crack and a rainbow
cleaves my mental sky, I see something
falling from one blue into another and then a gasp
of what I like to think of as pure white.

Long Goodbyes

I miss all of the long goodbyes
of my parents' guests
taking their leave by not leaving

when it was time to go. Someone would sign
Better go home we but hours would pass
around our round kitchen table

before anyone stands up.
Then others, sighing, would stand up
slowly and slowly walk

through our house, pausing
where the walls offered stories,
reasons to stay longer

and touch more things with our hands.
I remember how long,
how wonderfully they stood

unwilling to open the front door,
signing away with warm faces
and hugging goodbye again

before going gently into the night.
My family would huddle to watch
their cars' headlights roll away

but pause to flash in the Deaf way,
waving goodbye to our house.
How we children dashed inside

to light switches for our house
to wave back goodbye,
light to light bright in the night!

Now that I am grown
and have my own family, do come
for a visit but do not leave

when it is time to go. Sign, do sign
Better go home we and our hands
will make time go suddenly slow.

LYRICISM OF THE BODY

Alex Lemon

AND NOW I SEE

A man may see how this world goes with no eyes.
—WILLIAM SHAKESPEARE, *King Lear*

I woke to a radically different world on September 16, 1999. My brain surgery had gone well, but everything around me was blurred and doubled and jumping and excruciatingly brilliant. The vascular malformation in the pons of my brainstem had been dealt with, but I couldn't see the intensive care unit around me. My eyes looked like they were trying to pop out of my head and they'd rolled out to sides of my head. It was devastating—I was suddenly sitting in a wheelchair, cloistered in blinding fog. I was twenty-one years old. For years, I wore an eye patch (and sometimes still do) for the walleye vision, and it slowly got better, but the nystagmus and double-vision have never completely gone away.

But, as I've learned to accept this changed body, I've realized that visual changes have played a significant role in my poetic development. They've destabilized me, helped me embrace the unruliness of the world and accelerated the broadening of my imagination.

Without sight, I felt like the world had become an unknowable place. But the idea that I knew the world because I could see it was an illusion—an illusion of control. This destabilization was bewildering and beautiful and pivotal. The act of tearing everything down helped me become open to the possibility of everything, and that openness is a crucial element of writing. "I dwell in Possibility— /," Emily Dickinson wrote, "A fairer House than prose— / More numerous of Windows— / Superior—For Doors—,"and the architectural metaphor that begins in the first stanza of 466 is an excellent way to think about the complexities of a poem. Each poem is a building. Theoretically, each building has an endless arrangement of doorjambs and windowsills and steps, just as each theoretical poem can be built of an enormously complex arrangement of poetic elements. So, what do you want to build—another cookie-cutter sonnet in the suburbs or the gorgeous wasteland of the Watts Towers?

Everything I see is shifting, vibrating. That glass of water looks as if it's walking across the counter. Those flowers are rising, ever so slightly, out of the vase. They are fireworks the half second before becoming fireworks. The painting bleeds into the wall, which the person walking by has already bled into. Nothing is contained. Nothing is capped or limited. This porousness, in my eyes, is a striking move toward what Keats so admired about Shakespeare, his great aptitude for negative capability. It is "being in uncertainties," because that mug has no exact shape and maybe it is rattling over the tabletop. Then again, maybe it's not; maybe the mug is a suitcase and inside the suitcase is a door to your favorite dining establishment, The Manatee Hut.

I do not think that my visual disability has given me anything I couldn't have acquired with the "good" vision I'd been born with, but it sped up my poetic appreciation of the world. Specifically, not being able to see forced me into an extended stay in my imagination. Like shooting baskets or doing the crossword puzzle, the more time I spent on it, the better it got. My imagination ballooned; it became wonderfully corpulent. It became a place of safety and pleasure. And as my altered sight returned and continued changing, my imagination continuously expanded, but suddenly, the one constant in my life was that wildly spinning place.

So of course I see how many fingers you're holding up. A baker's dozen, right? Or hmmm, is that sign-language and why are you calling me a big fat liar? It's OK, I forgive you—you're wearing a lovely face and a neato-bandito T-shirt. I too heart New York, almost as much as burritos. Or, wait a second—is that my hand living inside your chest like a heart koozie? And one last thing, before you make me leave, I must say you look utterly ravishing like that, with your hair all on fire.

Mosquito

You want evidence of the street
fight? A gutter-grate bruise & concrete scabs—
here are nails on the tongue,
a mosaic of glass shards on my lips.

I am midnight banging against house-
fire. A naked woman shaking
with the sweat of need.

An ocean of burning diamonds
beneath my roadkill, my hitchhiker
belly fills sweet. I am neon blind & kiss
too black. Dangle stars—

let me sleep hoarse-throated in the desert
under a blanket sewn from spiders.
Let me be delicate & invisible.

Kick my ribs, tug my hair.
Scream *You're Gonna Miss Me*
When I'm Gone. Sing implosion
to this world where nothing is healed.

Slap me, I'll be any kind of sinner.

It Had Only Been Dead a Few Hours

What a strange paradise this is—
languid apricot trees & birds

of paradise. Tire-flattened
oranges in the alley & ants

in the hummingbird feeders.
Neighbors peek from the blinds

when the sprinklers torque on
& I cannot romanticize this

ultimate torture test. You say
your foot is killing you?—well,

hot damn, you are dead
nuts, right on. That is the essence

of all of this, isn't it? So let me tell you—
they begin as piles of bones,

the animals in my dreams do.
Each night, they clink & clonk

& rise like a time lapse video
of sky-scraper construction.

One animal turns into a man
& the man gives birth

to a dead dog. In just seconds
the other animals have rent them apart

& then, I'm awake. Night-
swallows knife through the morning

Alex Lemon

fog as I stand at the window
listening to the coyote song.

My entire body is killing me,
& I have witnessed my own death

& lived—I whisper my wagers
against disaster into the dark air.

Other Good

Anesthesia dumb, scalpel-paste
Rawing my tongue, I found
Myself star-fished in sky
Spinning days. I stared into my eyelids'

Bustling magic, the black
Of my hands. Oh, how darkness
Swaggered, dealt fluorescent-blurs
& the choke of the sea. *This is my everything—*

Bright shuddered my cheeks,
Shadows whistled through their teeth.
Hallways thrummed & snorted,
The surgeons in my brain

Pissed with no hands.
Each day nurses wore their best
Tin-foil skirts, buried
Their caresses in my side

While pillows whispered
In spite of your scars you are tickled
To death   of life.
I couldn't understand this

Always being held. Lung-machines
Sang louder. Wavesong & useless.
Midnights & swearing. Blue.
Who prayed for me—my thanks

But I can't keep anything down.
Who knew it had nothing to do
With the wind by how light
Flickered with falling knives?

ALEX LEMON

And No More May I Be

So this is calamity: calendula-
oiled hands cupping a mouth

that sings through the caving
away thunderlight as the weeks

keep swinging by—house finches
shivering groundward in the catgut

blight. Black boughs absent of any
living weights. In the rain a man

ducks into his coat to light a smoke.
The park bitter with echoing space.

The park freezing. In the rain a man
ducks into his coat like the split-

ribbed chest of a dead horse
swallowing a wet-cheeked boy.

Benches slick red. Benches freezing.
In the rain a soaked man

watching in the rain. In the rain
my hands pink hands numb

in the rain. Beneath the skin
a humming *is*. Geese wreathed

in their own winter-coming
breath. Skinhulled. Taut

skin bustling. Bottle caps old
buttons half-buried hard in the dirt.

Laurie Clements Lambeth

RESHAPING THE OUTLINE

Having dispensed with the neurological tests and their curious implements (pizza wheel for the sole of my foot, reflex hammer, tuning fork), having ceased the comparison of MRI results over ten years, recognizing the progression of my illness, the doctor asked what I'd been writing lately. I said I'd been writing about multiple sclerosis (MS)—about MRIs, areas of damage that turn from brilliant white spots to "black holes," irreparable. We had counted something like seven new black holes during the exam. I remember the doctor paused and lowered her head in profile, as though laboring to offer wisdom.

"I think you're very...intelligent, and very...creative," she said, turning her face toward me, "but writing about your MS isn't going to make it better."

How does one respond?

"Oh, I'm perfectly aware of that. I'm under no illusions that anything at all will make me better." I wanted to tell her that my writing and my disease have existed side by side from the moment I was diagnosed at seventeen, my new physical life giving birth to my life in words.

Poet Gregory Orr points out that while in English "to bless" is to confer divine benevolence on someone or something, in French the verb *blesser* means to wound. The two are linked, he suggests, beyond logic. This coincides with my experience; the disease that wounds channels in my brain and spine, that disrupts my ability to feel through skin, that distorts my vision, that tightens some muscles while weakening others, is indeed the blessing-wound that changed my thinking and brought me to poetry.

My first recognizable MS symptom—although there were others I didn't yet understand—was a numb left hand, as though plastic wrap surrounded each finger. Over time it rose up my arm, then down my left thigh. The outlines between things blurred. Unable to detect the difference between my skin and fabric, my thumb and a buttonhole, my hair and the elastic I stretched to contain it, I slipped into a dimension where there was little distinction between the outside world and the inner contours of my own body. I had planned to be a cartoonist, so most of my drawing was defined by outlines. And now this shading moved in, this nuance. About six weeks later the numbness subsided, but it left its physical traces that would rise up again, and more importantly, a permanent mark on my consciousness: outlines shifted, faded.

In the catalog to his 1809 exhibition of paintings in his brother's sock-shop, on view two hundred years later at the Tate Gallery, William Blake stresses the importance of the outline: "How do we distinguish the oak from the beech, the horse from the ox, but by the bounding outline? How do we distinguish one face or countenance from another, but by the bounding line and its infinite inflexions and movements?" He goes on to warn, "Leave out this line and you leave out life itself; all is chaos again." Chaos. There is indeed a chaotic quality to a disability that shifts and interrupts, leaves and re-enters one's life in new, surprising ways that at once echo earlier experience and carve new notches into the body.

Gregory Orr observes, in his essay "Poetry and Survival," that poetry has the power to take crises—loss, pain, illness, instability—and give them shape. To order the chaos in our lives through language: "Rather than the transcendence and abstraction counseled by philosophy and religion, the personal lyric urges the self to translate its whole being into language where it can dramatize and re-stabilize itself in the patterned language of the poem." Poetry helped me investigate and reinforce the blur I felt between body and world, and gave me the space to insist upon the bounding line's fluidity. In metaphor, for instance, I could bypass all that tenor and vehicle business and create images that were simultaneously literal and figurative, hovering somewhere in-between. It was this way that MS entered my poetry—not in subject, but in the ways it altered my perception of my body's place in the world, as though the outline of what I could call "me" was a broken line, permeable and wavering, and what was inside that perimeter was a shimmering transparency, at once me and not me.

For eight years I did not write about the disease, aside from one particularly rough poem in my senior year of high school. The subject was too expansive and tentacled, too emotionally unpredictable, too difficult to harness into free verse. Orr's description of the lyric poem's role as the provider of order via "patterned language" rang true for me. I needed the cage of a villanelle—so restrictive, in that very few lines can truly further the poem along, and yet so obsessive a form—to house the poem. In fact, even that high school poem was propelled by repetition, what Orr would call "the consoling power of repeated sounds." After living with MS for eight fairly uneventful years and being woken up one night by something like a seizure, neurons misfiring, arms and legs flailing beyond my conscious control, I wrote about the experience in my villanelle

"The Shaking." The poem takes on two possibly melodramatic hazards for poetry: love and sickness. Either could have gone horribly out of control, but the project of formal containment allowed for necessary perspective to tinker, prune, dissect and question, long after the poem was originally published.

As MS more fully entered my poetry, my experience of disability deepened, or vice-versa. They helped each other along. While I wouldn't go so far as to say that poetry is therapy, it is a means for me to take something that may not be considered desirable or beautiful (dragging a leg, losing the sense of touch), investigate it, sculpt it and create something outside of my body that is vividly physical, in subject and in form. I am moved to craft different formal responses to each somatic experience. In my first book, the most obvious formal departure can be found in the prose fragments addressing memory loss, low vision, ocular pain and incontinence. These subjects are difficult to handle in poetry without risking melodrama or perceptions of shock or self-pity, so it felt deeply satisfying to tighten prose into a voice that is at once stark and lyrical, then to juxtapose those fragments against more lyrically expansive poems.

Two poems included in this book, near companions if not for the time elapsed between each poem's composition, address the difficulty of communicating impaired sensation: "Hypoesthesia" and "Dysaesthesia." These narrative lyrics attempt to describe lack of sensation (numbness), or the feeling of pain without source, dysaesthesia: "wrong feeling." In each, there is a sense of the possibility of formal connection that is not actualized. This is not how their shapes were planned; I write far more organically than that. But the feeling in each is a sense of hesitancy, a disruption in fluidity, reflective of the inability to share physical experience, even at our most intimate or domestic moments. In "Hypoesthesia" this is actualized in certain long lines and sentences disrupted mid-stream and continuing mid-line in the next stanza, as though they were dropped straight down. In "Dysaesthesia" the slanted gutter down the middle performs the same task, except this poem is addressing pain, so its language and form are more halting, frantic. Their brokenness exists far more on the surface than in "Hypoesthesia," where the speaker finds some pleasure and gratitude in shifting her sensibilities.

In either case, fitting form to the poem, lending it shape and order, granted me a tremendous sense of power—not to change my physical condition at all (why would I want to change?), but to relay its essence and create a thing of beauty that speaks

LAURIE CLEMENTS LAMBETH

simultaneously about the individual and a more universal sense of alienation, all of us trapped in chaotic bodies, the potential of unrest ever-present in every body, which I hope, if the poem's shaped well and the reader willing to follow, will foster empathy, not sympathy, for the blessing-wound.

Hypoesthesia

Hypoesthesia: numbness, the absence of sensation. Absence often feels like something.
—INSIDE MS

All those years
I made love to a man without thinking
how little his body had to do with me
—MARK DOTY

For now (who knows how long now is) his touch is nothing but warmth and trace
trailing his hand up my thigh and around my stomach. I feel a little
something crystallize after each pass of his hand, then it's dust.

Whoever thought sex could be so literally senseless? The first time (*my first time*)
I cried a little because I did not want it, but gave to make my boyfriend stop asking.
That was a different kind of senselessness.

I wanted to cry this time, too, another first since the new flare-up broke:
feet, knee, thigh, stomach, hip, hollow of the back, neither my body nor my skin
but a loose-fitting carapace, bubble, prosthetic even.

                                                    Are you touching me,
I thought to ask, but instead watched as he kissed each part and caressed
and did what we do when I feel right. I didn't say   *I can't feel that,*
but let his hands and mouth travel.

For the first time in my life I let go of my body a while and looked down
with fascination at the man I love in the process of loving me—:
the way the window's meager light managed

to illuminate his nails with each finger's lengthening, how it raised
his tendons (like spines) before his knuckles into glow. Stunning
to see his eyebrows and lashes crush, devoted,

with each kiss planted along my belly, to feel only the cool afterward.
Strange that now would be the time I comprehend our otherness, these bodies
wanting more: luminous, impossible whole.

LAURIE CLEMENTS LAMBETH

The Shaking

I know I scared you last night by shaking,
the only time you were forced to share
a dream that shook me to waking.

Your left hand pressed upon my aching
thigh as it kicked and flailed; how compare
your strength to synapse whims, wild shaking?

You know my nervous system could be taking
over any time; disease is unfair.
Remember: it seems bad when you're waking.

Many times I've trembled when you're making
love to me, my round shoulders open, bare,
but never have I broken into such shaking,

when my body shows us our lives breaking
apart. Still, you hold me. Your kind is rare,
who know (or pretend) dreams seem worse upon waking.

Surprising you stayed: here you are, forsaking
quiet nights for me. Will you be there
when it worsens, my gait palsied with shaking?
Who could be strong enough to hold back its waking?

Seizure, or Seduction of Persephone

I convulsed so   hard I broke
open, broke   the earth,
erupted and   pushed out
a narcissus   by the roots.

It doesn't   matter where
the flower   broke on my body,
through the   skin, a pimple,
my head, or   the belly.

I could not   tell you.
What I can   say is this:
my limbs   flailed and seized
in the bed.   I watched, both

inside and   outside, skin
the sheet   of a Richter scale,
delicate   needles charting
the shifting   of earth's plates,

limbs all   speaking
unknown   tongues, plotting
maps and   pathways deep
into the   body. As he held

me still   in that bed,
how was   I to discern
if he then   learned
his way   through the flesh

LAURIE CLEMENTS LAMBETH

into my   need, or if
he chose   this blue moment
to come   out, rupture
the field   from within

my own   unruly body?
Seduction: nothing but
a man's hand   depressing
and a flower   jolting out.

Some void   here between my hips.

Dysaesthesia

When I tell Ian   my hands are on fire,

when I first pull   them from the warm bed

and release them   to the air's sting,

begin the morning   routine, measure

dog food, twist open   ridged lids of jars

upon which I scratch   my palms,

when I lift and unscrew   the milk bottle,

fingers sparking without   cause,

when I pour coffee, rubbing   the hands

on any rough surface because   they smolder,

when I tell him I watched myself   drop

the spoon as though in a movie,   not me

that wincing, palms turned up   and why,

their inner tremble radiating   holding nothing,

I remember James Dean

in the police department,   so angry

he pummels a desk, and   I said last week

when we watched it again,   *wait for it:*

he broke his hand there   *in the take—that's real pain,*

and I read my hand like   his, roiling under skin

while he clutches his wrist   in close-up,

when I hear myself gasp   and can't help it,

just the shock, I can say   *spark* or *burn*

or *electric*, and Ian asks   me if I mean

the hands are hot as in   temperature.

Not hot, just on fire.   Flameless, sourceless—

how else to say it   but fire, this mistake

creeping between   spine and skin? How to discern

this pain, these hands,   who operates them?

LAURIE CLEMENTS LAMBETH

Brian Teare

LYING MEDITATION

'm not a practicing Buddhist, but the longer I live with two chronic diseases, the more often I turn and return to Buddhist theology and poetry as ways of helping me to conceptualize and accept the unpredictable. I can't know when my body will be disabled or when my body will be able. Gouty rheumatoid arthritis means daily low-level pain in my feet and knees, but monthly there are days of significantly limited movement and yearly I experience crippling bouts of swelling that last anywhere from two to ten days. Celiac disease and a severe soy allergy mean that even a minor deviation from my increasingly narrow diet—due to poorly labeled packaging, "hidden" ingredients, cross-contamination, misinformed wait staff or my own ignorance—gives an entire day or more over to symptoms. Thus, while I wouldn't feel comfortable claiming a "disability" in the strictest sense of the term, the epithet "temporarily able-bodied" favored by some disability activists makes a lot of sense to me. "[B]revity is natural / it makes sense," writes Laozi in Thomas Meyer's translation of the *Dao De Jing*,

> a storm doesn't go on all morning long
> nor does a sudden shower all day

> but where do these come from
> from heaven and earth

> and even heaven and earth
> can't keep at it for long

> so how could human beings
> make anything last (p.28)

Buddhist wit and conceptions of cosmology, selfhood, embodiment and knowledge have been particularly salvific and salving because both diseases were initially misdiagnosed, the celiac disease and soy allergy going under the name of "acute gastritis" for over seven years of incremental debilitation. Not even knowing how to say what was wrong and often in psychic distress and pain, I spent a lot of time with, in Zen scholar

Charles Egan's words, "Existence and void...mixed up" (p.161). Finally being able to name my conditions meant being able to treat them; treatment enabled me to begin to perceive clearly the emerging dynamic in my life between ability and disability, even though I couldn't and still can't control it. One thing for certain: the alleged boundary between ability and disability is as pernicious a fiction as the alleged boundary between mind and body in Western culture. "Real is not real," the Yuan Dynasty monk Wujian Xiandu reminds us, "and not is not-not" (Egan: p.147).

Nonetheless, I've found that the more committed I am to an embodied consciousness, the more I find myself reckoning with contingency and paradox. This is a fact that even Western medicine is beginning to recognize—helped along by recent research in neuroscience. In *Descartes' Error: Emotion, Reason and the Human Brain*, Antonio R. Damasio asserts that "the self that endows our experience with subjectivity is not a central knower and inspector of everything that happens in our minds...mind arises[s] out of an organism rather than out of a disembodied brain" (pp.227-229). Damasio's description of "The Body-Minded Brain" is remarkable for its congruence both with poststructuralist ideas concerning identity's "always already" constructed quality as well as Buddhist notions of permanent flux and transformation: the representations your brain constructs to describe a situation, and the movements formulated as response to a situation, depend on mutual brain-body interactions. The brain constructs evolving representations of the body as it changes under chemical and neural influences. Some of those representations remain non-conscious, while others reach consciousness. At the same time, signals from the brain continue to flow to the body, some deliberately and some automatically, from brain quarters whose activities are never represented directly in consciousness. As a result, the body changes yet again, and the image you get of it changes accordingly (p.228). Since body and brain must act in concert continually to construct our interdependent sensations of consciousness and selfhood, Damasio argues, "we construct the mind of the moment"(p.229). Each time I read Damasio's book, I'm struck by the profundity of this phrase, a radical claim that might seem more at home in a volume of Buddhist theology than in a mass-market paperback about neuroscience. In fact, each time I revisit Damasio's phrase, I'm called back to Laozi:

> best is a mind not made up
> then that mind is everyone's...

BRIAN TEARE

live in this world breathe it in breathe it out
let the world dissolve your mind

it and everything in it fixes upon your eye
and your ear and needs your mothering (p.59)

This is how my own ongoing embodiment has led and continues to lead to a poetics deeply indebted to "non-normative" somatic, physiological and cognitive processes as the basis for poetic forms, forms frequently engaged with classic texts from both Western and Eastern traditions of wisdom literature. All along my body has been its own book of wisdom, articulating far more about the terms of living than my mind can always be conscious of. And at this point, it has taught me at least one lasting lesson in poetics: I *have* to write from a place of uncertainty and flux, despite my deepest desire for certainty and stability, because the nature of things—both interior and exterior—is transience.

Okay. Sure. On those days when I walk with a minimum of pain and digest my food without incident, I *do* feel "temporarily able-bodied," and I am grateful. But still those days when I'm unable to walk or digest my food without symptoms are totally impossible to accept with equanimity. Instead of assessing the situation and seeing it objectively as a part of a continuum of experience, mostly I am like Yongjue Yuanxian, the monk-poet of "Lying Meditation." One of my favorite poems from the Ming Dynasty, it places its speaker deep in the struggle of distinguishing between what is and what seems to be, his consciousness intricated in the phenomenological, body-minded brain that we all share:

On my seven-foot rope bed
with arms bent, I sleep with the clouds.
Existence and void are mixed up;
Saints and sinner are cast away.
Don't say there are no things at all:
A bright mirror floats alone in the sky. (Egan: p.161)

5 poems from
THE EMPTY FORM GOES ALL THE WAY TO HEAVEN

afternoon

clarity arrives
brief virtue

cloud cover
alters symmetry's

trellis and shadow

classic image
two late T'ang dishes

one flowering
one empty

illness asks
as though it were

an aesthetic choice
will it be mind

or body emptied

first brief
clarity before

a day's gray
scale study

BRIAN TEARE

old tin tub

soapy water
tilts over

its rim hits
linoleum

nice image

for nausea
washing hot

one end
to the other

I remember

my mother
poured warm

water over
how small

my body

has become
again

western window
eastern window
sickbed between

illness shares
its few virtues

with art pain
as anomalous
as imagination

in not being "of"
or "for" anything

even language
lacks the quality
of their solitude

pure process
like art illness is

mostly the mystery
of why one window
opens slowly

why one window
remains locked

hours without
words I can't

form space
contour can't
hold anything

interior my body
never empties

of what it has
to do ache
wavers in the tin

tub where also I
bobbed for apples

until my face hurt
and hunger can't
urge me a child

sitting in snow
to open my mouth

language returns
like Li Ho

on his donkey
wrote one line
per scrap he'd bag

and shake out
at day's end

to make *human*
and *earthen* one
horizon   poetry

sum of patience
forged in heat

loose barb
tip broken
cracked red

it sliced through
flesh once

Ona Gritz

A CONSCIOUS DECISION

I know why you write about me so much," my son, Ethan, said to me once. "It's because I'm so important to you."

Writing has been a natural response to parenting for me; a kind of overflow. In poems, I've sought the perfect word to describe the particular blonde of Ethan's hair. *Honey-colored*, I wrote, because, as it changes with the seasons, his hair takes on the various hues of that thick, sweet stuff lined up in jars. I've attempted to describe the still, not-yet animated face I glimpsed in the birthroom mirror seconds before he woke to the world. *Calm as milk in its cup.* I've written about the rifle he used at summer camp. How the hand that once lay splayed on my chest as he nursed has held an actual weapon. He's a teenager now, but recently I drafted a poem in which I witnessed his tentative first steps, noting anew how they mirrored my own palsied walk.

My palsied walk. Disability is another subject that frequents my poems, but not because it compels me the way motherhood does. Writing about it has been more a conscious decision than a matter of inspiration.

When I was a child, there was a brown paper grocery bag kept on the floor of my closet, on the left-hand side toward the back. Inside was a single shoe, ankle high with a leather strap above the laces, and a hole near the ankle where a leg brace attached. The brace was a thin metal pole with a leather cuff that buckled near my knee. I had to wear this contraption while I slept. Heavy and stiff, it got caught in my blankets and sometimes caused bruises on my knees. Though I understood that what I had was cerebral palsy, I thought of that shoe as my disability. More precisely, I thought of it as my secret inner ugliness. After all, it was kept hidden and mentioned only in private as my mother helped me put on at night.

My cerebral palsy is relatively mild. I lack fine motor skills in my right hand, but learned early to compensate with my capable left. *It's nothing*, I was told. I walk as though favoring a sore foot. *Barely noticeable*, people said. These comments were meant to be compliments. I was lucky, it seemed, because I wasn't *too* different. Because I could more or less pass.

True, there were times I was forced to face my limitations—coming upon a winding staircase with no banister—walking down a slick, icy street to get home. But mostly when I thought about having cerebral palsy, what I focused on was how people saw me. It pained me to think that someone might not find me pretty because of my uneven legs and awkward gait. I didn't know then that worrying over such things is a kind of luxury. My quirky walk gets me where I'm going. I can speak clearly, cook, shop, clean and use my good mind to read, teach and write. Scarcely hampered by it, I saw disability as primarily a cosmetic issue. That changed when, in my thirty-fourth year, I took on a job that was, in many ways, beyond my physical abilities.

The following tasks are near to impossible when you lack fine motor skills in one hand, and when your gait is less than steady: Positioning a newborn to nurse at your breast. Safely bathing that newborn. Swaddling him. Walking while holding him. Opening a refrigerator while holding him. Eating while holding him. Drinking while holding him. Preparing a meal while holding him. Answering a phone while holding him. Climbing stairs while holding him. Descending stairs while holding him. Pushing a stroller while holding him. Lifting a stroller onto or off of a bus. Lifting a stroller onto or off of a train. Keeping pace with a fast crawling baby. Keeping pace with a fast running toddler...

I've had cerebral palsy since the day I was born, but it wasn't until my son was born that I truly experienced disability.

The first morning after I brought Ethan home from the hospital, I cried to a friend that he wailed every time I put him down.

"I can't even fix myself a bowl of cornflakes!"

My friend, a mother of two, laughed like it was all too familiar. "Don't worry," she assured me. "Moms get used to doing things with one hand."

What she didn't understand was that the one hand I had that was capable of pouring cereal and milk, of using a spoon, was the same one hand that could safely prop an infant's head. Hardly anyone knew this about me, and I found that fact frightening. Faced with caring for my baby and myself, I no longer wanted to pass as able-bodied. I wanted to be looked at squarely, limitations and all, so I could get the practical advice and physical help I needed. For that to happen, I had to take my disability out from the bottom of the closet and claim it. My great discovery was that it felt good to open up. To say, *Actually, it's not "nothing," it's this* and begin to describe—first in conversation, and soon after, in poems—what it's like to live in my particular body.

ONA GRITZ

Hemiplegia

Left, my bright half, gets all of it...
soft sharp prickly wet lined.
But press your head against my right shoulder,
I sense weight but no warmth. Your cheek,
to my right touch, stubble free,
whether or not you shave.
Under my right fingers your silver hair
holds no silk, nor can I feel it part
into single strands. I'll tell you
how I know you in the dark.
Left whispers the details.
Right listens and believes.

No

The nurses shaped us into positions.
Cradle hold, football hold. My hands
couldn't take you to the right place.
Cerebral palsy I mumbled, apology,
explanation. As though those experts
of the body didn't already know.
Finally, they propped cushions around us.
Your lips touched my breast
but instead of suckling, you dozed.
This had the nurses worried.
I worried how I'd feed you alone.
That night, your wail woke me.
I scooped you up, found the nurse's bell.
When a new one came, I shyly
explained the pillows, the palsy.
"No," she said coolly and I stared.
"No. That baby needs sleep not milk."
I tried again: "he's hungry."
Shaking her head, she left our room.
I attempted the football hold.
The cradle. Tried setting up pillows
then sitting between them. They fell.
Keeping you in my arms, I paced, I sang.
We cried in unison, both of us
so helpless, so desperately new.

ONA GRITZ

Prologue

A beach block gets so quiet
with the season over,
the ocean louder.
Year-rounders grow restless.
Neighbors flirt and my father
who worked nights, the only man
around on those long afternoons.
Getting home later, missing supper,
spitting out words that made
my mother shut the window
against that salt, that cold.
You don't know where I been,
he'd bluster. *You don't know*
where I go—until she folded inside
where I was folded,
another unknown, forming.
She believed this caused
my cerebral palsy. Water
takes the shape of its container,
and we are mostly water.

Because You Can't See My Photographs

I seek out the past in voices, pulling you over
to speak with men whose words are edged
with my father's New Yorkese, or to hear songs
I listened to in his finned blue car. Sometimes,
I name shapes to convey what I mean. *Bowl*
for the feeling of standing surrounded by
mountains as a teen, *torpedo* for the rounded
point my pregnant belly made a decade before
we met. Once, I placed a friend's infant on your lap,
telling you my son had been heavier than she,
that his scalp smelled like sleep lingering in sheets.
I have box after box of pictures, curled rectangles
that are blank to you. Still if you could travel
back to the schoolyard in Queens where I played
as a child, I trust you'd recognize the girl I was,
you who tease her laugh from me so easily.

ONA GRITZ

We Are Everywhere

The first one I see, on Bleeker,
has a rigid leg that traces half moons
as she moves. The next, spotted on
Houston, uses crutches to swing
her whole self forward, a leap
for each of her boyfriend's strides.
Right now, a woman with auburn hair
and a gypsy skirt waits for the light
in a motorized chair. The walk sign
flashes green and, magnetized, I follow,
willing her to notice I'm kin.

Stephen Kuusisto

DIGRESSIONS ON POETRY, PROSE
AND A LINGONBERRY BUSH

Poetry differs from other forms of expression in two essential ways: it does not aspire to tell the literal truth and it can get at the truth with unreliable methods. Or to put it another way: you can glean the truth from a poem but the process is quasi-occult, like reading the entrails of birds. The Roman Legion always did this before setting out on a campaign. It's possible that by reading avian intestines the Romans bought themselves some extra time to hang around the capital and that, in turn, this would have improved the morale of the troops. Such is the incalculable power of art— even those who do not care about it can derive benefits from living in an artistic culture. But I digress.

Poetry is only concerned with a provisional kind of truth. I've been reminded of this lately because someone asked me after a reading at Chattauqua how it happens that my writing is so visual when I am obviously blind. I have been asked this question literally hundreds of times and I'll likely never elude it. I'm getting used to it. Yet I think that I would like the question more if I thought it had merit.

The problem is that people think literary writing is the same thing as journalism. It's as if the audience says: "Nonfiction has to be like a photograph." They don't know this is what they're thinking but this is the ingrown narrative assumption of our time.

The idea that nonfiction is a form of journalism stems from the years just after the First World War when photographs first appeared in newspapers. Suddenly "the image" was all the rage, even if you wrote for the *Kansas City Star* or the *Columbus Dispatch*. Ernest Hemingway wrote a paragraph in his notebook about the carcass of a dead dog beside a railway platform and in effect nonfiction was wedded to the camera, at least in the eyes of the public.

The thing my well-meaning questioners don't understand is that I'm not writing prose that's powered by the appearance of truth ("verisimiltude" is what Henry James called it). I am driven by the vagaries of poetry and the imagery in my prose is entirely unreliable though it feels clear for all of that. I do not write about what I see, I write about what I do not see with words that feel good to the ear. When I write about the morning skin of ice on a birch tree I'm saying it because it feels right, not because I've watched it.

When the great Spanish poet Federico Garcia Lorca wrote lines like the ones below, no one thought he was reporting how the moon really looks. He was writing a poem. He was concerning himself with the truth in an unreliable way.

> When the moon rises,
> Moon of a hundred equal faces,
> Silver coins break out in sobs
> In pockets...

One can get a good sense of the moon from Lorca but it won't look like the moon in the photo on the front page of the metro section, which is of course why we like poetry and why we wrap fish with the newspaper.

There's another reason people are fooled by the clarity of a blind writer's prose. Most readers have forgotten that language is essentially magical. All nouns are merely images. Man. Horse. Street. Lingonberry bush. If I can write it, or say it, you will see it. No wonder the ancients thought the poets knew something.

Letter to Borges from Houston, Texas

I fell down this morning, Borges. I blamed this on the pavement outside the hotel.
There is something about falling when you're blind, a kind of synesthesia occurs.

I fell slowly into a cold paradise of blue.
It was like falling into the world in the birth wind.

Do you remember that?

Falling like this is certainly a kind of nostalgia.
I had time to think.

"Only God can conceal God,"
That's what I thought.

My arms were extended like wings.
Joyfully, falling...

I should add that no one was awake to see me.
Borges, did you ever laugh in so much blue?

Stephen Kuusisto

Borges: They Are Knocking the Wind
Out of Me in Iowa City

Up late, reading alone, I saw how Minturno was fooled by the intricacies of beauty. Unfortunately at that hour there was no one to tell (as a friend once wrote: "Everyone I know is either dead or still asleep.")

"Don't talk to yourself," I told myself. "Don't scribble in the margins."

When Marsilio Ficino said that beauty was just shapes and sounds he was surely bathing outdoors.

Neo-Platonists ease their bodies into their warm baths. Close your eyes you can see Minturno bathing under the autumn stars.

& so I went to bed at last & dreamt of my first city—Helsinki, late fifties—the old man in the harbor selling potatoes from a dory. In the dream as in life that old man was wearing a red shirt, the first I ever saw.

Minturno: ideal forms are the source of our passionate failures.

The next morning I walked in the street and felt too many things to be judged a success.

A man on stilts was handing out fliers announcing the arrival of a circus. It was a French circus. The man was speaking French.

"Ah," he said in French, "you are blind."

He withdrew the flier and tottered away.

I resisted the impulse to shout after him in my high school French: "You sound like the first dull minute after a train wreck!"

The stilts made a metallic tic-toc on the paving stones.

"Tic-toc, train wreck," I said to myself, feeling my tongue dent the soft palate. That was my method of keeping silent. Tic toc...

Letter to Borges from Estonia

Where I go is of considerable doubt.
Winter, Tallinn, I climb aboard the wrong trolley.
Always a singular beam of light leads me astray...

After thousands of cities I am safe when I say, "It is always the wrong trolley"—
Didn't I love you with my whole heart? Athens? Dublin?

Solo gravitational effects: my body is light as a child's beside the botanical garden's
iron fence—
But turning a corner one feels very old in the shadow of the mariner's church.

I ask strangers to tell me where I am.
Their voices are lovely, young and old.

Yes I loved you with my whole heart.
I never had a map...

Coordinated, Platonic movement in deep snow...
Crooked doors & radios in the bread shops...

STEPHEN KUUSISTO

Letter to Borges in His Parlor

What will become of you
With your Anglican heart & old furniture?
Are you waiting for insects at the geraniums?
What is there to love anymore my friend?

Some days I too don't feel like going out.
Secluded with my gramophone
I play *Flores Purisimas*, zarzuela,
Caruso—over & over...

Once, years ago, I got lost in the vast cemetery of Milan.
I had my dog; I was taking roses to Toscanini's tomb.
It was an ordinary day,
Men were digging graves.

Confounded in the ballyhoo *Italien*,
The tombs carved like sailing ships,
I talked to perfect strangers:
Women alone with grief,
Men walking "on doctor's orders."

It is good, Borges, to have a mission, don't you agree?

Only Bread, Only Light

At times the blind see light
And that moment is the Sistine ceiling,

Grace among buildings—no one asks
For it, no one asks.

After all, this is solitude,
Daylight's finger,

Blake's angel
Parting willow leaves.

I should know better.
Get with the business

Of walking the lovely, satisfied,
Indifferent weather—

Bread baking
On Arthur Avenue

This first warm day of June.
I stand on the corner

For priceless seconds.
Now everything to me falls shadow.

STEPHEN KUUSISTO

Sheila Black

WAITING TO BE DANGEROUS:
DISABILITY AND CONFESSIONALISM

I have XLH, commonly known as vitamin-D resistant rickets because the symptoms mimic those of nutritional rickets—sharply bowed legs and an unusually short stature. "It is usually classed as a form of dwarfism." I was over forty the first time I read that—on a description of the illness posted on-line from the Merck Manual. I was shocked. "Dwarf" had been a word that I had never heard or used in reference to myself. But it made sense when I thought about it. Still, it was hard to say: "I am a dwarf."

When I think about why I am drawn to confessional poetry—confessional poetry which M.L. Rosenthal first defined as consisting of "sexual guilt, alcoholism, repeated confinement in a mental hospital" among other subjects—I think of my disability (p.7). Rosenthal asserts that in "confessional poetry" such "difficult" subjects are "usually developed in the first person and intended without question to point to the author himself (herself?)." I do not like my automatic association of disability with shame, but there is no question it is there. The first time I read that my illness was "a form of dwarfism," I suffered a sudden hot flash—my cheeks reddened, my palms burned—I felt somehow ashamed of myself. Even though—as my disability is a genetic one—I bear no responsibility for it whatsoever.

When I was growing up my mother used to say that the cause of my illness—she called it "my illness" or, more commonly, "my legs," as in "the reason your legs happened to you"—was that when I was two months old, I caught the red measles. She said my fever rose so high "it must have done something to your DNA." In fact, this explanation makes no sense. No fever can change the coding of the DNA. My mother insisted this because she said "there is no other record of anything like this in our family." Only years later, did I realize why she kept repeating this story, because it was a way of saying what had happened was *not her fault*. Later, when she came to understand that XLH occurs often out of the blue—due to spontaneous and unexplained mutations in the genetic structure—she appeared to accept it, but I could tell she did not find this as soothing an explanation as the red measles. I could not understand her guilt until as an adult I reviewed my old medical charts. I discovered that when, as a young toddler, I began to exhibit radical bowing of the legs, the doctors believed the reason was that my mother was not feeding me properly. They ordered her to keep charts of every meal she fed me. They asked her if she was lying when she reported giving me milk many times a day. Shame and guilt, the rock-bed of the confessional.

In recent years, confessionalism has become a favorite target of a multitude of poetry critics, often employed as a symbol of all that is wrong with poetry. Among the accusations: confessionalism relies too much on the poet's own experiences; it reflects a "reality television" aesthetic in which artistic power is predicated on the revelation of lurid secrets or personal trauma. Yet the silencing of or scorn for such so-called charged material is often itself a kind of corrective repression. As a few perceptive critics such as Cate Marvin have pointed out, dismay at the confessional is often specifically addressed at the more powerless (women, minorities) who seek to marshal its power. Furthermore, the direct association of confessional poetry with "true confession" is naïve and problematic. In "Female Trouble: Women's Transgressions in the Confessional Mode," Marvin writes:

> ...confessional poets set up their camp smack in the middle of the dangerous border that separates the poet's lived experience from the poem he/she has created. However, what makes the project exciting and dangerous is the poets' refusal to remain faithful to the truth, as opposed to offering strictly biographical revelations. Confessional poetry is never earnest; rather, it is mercilessly manipulative of the reader...(p.31).

Put simply, the confessional poem relies for its charge not simply on the presentation of problem material, but rather on the self-conscious presentation of it before a specific audience. In this sense, the confessional poem is much closer to the dramatic tradition of poetry—the dramatic monologue, the staged scene—than it is to a simple narrative of truth. As a result, confessional poetry, far from being dominated by the personal, often becomes a place where the personal and the political intersect in surprising, exciting and potentially subversive ways.

As a person with a visible disability, I have often felt intruded upon, defined and even circumscribed by the gaze of others. As a child, I don't believe I truly conceived of myself as *disabled* or *different* (the word for what I was in my day was *crippled*) until I started

SHEILA BLACK

school, at a Catholic convent in Rio de Janeiro run by an order of mostly English and Irish nuns. Here my legs were immediately tagged as a sign of God's will, God's mystery, even God's love. Yet for all the talk about how God loved everyone, and people like me were somehow special proof of this, I also attracted an uncanny amount of hostility. In my class was a boy named Gabriel who was in the most classical sense *beautiful*. He had golden hair; he was tall; he had a crooked and somehow endearing smile. Everyone appeared to turn to him as sunflowers turn to the sun. And he, from the very first, hated me. The mystery of his hatred grew as vast and immutable as the mystery of how day turns to night. In the playground—a cobbled courtyard surrounded by a thin fringe of grass—he would follow me chanting, "There goes ugly girl." Once he and another girl asked me if believed in fairies. I said I did. He picked up a stone and threw it at my cheek. When it cut me, and I bled, I went to the nuns crying. He said I was lying; I had tripped over my own crooked feet. The nuns believed him, and I—why did I do this?—recanted. Later that year, I would read little picture books about the lives of lions; the "natural order" of predator and prey. All of this would make some kind of intuitive sense to me, but it was a sense that bordered on despair. There was an order, an order I did not understand, hooked together with Gabriel and me, with God's mystery, God's judgment, God's order, and I was on the wrong side of it. "Don't stagger like that," our teacher, Sister Agnes, would say to me with irritation as we lined up for morning prayers. "Of course you can't help it, I suppose, but it does seem to me you could at least try to put your feet straight and walk like other people."

I think about why I tell this story—a "true" story more or less—or why it might have meaning. The story for me is obviously how I was a victim, but if it stops there, it is not a story with much lasting interest or value. It is perhaps more interesting as an allegory of power—Gabriel and I as symbols of forces beyond us, positions we have in a sense inherited—the ugly "crippled" girl, the beautiful "golden" boy. Yet to tell it as pure allegory leaves out the hot, dense, embarrassing, complex ways in which we as individuals reacted to the situation. Often that year I tried ineffectually to win Gabriel's and, by extension, my teacher's approval. I tried by wearing my school uniform longer than was the custom. By putting straight my crooked feet as often as I could remember to. By pretending to like and admire whatever they liked and admired. I am sure they tried too. Gabriel's cruelty to me—how ironic that he should be named for the archangel—mounted as the year went on. Yet was it entirely personal? I can't imagine it was. He too was performing for an audience, carrying out a role he felt bound to play—or perhaps he was just poking at me as you might poke at a hill of ants, out of childlike curiosity. What will they do? What does it mean that they live, too, in this world, but appear so *other?*

Late in the year, Gabriel accused me of deliberately kicking in the tall, ruby-colored stained-glass window of the school chapel. I knew I was in big trouble when a group of nuns came bearing towards me across the playground like an Armada of black ships. I panicked—and ran out of the school grounds. A group of street people caught me and dragged me back through the school gates. At first, the fact that I had run (barely run, actually, since I was at this time extremely bow-legged) was taken as evidence of my guilt. But when the Mother Superior asked that I recreate what I had done, I could not lift my leg high enough to reach the window. And it became apparent, because of the precise way my legs were twisted, that it would have been "physically impossible" for me to have kicked it in. Gabriel was in disgrace. Yet the pleasure of victory I might have been expected to feel instead had the ashen taste of the worst kind of defeat. I often thought years and years after I would like to write a "confession" of how I had kicked in the window, except I hadn't. I had never even conceived of doing such a thing, until I was accused of it. Yet I could not help feeling that the whole incident echoed or reflected something inside me—I was angry, and I would have kicked that window in had I been able, had I been braver, had I thought of it. I recount this simply to express the ways in which the truth of experience, or its inner meaning, tends to blur or bleed over the more you contemplate it. Hated because I was different, that very hatred transformed me into someone who hated.

As a poet, a storyteller, I am attracted to the unruly and confrontational elements of the confessional, to the ways it complicates personal truth through a presentation that makes the audience continually question whether the speaker is to be trusted. I think hard about why this element of unreliability, the trickster aspect of confessionalism, appeals to me. And I think the answer has to do with the positions historically available to the person with a disability—or, more pointedly, the paucity of those positions. For instance, in the story above, no matter how I try, I cannot see myself as anything other than "crippled." The most striking thing about me as far as this story is concerned is the fact that I have crooked legs.

Like many people with a disability, I am always slightly amazed to realize I have suffered more from other people's perceptions of my condition than I have from my own

SHEILA BLACK

real "disabilities." I do not remember ever staying up all night wringing my hands because I would never run a four or even a ten-minute mile. On the other hand, I have spent many useless hours agonizing over how people might react if they ever saw me in a miniskirt. As a poet, what influence this has had on me is both hard and easy to track. I tend to write in a kind of supercharged rush—images of violence and/or horror laid up right against images of beauty and/or tenderness, as if the two were part of the same continuum, as if the two could be forced together, blurred into one another, or represented contradictions that must find a way to co-exist because they could not be resolved. I do believe this comes from the experience of living with disability—or living with a disability in a world that circles around ideals of "normal." A world in which I am always the piece that doesn't fit and also a body that speaks or argues loudly—even against my will—about the problems with such normalizing structures. Furthermore, these are structures I have certainly internalized in my own attitudes about my disability. I believe my disability matters because I know it matters to other people. At the same time, I tend to believe—imaginatively?—that viewed in perspective it is just one fact about me, and not always a particularly important one.

I love the confessional because it allows such contradictions, such instability to be front and center. It allows feeling and extremes of feeling within an ideological context, but one which is inherently unstable, one in which the message is never entirely anchored. As Cate Marvin notes:

> The confessional project may be of particular interest to women because it allows them to misbehave on the page, to reconstruct their identities, to display the power of their intelligence through language, to speak their minds without being silenced or interrupted...and to, ironically, say what they really mean. In confessional poetry, there are no rules...(p.46).

By "no rules" Marvin suggests that the confessional, by offering the ability to occupy multiple intimate, apparently "true" positions vis-à-vis the charged "issue at stake" also offers the possibility of an imaginative transcendence. In the case of feminist poetry, confessionalism offers a means of escape from the polarities of a discourse of femininity that limits or encodes the female speaker. The confessional often achieves this through ruthless and even extravagant staging of a charged emotional moment. The most striking example is perhaps Sylvia Plath's "Daddy," which compares her experience of an absent or repressive father to the Holocaust—a comparison that is clearly hyperbolic, offensive and meant to be so, but also, compellingly in the poem, "imaginatively true" for the speaker herself. The poem is a kind of psychic theater, but one which in its staging casts new light on "the world as it is," suggesting the necessity of a reconfiguration of female power and how it functions (or doesn't) within a patriarchal system. The radical, even unhinged, claims the poem makes thus become an affirmation of the imaginative and real power of the speaker—who speaks with almost Promethean fervor out of a desire to re-vision or recreate herself.

The parallels with disability poetry are obvious. Often the dilemma for the disabled poet is how to say what you truly mean in a context in which disability is either silenced and denied, or conversely, given such overwhelming importance that the human being becomes subsumed by his or her condition. Lennard Davis points out that the target of the poetics of disability must perhaps ultimately be the structures of "normal" in which the disabled speaker is conceived and constructed as a perennial other—and usually a lesser (Davis: p.3). This, for me, is the project the confessional most animates. When Marvin states that the confessional at its best or strongest "is defined by its artifice," by "its ruthless desire to convince us its untruths are true," she suggests how the confessional often uses "artifice" and "untruth" to allow a marginalized speaker to radically reconfigure his or her position. By allowing its speaker the dangerous freedom to be, or appear, extravagantly personal while making a wider critique of social artifice, social untruth and social control, confessionalism often becomes, as Marvin puts it, "a true expedition into the imagination" with the potential for tracking multiple modes of our liberation.

Sheila Black

Playing Dead

Begin by imagining
a failure of will,
the boundaries of the body erased
like lines on a chalkboard.

You might picture the usual things:
night sky, waveless sea,
the greeny depths
which plummet to pure dark

or something as small
as a single square inch
of soil, packed with rotted
leaf, root scrap, cracked

shell, the molted wing
of a specked moth, a handful
of sand, a handful of dust;
it all comes to much the same.

It is the absence of conscious
motion that takes getting used to,
no sound but the slow
settling, the ripening of decay:

burst liquid, gelid light.
The old story of how stars
are born of frozen dust
and radiance

from this house of bone.

SHEILA BLACK

What You Mourn

The year they straightened my legs,
the young doctor said, meaning to be kind,
Now you will walk straight
on your wedding day, but what he could not
imagine is how even on my wedding day
I would arch back and wonder
about that body I had before I was changed,
how I would have nested in it,
made it my home, how I repeated his words
when I wished to stir up my native anger
feel like the exile I believed
I was, imprisoned in a foreign body
like a person imprisoned in a foreign land
forced to speak a strange tongue
heavy in the mouth, a mouth full of stones.

Crippled they called us when I was young
later the word was *disabled* and then *differently abled,*
but those were all names given by outsiders,
none of whom could imagine
that the crooked body they spoke of,
the body, which made walking difficult
and running practically impossible,
except as a kind of dance, a sideways looping
like someone about to fall
headlong down and hug the earth, that body
they tried so hard to fix, straighten was simply mine,
and I loved it as you love your own country,
the familiar lay of the land, the unkempt trees,
the smell of mowed grass, down to the nameless
flowers at your feet—clover, asphodel,
and the blue flies that buzz over them.

Reconstruction

I think of the trees there first:
how large and tender
they seemed, breathing green
above the brick colonials,
the loneliness of other people's windows,
glittering under the sulfurous
street lamps, past midnight
when the pills stopped
working, and I could feel
my bones knitting themselves
into a new shape.

The rings of trees accreted
slowly, one by one,
spread ripples from a dropped
stone, the healed bones hardening
a different white on the x-rays,
not even a ghost of the form
they had been.

The codeine was blue, shaped
like a small bullet.
My mother did not believe in such simple
relief of pain. She had stayed
awake even when we were born,
seen us slide out bloodied.
Where had I gone wrong?

All summer they brought me trays
of food, bowls of plums
shimmering with water, cooked
spinach, a limp sea of green,

said, "Eat," but I was wary,

remembered the myths I had learned:

If you take a single seed
you will stay down here forever.

I swallowed the pills furtively,
felt myself plunge, a girl
down a well, my own voice calling
back at me from the curved walls.

I was remade, and I fell,
searching my old self
in the trees above our house,
their age passing through me,
their green hearts blooming in me.

All I wanted was to remember everything,
the way a child asks questions
to resurrect the moment of origin,
the expression of a face
before it is born.

SHEILA BLACK

Objects Waiting to Be Dangerous

Do I get tired of the stories
I know or the ways
I have of telling them?
Today the sun shines
with that piercing autumn clarity.
Silk trees fray along the roads,
pink and white threads
darkening to burnt sugar.
And on the river banks
swallows gather in great numbers,
filling the branches of the dry cottonwoods.
They will fly south to the sea,
trace the hip of the land
over plains and mountains
to Venezuela or beyond.

Driving down the old Highway 66
at noon, I hear them chatter
through a hedge of mesquite.
How they ache to leave and how this season
fills me with pestilent longing—fretful,
tiresome so I jerk the wheel too sharply,
raise dust devils in the road,
imagine crumpling metal,
some kind of annihilation,
meanwhile all this life in hands,
so easy to waste, so hard to taste each bite.

Rilke said the beauty which is next to terror
is the trace of God
in the world, but I can't find it,
and so I drive and watch

SHEILA BLACK

the swallows lift from the branches,
flutter over the water in little clouds
that rise and fall like waves,

a feeling rising in me
so shapeless and yet so sharp,
I can't keep my mind in one place,
but dart around, hunting,
pecking like a women who can't find the key
to her house but is sure it's right in front of her,

right under her nose, so close that
all she needs to do is put out her hand
and she will touch it.

SHEILA BLACK

Raymond Luczak

LISTENING SIDEWAYS TO THE BEAT OF A POEM

With the gift of deafness, you learn to listen better than anyone. It has nothing to do with sound, and yet when you pay close attention to everything but sound, it does.

•

Although I began writing poetry at the age of eleven, meter wasn't on my radar. I started out writing limericks, a five-line form that required the counting of syllables and accommodating of end rhymes. A word was just a building block, its resulting line a room, and the poem a tiny house all by itself on a prairie. I built many houses that way. It was fun and easy. Not much thought required, really.

That was how I saw my life in Ironwood, Michigan. A former mining town, Ironwood barely had 5,000 residents. We were all familiar strangers.

•

Once my hearing loss was diagnosed when I was two and half years old, I was instantly outfitted with a bulky hearing aid. Sign language was forbidden. I learned to speak. I didn't realize until years later how much I wanted to sing instead.

At the age of thirteen, I discovered the Bee Gees singing harmony against a pulsating disco beat on a jukebox in a bar. That changed everything.

Suddenly limericks looked tired, repetitious.

I examined lyrics of the latest Top 40 songs on the radio, and imagined myself something of a songwriter: I wrote lyrics to imaginary music. Disco music was a godsend because its beat rarely varied. It enabled me to follow the beat and gradually solve the mysteries of melody, chorus and emotion. I would be glorious on the dance floor like John Travolta prancing about in *Saturday Night Fever*, and everyone would be my friend.

Unwanted and misunderstood as the only deaf student in the entire Ironwood Catholic school system, I sought refuge in the loom of words where I spun tapestries, an ever-tightening cocoon against the taunts and laughs of those hearing boys in my classroom.

I saw how they talked about music. I read *Rolling Stone*, *Creem* and other music-related magazines so I could be ready to partake in conversations about the latest hits. I borrowed library books on the history of pop music. I sought out used vinyl albums and barely scratched 45s at the local thrift store and garage sales. I always came home to listen to DJ Casey Kasem announce the latest Number One hit of the American Top 40 on the radio every Sunday afternoon. One day I would be accepted as one of these hearing boys.

That never happened, but at least I had assembled a killer record collection.

•

Not long after I heard the Bee Gees for the first time, I had sex with an older man in a public restroom. I was fourteen. I was the instigator. There was something about his eyes that told me he was lonely too. Even though I didn't understand the protocols for anonymous encounters between men at the time, my instincts took over. One of the many things that had confused me, because it made me feel different from the others, became clear as day. I didn't know there was a name for it, but I knew it had to be a secret like so many others I'd kept inside. Lonely people have the most secrets of them all. Being unwanted is the ultimate mark of shame.

•

I stopped writing poetry for a long spell. I wrote plays in which I starred as the most popular friend of them all, and everyone else in my life were only players. I never showed them to anyone.

I never wrote about my deafness, the single defining moment of my life. It just didn't exist. I didn't have the proper vocabulary to help explain those things in my ears.

•

In May 1980, I caught sight of an older man finger spelling with a girl while he was sitting on a bench outside Hulstrom's, a candy and convenience store on the edge of downtown Ironwood. Once I saw his expressive face, I understood.

I didn't have to decode his face in the same way I always had to with hearing people. He was an open book, which didn't require lipreading.

I sought out the manual alphabet in a book and learned it in secret.

As a lonely boy, I found the intoxicating desire to learn signs the most important secret of all. I loved how these magnificent handshapes could disappear into the gloves of my skin.

RAYMOND LUCZAK

No one would know how proficient I'd become with finger spelling words without thinking.

I knew I was deaf, but I didn't own the word. I merely had "a hearing problem."

I was terrified at first, but I forced myself to meet "Gramps" Morrison. He lit up when he saw my earmolds. He gently showed me the right way to hold up my hand when I finger spelled.

This, I thought, was how things should be done: a deaf person showing another how to live a life.

•

I told my parents I needed to learn sign language.

They were not happy.

My speech therapist arranged for me to meet with a hearing woman who knew sign language. She brought over a thick binder of mimeographed signs. It was clear from her lesson plan that summer that I would learn a chapter per session. I ended up learning half the book in our first session. I couldn't get enough.

She was agog.

I asked her to try different signs so I could read them.

She was stunned that I didn't have a problem following her signs.

Excited, I biked to town and looked for Gramps. I began signing.

He looked confusedly at me.

I felt hurt. What had I been doing wrong? My teacher said I was good with my signs, wasn't I?

I didn't realize that the signs I'd learned had come from Signing Exact English (SEE), a bastardized version of American Sign Language (ASL), that was created as a system— not a language!—designed to teach deaf kids English. I didn't know then the pitfalls of learning signs from a hearing person who didn't know anything about Deaf culture.

•

By then, I began expanding my listening preferences. I wasn't interested in Chic and Donna Summer anymore. I wanted something edgier, like Blondie's classic album *Eat to the Beat*, and musically diverse, like Paul McCartney's *Tug of War*. I continued to create handmade books of poetry, which I never showed anyone.

Then I was given a chance to change my life. I didn't have to go to Ironwood Catholic High School anymore. Houghton, a university town two hours away, had a deaf program for high school students. I wouldn't be the only one deaf, and they used a combination of SEE and speech for communication. My long and lonely wait was over.

•

The more I learned signs, the more organic my poetry became; the lowercase "i" became an assertive "I." It was as if the aspiration to become hearing through my mastery and understanding of the current Top 40 songs no longer mattered. I still listened to music, but I was now listening to the other music within.

I wrote poems about the boy I loved, most of which I destroyed in fear of being found out.

But not once did I write about being deaf. That did not happen until the fall of 1984 when I went to Gallaudet University. I discovered ASL, the deaf LGBT community and literature.

There, the puzzling signposts on the road of my life made sense all at once. Yes, I was deaf. And gay. And a poet. I hadn't been on the road to nowhere!

Using ASL freed me at last. Being able to understand completely what was being said gave me invincible wings.

It enabled me to have the courage to *look* different and not worry about what others thought of me. I wasn't going to try speaking at the same time with my signs. I wasn't going to try signing in the English word order. And I wasn't going to hide the fact that I was deaf—and gay—in my own writing.

My life has been a highway after I took that exit to Gallaudet.

•

Switching lights between English and ASL constantly fills the shadows of a phrase or an expression. The way to describe something in English would be described very differently in ASL. I write in English, but I dream in ASL, or at least, I don't recall dreaming of myself speaking. ASL unleashes my emotion, and English tempers it. This tension between these two disparate languages informs all my rewrites because I borrow nonstop from each language without thinking about it. If I have trouble with a line, I sign it and rewrite. Sometimes I find I have to invent new ways of describing things in English because ASL is often superior to what's possible in English.

RAYMOND LUCZAK

Writing a poem is never straightforward. Yes, there's the setting down of lines, at first a ramble of images and words. Yes, there's the constant pruning of words and stanzas to achieve a certain look, a mood. But I am always listening to the poem's melody itself. What's its time signature? Emotional pitch? Can it be shorter and yet dense like one of the memorable singles produced as a "Wall of Sound" by Phil Spector? Like a jazz musician long used to hours of on-the-spot improvisation, I rewrite as if onstage. My melody must sing, sing, sing!

I do not hear as well as I used to in the days when I discovered the Bee Gees for the first time, but this doesn't bother me. My heart still knows how to listen, and that's the most important ear of all.

Consonants

1.

Standing in the choir, I watch
out of the corners of my eyes
my classmates singing from their books.
I try to hold my silent vowels
as long as they do before
I blink my eyes and miss
the beginning of their next note.

People in the audience who know me
struggle to hide their smiles
when they catch me in the last row.
My mouth movements must be out of sync.

I want to fall backwards,
off the bleachers
into the Montreal River,
floating amidst its mist
of dragonflies sewing the air
and cattails knitting
songs that I need not sing.

Everywhere I see their voices
never in tune. I exhale in relief.

2.

Mrs. Fraites, my speech therapist, peers
over her bifocals into my eyes. "Do that again."

I try to reel in my tongue,
lock up its sides rising up like the valley
inside the cavern of my mouth.
I hiss "st."

RAYMOND LUCZAK

"Try again."

"St. *St.*"

"The front of your tongue's too close
to your teeth." She draws a map
of my tongue encircled by a moat
of teeth, pinpointing just how far back
I should wait before I volley the sound.

I try again. She smiles.

3.
Consonants are cannonballs I cannot hear.
People hearing me for the first time search
for the solid sounds spanning the bridge
of vowels. Some of them give up.
I am an unnecessary detour,
a road construction annoyance.

4.
"*Errrrr,*" I stress. Today
is another war between "r" and "w."

I am starting to realize how cursed
I am with my first name.
I have long spoken my name as "Waymond,"
forgetting often to curl up the tip of my tongue
for the preciously elusive jewel of all consonants.

"W" requires no thought: "We," "will," "weak."
But the "R" demands focus: My tongue aims,

a rifle pointing at the sky past my teeth,
not to overshoot the eaves.

The consonant "w" is an eagle soaring,
its wings spanning all below.

The consonant "r" is a hummingbird.
One mustn't blink lest you never catch its thumbnail wings.

Instructions to Hearing Persons
Desiring a Deaf Man

His eyebrows cast shadows everywhere.
You are a difficult language to speak.

His long beard is thick with distrust.
You are another curiosity seeker.

His hands are not cheap trinkets.
Entire lives have been wasted on you.

His face is an inscrutable promise.
You are nothing but paper and ink.

His body is more than a secret language.
Tourists are rarely fluent in it.

His eyes will flicker with a bright fire when
you purge your passport of sound.

Let your hands be your new passport, for
he will then stamp it with approval.

A deaf man is always a foreign country.
He remains forever a language to learn.

Ablutions of the Tongue

Forgive me, Father, for I've committed a venial sin
while an altar boy at St. Michael's. I dreamed
entire congregations struck dumb, their eyes wild
with fear and helplessness. I would step down from my cross
and free birds of paradise from my hands,

their plumage catching glints of pure prism,
wordlessness an art to behold. Utterances, now noise
pollution, would catch wind and swirl high above their heads
while they tear at their own throats, commanding
a single sound of importance. I would stand still,

waiting for the blood on their fingernails to cake.
Their sobs would slow into hiccups of what next.
The only one smiling, I would take off my surplice
and unzip my black cassock like a butterfly
casting aside its childhood of drabness.

Down the aisle I would walk out the back
of St. Michael's and see people in great shock
of finding their own voices gone to the heavens.
For days afterwards I could pick out my new friends
on the street. They were the only ones smiling.

RAYMOND LUCZAK

Hummingbirds

Our new Sheet Metal teacher left
us boys alone in the cafeteria.

My notebook was filled with
sugarcubes of want.

One of them said, "Hey you!
What you doin' over there?"

My fingers were only
hummingbirds in a small cage.

I sat up and freed
my deaf voice, my hearing hands.

They fluttered under my chin, in
front of my chest, everywhere.

The boys' eyes narrowed like a cat's
for a minute. Then they stood up.

My voice faltered as I felt
their fierce wings beating.

"Fairy! Look at his hands
swishing in the air!"

Lilacs' fragrances melted
under globs of solder.

The boys flaunted limp wrists. I shot
all my birds in mid-flight.

Raymond Luczak

Anne Kaier

RIVER CREATURE

One October afternoon about ten years ago, I sat fingering the bark of the yew tree that dominates my small Philadelphia garden. As an evergreen, my yew is prized in the city, and it's been allowed to grow freely, reaching nearly thirty feet. Its bark bunches in rough clumps where the branches fork. On the trunk, it peels in copper-gray strips. The tree's skin is rather like my skin. Only the tree's is normal and mine is not. Mine also flakes and mottles because I have a rare skin condition called ichthyosis in which the skin does not shed normally, but clots and peels perpetually. It's genetic, chronic and inelegant.

That afternoon, once again, I had been looking for a way to talk about my skin in the poetry I'd recently begun to write. How, I wondered, should I handle my flawed body? What attitude do I take? What language do I use? The answers did not come easily. All my life I had been taught to ignore my skin condition, to pretend—against manifest evidence—that the problem didn't exist. Schooled in silence on the subject, I had to develop a stance about my ichthyosis and then find the voice for my first poems that reflected the fact of my condition. The poems didn't simply pour out. I set out very consciously to choose certain seams of metaphor. How was I going to talk about this body which flushes with an unnatural redness and cracks in patterns like a desert pool drying in the sun?

I knew what attitude I did not want to profess. There was no way I'd let myself be sentimental. No nonsense about how God or some wise power gave me this disease for some greater benefit. I remember once going to the confirmation of a friend's daughter. One of the confirmands was a child with muscular dystrophy. The bishop looked out over the rows of preteens in their thin dresses and dark suits and told us that the child with muscular dystrophy was actually lucky that God had given him this burden, luckier than the kids who could easily run. In the back of the church, I seethed and swore to fight such attitudes, which were implicitly patronizing, glossing over the difficulties of being different—much as my own trained silence on the subject of my illness did.

Of course, I certainly wasn't about to treat myself as a freak either. I flinched when I read that, as late as the 1950s, someone with ichthyosis allowed himself to be called

Alligator Man and made a living as a sideshow attraction in the Ringling Brothers Circus. Even today the TLC channel regularly features people such as conjoined twins who have unusual bodies, and encourages the audience to treat such people as freak-show performers.

It has been easier for me to know how I wouldn't present myself than to know how I would. In searching for an answer, I wondered what other writers and artists did. I'd been taken with the story of how the nineteenth-century French painter, Jacques-Louis David, portrayed the fanatical revolutionary leader Jean-Paul Marat, who was murdered in his bath during the French Revolution. Marat suffered from a debilitating skin disease called dermatitis herpetiformis, or Duhring's Disease. For relief, Marat spent as much time as possible in a medicinal bath, plotting the deaths of his enemies. On July 13, 1793, a young woman in a rival faction gained entry to his bathroom and stabbed him. David, who admired Marat, immortalized this scene in a famous painting. Simon Schama calls this painting a lie because David has transformed Marat into a hero. His skin looks clean—his arms muscular and firm. If David had wanted to portray Marat as evil, implies Schama, he would have shown the man's skin as red, blistering, scaly. The sins of the soul would have shown themselves in the flaws of the body. I hope I am not alone in finding this a positively medieval equation.

Although I don't think my skin has ever quite prompted anyone to think of me as morally corrupt, I've often encountered fear. Like many people with ichthyosis, I was stared at continually as a child. Other kids were frightened by my scaly skin and scarlet face. In summer, because ichthyosis plugs up my sweat glands, I lack the cooling, if cloying, moisture of ordinary sweat. Warmth builds up in my body, and my face can turn a dark purple-red.

One August afternoon, when I was about eight, my mother and I walked along a hot sidewalk toward the local supermarket. On that treeless concrete path, the heat caught up with me and my pounding heart turned my cheeks a deep scarlet. Two boys on bikes pedaled by, then slowed, swerved and circled back. One leaned forward yelling, "Look at that girl," to his pal, "her face, man—that's a sin!" I could feel him circling nearer, his bike wheeling up onto the pavement. I ducked my face away. The supermarket door stood three yards ahead. As I pushed through the heat, willing myself to keep moving as he taunted me, my mother spun around on her strong legs.

"Look at that boy!" she spat out. "Who does he think he is?" I heard the bikers brake, wheel off and rattle down the street. She followed me through the glass door into the cool store. With her hand on my shoulder, she leaned down and practically hissed in my ear: "Did that boy wound you?"

I didn't know how to answer her. The intensity of her love was almost as difficult to bear as the boy's jibes—and more familiar. I wanted to shake them both off. So I mumbled "not really," and ducked beneath the family code of not talking about my skin—a code which she had just broken.

Years later, as I began to write poetry, I thought back to that scene and wondered what kind of primitive fear lay behind the boy's pointing finger. Was he worried about catching the disease? Was he disturbed by the sight of a child who looked so rivetingly different—or was he reacting to some itchiness in his own boyish body? All the above, perhaps. I also asked myself how I could handle that kind of fear—not on the street—but in my readers.

If the people who read my work were afraid of skin disease, if they even thought that my condition was the reflection of a polluted soul, how, I wondered, could I ever neutralize their fear? How could I make them see me clearly? I knew that the way in which I characterized my body would affect the way I invited others to look at me, know me, accept me. I didn't want to be feared. I didn't want to inspire only pity or horror. I wanted to write about my skin in a way that would assuage terror, tame it. But first I had to tangle with my own feelings about my body.

In the end, like poets from forever, I turned to the natural world. Here were pools of metaphor and a way of looking that I could use. The yew tree, I thought, peels and is beautiful. Its bark whorls like the clumps of skin between my toes. Sitting next to it, I stretched my hand out to its trunk and the scales on my palms met its rough bark.

I think that afternoon with the yew tree gave me a beginning, a sort of permission to write poetry about my body. Using language drawn from nature, which, of course, can be intensely cruel, gave me one way to show myself—to myself and to others—as part of a larger current of life. It also gave me a way to depict myself without false sentimentality, with a kind of clinical accuracy. In a poem "Cossetted" that I wrote a few months later, I pictured myself as a baby in the rushes like baby Moses, but also as a river creature—scaly, strange and beautiful.

The river creature image, with its suggestion of strangeness, of alligators, and above all, of water—which is life to my dry skin—gave me a way to talk about my body as a living, natural creation. The link to the baby Moses—hubris by any standard, I suppose—gave balm to my ego and refuted those who would associate flawed skin with moral evil. Once I had the river creature image, I could go further, could describe my own face very precisely, sparing neither the reader nor myself. To write like this was a great relief. I could finally confront the realities of my condition, yet see myself as a part of the eternal natural world. No longer an anomaly, I too was part of all creation—and I had the language to prove it.

Cosseted

1.

In my fantasy, the organdie dress
bought to cup flawless cheeks
fills with a baby whose skin mottles
with scale, clumps in ridges on her back.
She's a river creature,
washed like the infant Moses
from some muddy mutation,
a gene gone awry in the womb.

I coo and tell her she's pretty in her eyes
and in my eyes, in her dress she's pretty;
she smiles and her smile breaks into fissures
at the corners of her lips.
I wipe blood from the cracks and never mind
that her dress is stained.
I pick her up as tenderly as any mother, as any father.
I tell her she's pretty and she smiles.

2.

In our seashore town,
anger hit me like a hot dry wind.
It's a cruel place for anyone over thirty,
for anyone with a skin disease.
Shoals of girls in bikinis
swim along the beach.

As a child, playing in the sand,
squinting at my chest,
jumping around the truth of my legs,
words screened my eyes:

ANNE KAIER

no, no, no, that's not me
there's nothing wrong.
My playmate said: "You were burned."
Was I? I wondered.

3.
Loneliness shrouds this child;
she can't beat it back.
It shades her from the moment she enters
her mother's glittering party
in her best blue dress,
scratching her arm.

4.
In my dream, Mother and I share
red wine in a plush room, while
a half-naked child shivers on a hillside,
her buttocks sluiced with rain like a gelatin print.
I watch her crawl into a hole,
thinking at least she has red wine in her,
the memory of something warm.

5.
On a business trip to the flaming South,
I heard my client ask:
"Will you meet my daughter? She too has ichthyosis.
She's thirteen, plays alto sax, likes
Mexican food."

An hour later, I reached past her parent's love, past
the beaches of our thickened skin
and furtive glances at each other's legs,
to clasp and stroke her grosgrain hand.

ANNE KAIER

Accoutrements

1.

Commissioned, I brought my mother's
perfume back from France,
Guerlain Mitsuko, in a
brown Art Deco box.

"Do you know this scent?" She knew
I did.
"Dad loved it."

In sweater drawers,
negligees, the back
of her neck.

2.

She knelt with cotton gloves
to fit the first sheer stockings
on my shrinking legs
where my jagged skin
threatened the silk.

3.

A snakeskin mirror
peacock blue,
I bought in Paris lately,
ornaments my hand,
like womanhood smoothed out.

ANNE KAIER

4.

In the deep porcelain bath,
bands of skin tighten my thighs.
Skin shards rear,
torn again and again,
always for the last time,
other scales mottle like peacock eyes.

5.

Tonight I pump
breeze through a Spanish fan
with boxwood scent.
I cool my face before
the fire of strangers, hiding
behind the dancer's fan,
her shock of black
hair, her yellow boot.

The Examining Table

1.

My skin cracks like scorched earth.
A rash beneath my breasts shames me.
I hide in bed. I hide in the sun.

2.

In my dream, a woman juts scarred arms,
like fissured wood, towards me.
I stroke her burnt-red hair,
her head an African goddess,
my hands wet, electric.
"Feel my arms," she says, "feel them."

I cannot finger the ridges where
knife, lash, electrodes
slashed her arms.
"Touch my wounds," she says.
I cannot move my moist hands off her head
to stroke her skin and cling there.

3.

Yet, in the hospital parking lot,
my heart jumps in my throat
as I walk to the annual meeting
of the Philadelphia Dermatological Society.

In the examining room,
I'm Case #18: ichthyosis.
"You're the star of Philly Derm," the resident says—
"the only full-body case."
Even the lepers show only extremities.

The kindly doctors
gather round, thumbing
their casebooks,
asking: "when did your condition start?"

Like Susanna with the elders,
I tell my story,
swinging my legs against the metal table.

In childhood, standing in Dr. Shelley's office,
I stretched my arms to his soft, scientific gaze.
My body came along with me who looked and saw and did not see.
But now, on this day,
I sit on the edge of the examining table, nakedly me.
The ridges of my skin stick
to my arms and I am one with them.
I sit whole on the table edge, Case #18.

4.
I have broken the old taboo,
named my affliction,
called it mine.

5.
In the Inner Harbor,
walking by the water,
I flirt like a girl
with a strange guy eating a baloney sandwich.
"Sit here by me," he says.
He names the tugboats, wharves, the water taxi.
And so we sit,
looking out to open sea.

ANNE KAIER

Hal Sirowitz

ZOMBIES ARE LOOSE

Having Parkinson's in a marriage is equivalent to the old Hollywood B Movie, *I Married a Zombie*. I got to like being a zombie. It was ultimate bliss. I didn't have to respond to safe conversations, like "Who do you think will win the Oscars?" Instead of saying in an obtrusive manner, "Frankly, my dear, I don't give a damn," and walking away in my best Clark Cable imitation manner, I just make sure my Parkinson's mask is on tight—the other person can't see through the cracks—and go to Neverland. If in sports, the best offense is a good defense, then I'm way ahead on any count. For years, I dabbled in Zen meditation. But I never knew Nirvana until I got Parkinson's. It's like being in the womb again. There's no pressure to respond. Because you can't.

It shouldn't be discouraging being diagnosed with Parkinson's. It's like a chance to be an extra in a John Carpenter movie, *Invasion of the Body Snatchers*. Your body is literally snatched away from you. You're not given a new body. It's just that the old one is different. You have a blurring of the usual sensations, and then new ones, like genuine hallucinations, not inspired by LSD or any other hallucinogen. I used to see people in cars. But when I got closer, I'd see it was just the head seat. Those hallucinations kept me from being lonely, because as soon as I discovered one person was just a mirage, the next car seemed occupied. It'd go on like that until I'd come across a real couple in their car seats smooching. I'd quickly look away before I was caught spying. As a Parkinson's zombie, you don't lust for someone's blood like the typical Hollywood version of a zombie; you just lust to be alone. You're no longer social. You just want quality time by yourself so you can avoid "the slings and arrows of outrageous fortune," to quote Shakespeare.

What does a Parkinson's mask looks like? It looks no different than the faces of exiles. Their pain at losing their homeland is expressed in their faces. They don't look at you or the camera. They have that faraway look as though they're back home, inside their communities again. Whereas the Parkinson's patient looks as though he's losing his body. It's not unlike a mask by Picasso (who was influenced by African masks). What I'm saying is that it's not an exterior look. It's like looking in the mirror, but the mirror is black—it doesn't reflect you or create new sensations in the viewer. It's like looking at someone and getting lost in their alternate universe.

There are other ways of acting obtuse, but Parkinson's provides the best excuse for being that way. You can frustrate your friends and further hinder your enemies by crawling into that turtle shell specifically designed for you by the disease.

I've been accused of shoplifting two times—pre-op and post-op. I didn't think I was doing anything that might have warranted those accusations, except for maybe knocking over one or two items. But I'd always pick them up, placing them in more or less the exact spot where I thought the collision had occurred. In one store, the clerk spoke to my wife like I was invisible.

"What disease does that guy have?" she said. "My aunt had Parkinson's, and she didn't look as bad as him. He must have one of these new types, like one of those viruses going around. I've never seen that type of Parkinson's. Do you think it really is that? It could be something worse."

Post-op, I was in a 99-cent store, looking for bargain books. They had *Conversations with Groucho Marx*. I thought he was dead. He was, but that didn't stop the book company from making a few bucks. He was talking like he was still alive. The security guard approached me and told me to open my coat. I wasn't sure whether I had a shirt or just an undershirt underneath. I soon found out I had a shirt. She had unzipped my jacket. When she walked away, at first I felt relief, then anger.

Just because I wear a Parkinson's mask doesn't make me a criminal. Not everyone with a mask is bad. Look at the Lone Ranger. Look at Superman. Doesn't the Lone Ranger wear a mask? Doesn't Superman have a hidden identity? The good don't just die young, as Billy Joel sang, but also get accused of shoplifting.

A Step above Cows

I read somewhere that a cow
can only walk up stairs but
not down. Even though I have
Parkinson's, I'm a step ahead
of a cow. I can walk up or down
without much trouble. And the
one time I fell, I was walking up
but lost my balance and fell down,
which proves that I'm not
a cow, because for a split second,
I had the choice of where to fall—
up or down—and unceremoniously
took the down route, because it
takes you faster to where you
want to go—at the beginning
of the stairs, so I could do it right this time.

Legal Drugs

No one knows how you get Parkinson's.
It could have been from the Thorazine I took
my last year in college when I was depressed
about the possibility of being drafted to fight
in the Vietnam War. Taking the Thorazine
was like hitting yourself on the head
with a hammer and the reflexive result
was it'd drag you to sleep no matter how
wired up you were. I gave some
to my druggie friends when we met up
at Washington DC to protest the invasion
of Cambodia. They said Thorazine was
a chaser, like taking a shot of tequila
after gulping down a pint of beer. It calmed
them down when they went cold turkey. They
couldn't believe I was getting Thorazine
for free when they had to pay street prices.

A Famous Ball Player

When I was first diagnosed with Parkinson's
I was happy my symptoms—limping,
trembling—had a name. Who'd
want to suffer from a nameless disease?
At least if one had Lou Gehrig's Disease,
one could identify with the great Yankee
first baseman. Sir Parkinson excavated
dinosaur bones, then assembled them.
Not that I'd want to trade my disease
for Gehrig's, but at this point in my life I'd
rather have a ball thrown to me—
at least I've caught balls before—than
have to deal with an extinct species.
The subject of extinction is too close to home.

Hal Sirowitz

Avoiding Rigidity

"It's the medicine that makes me shake,
not the disease," I said. "Then why
take it?" she said. "If I stopped, I
wouldn't be able to walk," I said.
"My body would become rigid."
"Rigidity seems better than
all that shaking you do,"
she said. "I'd rather shake
than not be able to move,"
I said. "Each to his own,"
she said. "But if you were rigid,
I wouldn't have to worry
about you accidentally
hitting me on the head." "But if I
couldn't move," I said, "what
would we do to make time pass?"
"We'd do nothing," she said. "We do that, anyway."

Lisa Gill

MAPPING CAESURA: THE ENCOMPASSING BODY

O n the median in the stretch of Route 66 that runs through Moriarty, New Mexico, a cardboard sign read *Craft and Gun Show*. I couldn't help thinking that was a fair assessment of gender roles in Torrance County. Add a Christian cross, a rodeo belt buckle, a big rig and a tractor and you would sum up my expectations of the entire community where I chose to make my residence.

For eight years I lived in a house fourteen miles from the crossroads that constituted "town." The structure abutted a ranch with 11,000 acres of piñon/juniper grasslands populated only by wildlife and a few cattle. As close as I ever got to knowing any of my "neighbors" was to exchange a book of my poetry for a tow after getting my car stuck in deep snow. The help came with a mandatory ninety-minute history of the valley. Loneliness was rampant in the region, though I tended to call it solitude and protect it.

Much of the community lived as I did, tucked down dirt roads in little enclaves of rural sprawl in various states of disrepair, with windmills spinning, tires on tin roofs and barns—or some type of outlying shacks—on the property. Sometimes I suspected that the preponderance of little decorative Christmas trees made from paper clips that I witnessed on the tables at *El Comedor* was just an incidental result of isolation and a median income of $13,000. Twenty percent of Torrance County's population lives below the poverty line.

If I felt at odds with much of the political and religious slant of Moriarty, as an unemployed, disabled poet, I fit the economic demographic squarely—but cheap rent wasn't what enticed me out there. *I loved the land.* My relationship to the environment, however, was almost as parasitic as the plump crimson cochineal feasting on the prickly pear: I needed nature.

I needed—for medical reasons—to be able to go for a walk between juniper and piñon, look down and spot white mold on a pad of cactus, kneel and peel the webbing gently back between spines to reveal the coveted species of small, oval insect that has been used to make blood-red dye for centuries.

Last century, in 1980, the American Psychiatric Association added a new diagnosis to the Diagnostic Manual of Mental Disorders. In 1990, while living in Albuquerque, I was given that diagnosis: post-traumatic stress disorder (PTSD). The disorder is a cluster of symptoms that happen as a result of severe traumas, like war, like rape. At twenty, I was given the diagnosis due to symptoms following a rape. When I was twenty-three, an attack by a lover exacerbated my illness and I gave up. I left the city. I was afraid and so I ran. I ran away from 521,000 people.

If I was literally afraid of stalkers and predators, I also found Albuquerque's light and noise pollution taxing. One of the symptoms of PTSD is hypervigilance, a heightened intake and awareness of all sensory stimuli. My body was perpetually on alert, my mind overburdened with information. I needed solitude. I needed peace. I needed rest. I needed to be landlocked, carefully buffered from overstimulation, and then I could endure.

And I could write.

For seventeen years, five books and several manuscripts, I hunkered down at my typewriters or computers in various small structures in communities outside city limits: Carnuel, Cedar Crest, Alameda, ultimately settling in Moriarty. With or without power, with or without a paved road, near the Rio Grande, by an alfalfa field, beneath a steep rocky canyon, nestled in the piñon/juniper spreads at 6,500 feet, my symptoms subsided.

Or at least, I had a safe place to retreat to after commuting an hour for city interactions. I had a quiet place to collapse after rounds of insomnia. I had a place to write——and I had poetry as a "place" to think.

My ink-based contemplations were nurtured by both distance from the city and proximity to a more visceral and sensible—or sense-making—environment. Resonance matters. What I found in the natural world was a mirror to what I knew. While manicured lawns and coiffed landscaping offer me only an unreliable façade to cling to, a rock bed in a natural arroyo practically coddles me. Even a coyote kill, sun bleached in a matter of hours, leaves me duly somber. And calm.

Honesty aids any relationship.

As does clarity.

In August of 2003, it was unclear what was happening to my body: my feet went numb after a long hike carrying a twenty-five-pound tree trunk back from the upper mesa. What began with a sensation of small metallic pins and needles in the bottoms of my feet became—within days—wooden, my legs fallen logs, dead lumber splayed on the bed (and in the hospital) waiting to be "cured." Or seasoned.

Being diagnosed with multiple sclerosis (MS) can actually cause PTSD. Fear is off the charts. Lesions in the brain can—and do—wreak havoc on almost any neurological function. I lacked sensation, had tremors, grew weak, fell, suffered vertigo and became unable to read for three months. My cognitive function fluctuated. One night I cooked dinner for twenty-four hours and nearly burned the house down. And yet, still, I had nightmares and flashbacks. Past traumas vied for my attention with present traumas.

Given my new diagnosis, MS, doctors enrolled me into day programs for my previous diagnosis, PTSD. Their logic required that I control the stress of flashbacks and memory so as not to exacerbate the MS. The two diagnoses are twined together. My body and my mind are twined together. I am twined to the land. Everything is "comorbid." Each environment sings with diagnoses.

From my bed, I looked out the window at cholla—blossoms and spines. I studied wildflowers while laid up. I researched medicinal herbs between sessions of physical therapy. I stared at a topographic map on the wall. I walked (just barely) out my front door, watched the sky and wrote poems. During the first year of disease, land was lust. Or land was love, unrequited. After a course of steroids, rounds of physical therapy and a full year, I was in remission.

Even in remission, MS defines land. I walked the cowpath that paralleled the backs of the houses in Deer Valley and on towards the great basin where a two-track visible by satellite intersected my path at a water tank and feed station. The route was level, easier than the hikes up the ridge I used to take. Even the coyotes shared the trail, and I poked at their scat with my cane to see what kind of diet they'd been consuming; I poked at their scat with my cane because I could. The gnarled, once-trimmed juniper with a remnant of barbed-wire fence wrapped around its trunk is where I sat down. And then, after resting, I walked home. I absorbed the environment: gumweed, paintbrush, a small stead of scrub oak, everywhere snakeweed and yucca.

A few years later, a goathead meant a flat tire on my wheelchair, while dried, hoof-trodden caliche demanded a wheelie every arm pull. Stairs became a cliff face: my Moriarty house had three. With pain I mustered them, even when I used the chair for distances. The following winter, after a partial recovery, the woodstove nonetheless remained conspicuously empty, the woodpile by the shed full: my use of propane doubled. I kept sticking with the house, with the land, with the fear I'd have to leave, with the fear that I'd want to leave. I kept sticking it out even though opening a refrigerator door had become painful, and I knew I wasn't going to be hauling any more

Lisa Gill

wood. I had wanted to hermit. I had hoped to die rural. I left the city because of one disability and I couldn't admit that a second disability was going to drive me back. I couldn't admit that I was going to have to leave the land because I was afraid. I was afraid I couldn't take care of myself in isolation. And I was afraid of the alternative: people.

And then one day I got up from my desk to find a rattlesnake coiled on the brick floor of my living room. This was a new incarnation of fear: *danger without malice*. I spent two intimate hours with the snake and something snapped. A pendulum in my head swung clean from people *as predators to people as potential support*. I called the sheriff. A deputy came and helped me catch the snake and release it off the property. And then I wrote poems to the rattler. For months. The snake in my memory was my guide, lover, prophet and teacher, allowing me to tackle with words my fears and griefs, my loves, allowing me to gain perspective. The result was a verse theater piece, *The Relenting: A Play of Sorts*.

By the time the book was released by New Rivers Press, fish-eye cameras tracked all my entrances and exits. I had moved into a "green" building right smack in the middle of downtown Albuquerque. Leed Platinum. Energy star. Mixed-income. Subsidized. Rent cheap as the sticks. I neighbor the train tracks. I neighbor the bus station. A movie theater. A rescue mission. I have neighbors. I have friends, an actual community of artists and writers.

And still, I pause in the parking garage to examine a four-and-a-half-inch beetle. By the time I get to the third floor of the apartment building, my head swims. The sound of the elevator disrupts my equilibrium, and I brace myself against falling. I brace myself against grief. I remember catching a head-whipping skink, holding a towhee, the night travels of stag beetles across the concrete slab of my bedroom floor, a hawk on a fence post. I forget to make any urban identifications.

I listen to the traffic and train whistles. The church bells and disembodied "fuck yous" that rise through my window. The siren songs.

I feel safe. I feel happy. I feel sad.

I write it all down.

Sometimes on First Street, I see a hummingbird under the overpass or a homeless person in the bushes scrounging for something stashed a while earlier.

from The Relenting: A Play of Sorts

WOMAN (speaking to SNAKE)

I wish this moment were simpler than a woman trying to negotiate
with a snake.

Desert Carnivore, I'd love to give you an excuse
   that would pass in school or for a missed lunch date.
Yet, I already know better—I have always known better.
When don't justifications pale or do some grand disservice to something
that could be as honest as acknowledging divergent priorities
or accepting an everyday failure?

Here in my living room, my sad and mundane story merits no regard:
   disabled woman who just a few months back got out of a wheelchair;
    woman who's likely to need it again.
There is no place for pity.
You don't care whether or not today is a good walking day,
might prefer to bring me down,
encourage disease to disown my arms and legs,
leave me living torso.

Already you rib me,
your dexterous body nothing but internal spokes attached to a skull.

Am I any different, chest heaving?

•

WOMAN (speaking to SNAKE)

Sure enough what's untouchable is desire:
thirty-six of Botticelli's curves in a museum piece roped off,

fragments of roundness that loop in the imagination of pure shape,
visceral wish to touch.

You are not snake, you are abstraction of circle.

I'm tempted; I'm taunted.

The alarm of your tail resounds already in speculation
and yet, look at you—
                              peaceful coiled hush.
My mind stretches towards you,
inches around the maze of your spine,
and meters away from you,
recoiling,
my own body S-ing.
                              This apartness,
this knowledge of essential separation pains me plentiful.
Logic and sensuality ride the length of my spine,
                              twined together,
a braid of wish and wash:
            I do not want to be punctured;
            I do not want to puncture.

This barrier of physical distance,
a mere three and a half feet,
could be broached with a feather
from the dove that breaks morning
on the line outside the house.

Peace?
Stasis?
Fallible seduction?

I cannot frighten you. I will not.

Wicker-Work: A Sestina for Zukofsky

In the mental hospital I am a fan of your interpretation 1
of torsion. Bar nothing I know poles— 2
some flat-martyred mind split down the center by light, 3
bilateral symmetry. Doctors leaf through MRI films 4
and think thoughts split between aw-shucks compassion 5
and abject snooping. My brain is luminous, 6

scooped with polka-dotted-lampshade inflammation. 6
Chomp chomp goes the T-Cell—spotted elucidation— 1
of everywhere myelin is being pawed over. Concern 5
is merited—multiple sclerosis leaves my brain divided 2
into little bubbles of dysfunction, cartooned 4
into increments of prayer: bulb-3

ous head of a green thing. Photosynthesis 3
makes light 6
of the-locked-up-get-let-out-onto-the-poor-picture- 4
of-a-high-walled-courtyard—grass!!! We conceptualize 1
cigarettes, scratch our nicotine patches, pace two 2
directions. Back and forth, sympathy 5

strut. "Can you tell me what it's like 5
to off yourself?" Sad guy says. I respond, "Not bright— 3
but your logic errs! I didn't vault 2
over *over*!" That, after the fine art of admission, radiant 6
mouth saying, "Sure, I'm suicidal." I don't understand 1
why the intake nurse needs that motion picture 4

Lips Lips Lips Lips to let me in. Silver haired screen 4
with her protocol of limiting access to the ward we love. 5
What food! What art therapy! Puddin' analysis 1

LISA GILL

of sadness, as iridescent 3

as dreams of escape will become, turnstile gleaming 6

with sweaty prints of our fingers, tipped towards any axis 2

rotated counterclockwise opposite 2

to despair. Oops. The lair of sentimentality flicks 4

aside newsprint. Self-pity is a bugger on my chest, beam- 6

ing. I stumble in all sub-atomic-ways. Brain care 5

is mandatory or I get legs as logs. So sad. That's flare. 3

I'm sher 'nuf sick though comprehending 1

disease is polenta. 2 Too mushy. Meaning 1

one big screen 4 for all patients. We dazzle 3

in the blue glow 6, sicks of the contemporary ward. 5

My Inquietude Constrained Briefly
by Louise Bogan

Not marble, I am rather quartz and mineral cement,
sandstone the wind takes down,
daily hourglass, exposing mica, sun-flecked debris,
erosion's bitter crown.

My mind harps on the form that might contain
topsoil wearing thin, the self
made vulnerable as any remote landscape
slipping off the continental shelf

into depths of phosphorescent display. Meter
can't curtail the way
thoughts overgraze emotion, the body abraded
particles on some slick slope. The decay

of restraint rocks me, high
desert or lowland. In the adolescent pit
of a mine, I stooped to pick up flint
and released sea, eternal, unfortunate red emit.

The *Undering* and Other Great Inhumanities on 3.6 Acres

for Wendell Berry

Remonstrance is no use. I already live
where a downed fence is a plastic tube
running under my dog's skin, draining
the wound. Even the armchair in the den

held a slumped cottontail, smooth gray
spindle of intestine protruding from a solitary
puncture wound. It's peaceful here. Javelina
snouting the hurricane fencing, sunbeaten

days and every night sky, even clouded,
lit with stars unknown to the city, stars
vanquished from the sight of the dead
or overmedicated. There are so many types

of erosion. I lament not the cholla blossoms'
pink descent nor the hot yellow stream of piss
released from my dog after the second
injection. In the yard I sit listening to a blade

of grass crackle and bend under the weight
of a grasshopper. Death plagues me, the way
plagues and blights come and go, daily
happenstance. My brain, however, is subject

to ravages best documented with technologies
of the damned, profane knowledge of black
holes that are not made with a post hole
digger. I labor against all of it, even the sluice

of emotion that might run me off my own
land. The straight lines of my toil reap
no pinto beans, no edible crop, no rodeo,
and still, I hold out this might matter, might

keep me from aggrandizing the eventual
lullaby of grass plot, earth-turning, stone-piled
undering that we all must know, the death
that may or may not be natural when the mind

erodes faster than the ranch behind my house
under hooves of cattle. Did you know disease
is not anything other than a living entity?
A harmony of preservation and destruction,

neurological cobbling together of being and not.
I lament the erosion of my mind, the way effort
alone will not let me live my values, how
I have to ask doctors' help to keep me living

rural for as long as I can before the inability
of my legs or eyes or cognition will lead me
back to some sad city, overstimulated shelter
from everything that ought to be allowed

to take my body down like any other coyote kill.
This would be my "wish to be generous," to bow
sometimes to mystery outside the hospital, to let
my blood spill on the prickly pear, fruit-bearing.

LISA GILL

TOWARDS A NEW LANGUAGE
OF EMBODIMENT

Norma Cole

WHY I AM NOT A TRANSLATOR—TAKE 2

I was going to talk about why I am not a translator, but I'm not. I do translations, I've done many, mostly from French to English, but I still don't think of myself as a translator.

I had given a talk on translation at Suzanne Stein's sublet in San Francisco a year and a half ago, to friends who had gathered around her dining table, a talk titled "Why I Am Not A Translator" that began with a list of subordinate clauses I handed out, starting with "what," as in "What Rosmarie Waldrop has to do with it," "What Claude Royet-Journoud has to do with it," "What Stacy Doris has to do with it," "What Etel Adnan & Simone Fattal have to do with it," etc. Every one of them had gotten me to translate any number of books, but it was always so much more than what one thinks of as translating. Sure, it was pretty much straight-ahead translation—if you can say "straight-ahead" for the kind of experimental poetry I work on—but it was more exciting, more irritating, more crooked. More about editing than you'd think. But mostly I thought—and think—about it in terms of poetics.

At the same time as I was thinking about translation, about AWP and about this ten-minute talk I am actually starting to give right now, I was reading René Daumal's *Rasa or Knowledge of the Self: Essays on Indian Aesthetics and Selected Sanskrit Studies*, particularly an essay called "To Approach the Hindu Poetic Art." As some of you know, René Daumal was a French writer born in 1908 in Charleville, the same town where Arthur Rimbaud had been born in 1854. Daumal, a writer of the avant-garde, who penned, among his many essays, poems and novels, the acclaimed unfinished novel *Mount Analogue*, at sixteen taught himself Sanskrit, wrote a Sanskrit grammar and translated some very important texts, including the *Chandyoga Upanishad* and the *Bhagavad Gita*. With failing health, hiding out in Paris during the Occupation with his wife, who was part Jewish, he died of tuberculosis in May 1944, just two weeks before the Allies landed in France.

I was reading Daumal's essay and thinking about my class at the University of San Francisco, and about the course in "Visionary Poetics" I'm teaching, and about the things I wanted to make sure to discuss with my students, and I ran across these sentences:

The existence of thought without words but not without forms is nevertheless necessary, for example, to all translation work. Every good translator does his utmost, without actually realizing it, to translate his text first into *sphota*, in order to translate into the second language; but he would be an even better translator if he were consciously aware of this process.

I'd obviously run across these sentences many a time before, but suddenly I started to think about them in a more concentrated way.

First, the word *sphota*, what does it mean? We have to go back a paragraph: "Is there, between words and things, a rapport of simple convention or an eternal appropriateness?" In other words, the rapport of simple convention means the normal words syntax depends upon, like prepositions, or "sonorous words" (dhvani), the onomatopoeic and alliterative, as in:

> Hark! Hark!
> The dogs do bark!

whereas the eternal appropriateness means ideas that pre-exist words and objects. Word-seeds. *Sphota.*

Ideas that pre-exist words and objects. A test case in neurobiology: when I had my stroke four years ago, two areas of language were affected. One was a motor problem. Speech production was knocked out in the brain. Therefore I couldn't talk at all. And I've had to refigure, little by little, how to make speech occur with mouth, teeth, tongue. Think of Christopher Reeves in the swimming pool, trying to make his legs function. And then, for many people who've had strokes, the brain swells, doesn't settle for a while (perhaps two or three months), so we have aphasia and can't think of words: the words for up or down; the simply conventional words; and the words that stand for ideas. I am here to tell you that one has ideas even before one has the words to say them. Ideas, or images. No tabula rasa.

So, that being the case, "every good translator does his utmost, without actually realizing it, to translate his text first into *sphota*, in order to retranslate it into the second language..."

NORMA COLE

I am not altogether happy with this. I mean, why shouldn't one pass from the word in the first language straight to the word in the second language, without even thinking about ideas?

"I'll reveal for you, in words as simple as mooing," says Mayakovsky.

> "I would like
>> to live
>>> and die in Paris"

he wrote, translated by Stephen Rudy.

> "I would like
>> to live
>>> and die in Paris
> if there weren't
>> such a land
>>> as Moscow"

and you can't change that line, Mayakovsky said. It would not be the same if you were to write "Berlin" and "Warsaw," for instance.

Or Dixie. To live and die in Dixie.

Roman Jakobson, the genius of structural linguistics, among whose great works are *Verbal Art, Verbal Sign, Verbal Time*, has written "...the speaker selects words and combines them into sentences according to the syntactic system of the language he is using; sentences in their turn are combined into utterances. But the speaker is by no means a completely free agent in his choice of words: his selection (except for the rare case of actual neology) must be made from the lexical storehouse which he and his addressee possess in common." This is from his essay, "Two Aspects of Language and Two Types of Aphasic Disturbances" (*Language in Literature*, p.97).

Paris and Moscow, Berlin and Warsaw, both dyads would be available from the lexical storehouse, but, as we know, one expresses Mayakovsky's idea, the other does not. "The 'body' of the poem is created from 'sounds and meanings'," (Jakobson) whether it is a translation or not. But it's all translation anyhow. Crooked translation.

Speech Production: Themes and Variations

exhibit
exhibition

ribbons
vandals
the ribbons of vandals, the vandals
of ribbon, scissors of ribbon,
ribbons of scandal

sculpture of
ribbons or
strips
strippers
strip clubs

exhibitions: temporary inhibitions, *my semblables*: collective guilt: don't leave
your filthy shirt, your own fifty-yard line. What would be the motive in that
"kind of temporary performance"? (Christo & Jeanne-Claude)

quote
quotation
quit
quoting
quit it
unscripted
quoted unscripted
quote script?

script quote

Why do I like it under the trees in autumn when everything is half dead?
Why would I like the word moving like a cripple among the leaves and why
would I like to repeat the words without meaning?

physics
physical
physicist
metaphysical physicist (string theorist)
psychoactive physicists
psychotic episode

Sonata: a musical composition in contrasted movements

constellation
stardust
nuclear glow train, Yucca, Nevada
rotate the exhaust
on second thought

Did you *make* that: the sheep, yarn, afghan? birds, feathers, pillows, book-
shelves, (trees, nails etc.) the books on them, the slides (yes), their glass
mounts, tray, projector? lamps, record player, records (vinyl!), occasional
tables, desk, chair, papers? their colors and weights, sizes, like that candy
wrapper? notes (perhaps), postcards, newspapers, my cane, myself?

C.S. Giscombe

ON A LINE BY WILLIE MCTELL

Start with railroad music, start with "Statesboro Blues" because it claims southeast Georgia as its stage, because specificity takes its listener to something else. Willie McTell sang, in 1928, "Big 80 left Savannah—Lord an' did not stop—You oughta saw that colored fireman—When he got them boilers hot!"

No narrative to the song—about traveling, about sexual possibility, about the colors of race, about the ambiguous hand-downs of parents. Probably the Midland Railway, the old line over the fifty miles from Savannah to Statesboro; probably a reference to the "massive" eighty-inch driving wheels on some powerful classes of steam locomotives.

There's beauty to the railroad, this is given; the railroad's a received form—its "aspects and indications" regarding semaphores, its yard limits, its code of horn signals, the certain ways *movement* is permitted, and within that permission, restricted. In central Pennsylvania, in the first years of the new century, I trained as a brakeman using the NORAC rulebook and later became a petty railroad bureaucrat and worked with people in the industry and the regulatory agencies. Along with others I ran a tourist railroad, centered in Bellefonte, PA, and some of the fellows joked that we were playing train when we went out on the line, but the equipment was real and, because of that, "unforgiving"; and our operation was, like everyone's, governed by rules. We traversed the superstructure, the General Railroad System of North America, the big map that shows the tracks to be in fact all connected, from Hay River to Savannah and Miami and, via Laredo, down to Lázaro Cárdenas and Veracruz and down east to Bangor and out west to Coos Bay and Prince Rupert; including the Bellefonte Branch and the sixty miles of ribbon rail we shared with freight traffic—coal trains—from Lock Haven to Tyrone.

No firemen on our runs. As brakeman I would swing off to line switches, flag crossings, crank on (and release) the handbrake, set and remove the chocks, conduct the air test. The issue of railroad firemen is complex—the position survived the mid-century conversion of locomotive power from steam (with its fireboxes that, as we would say in Pennsylvania, "needed to stoked") to diesel but by then the pool of firemen, through a series of labor agreements, had been limited to "promotable men." A. Philip Randolph and others fought this in public, with mixed success. There were black brakemen but, as *Time Magazine* said, in a piece about Mr. Randolph's fight in 1943, "Almost the oldest tradition in Southern railroading is the Negro fireman." Post-war railroad hirings of black firemen and brakemen are documented in brief articles, often with pictures, in *Jet*. So wasn't I the colored brakeman? Yes, but usage and familiarity are what define and govern—stake out—our positions; fireman was the *storied* job available in engine service, what *Time* described as "the best paid, most aristocratic job a Negro can aspire to in the South." Promotable men were white men—one rose from brakeman or fireman to engineer or conductor—and my experience of engine crews is that they are still white, with obvious exceptions, and male (with obvious exceptions); I've seen exactly four black engineers since I began keeping score in 1962 or 1963 or 1964. Engineer's on the right side of the cab, head-end brakeman on the left. As brakeman I would converse with the engineer about track conditions directly ahead—we'd agree that the automatic crossing protection (flashing lights) was working, that switches were lined correctly, etc. I'd watch for foot traffic, kids playing on the railroad, I'd watch for hunters, for people in cars. Much there involved in getting those boilers hot. Why *should* you have seen that colored fireman? Showed his color (but that usually means something else). The adjective "colored" is added for emphasis in the song but it was also a cultural reference, casually made, not an intensifier at all but a *casual* statement of the underpinning of the whole structure of everything in the United States. As a colored *brakeman* in 2003 I was so anomalous I may as well have been white. But I wasn't.

Later I applied to be an engineer and had my eyes and hearing checked and allowed the national inquiry into my forty-year driving record. My student engineer license came in the mail, signed by the superintendant of our operating partner. Months before, I'd made it through his rules class, an all-morning event, and passed the written exam. In my other life then—those years in that place—I was a member of the faculty at Penn State, one town over in State College. But this was Bellefonte, the county seat. One day, as we were taking a half-full train up to Pleasant Gap, PA, my engineer—Steve, the man with whom I'd been paired when I commenced my training—said, "You run it for a while," and I did.

The horn was a problem. It was a piece of rope that hung straight down next to the windshield. Signaling the intention to move forward (two short blasts) or to back up (three short blasts) was fine but the familiar signal for grade crossings was more complicated to execute—as every schoolchild knows, it's two long blasts, a short and another long and "is to be prolonged or repeated until engine or train is on the crossing, or, where multiple crossings are involved, until the last crossing is occupied." The problem was that the engineer should take the equipment through such with his hand on the brake. Fair enough, but a childhood accident cost me my left arm some decades ago and it's been a series of prosthetic devices ever since—they've worked well but the horn was a problem. There was the likelihood of slippage if I used my steel hook to grasp the brass brake lever; and if I kept my right hand on the brake, the dangling, dancing rope was hard to pluck, with the hook, from out of the air. So I went to Home Depot one morning before reporting for my shift and bought an S-clip and a length of new rope and—with the help of a young man, Timmy, who helped out in general—extended the cord. That is, Timmy and I added a loop, a long down-hanging U across the top quadrant of the windshield, an easier target for my hook—gross movement skills as opposed to fine movement skills, less difficult to pull on and make a joyous noise with, easier for me to pipe wildly down the valleys. Two dollars worth of parts. "Now we're ADA compliant," said Steve.

Is this disability? My mechanical-man self ensconced in another machine moving across the surface of earth. My cyborg, my amputee, my centaur, my rolling man. *Type of the modern! emblem of motion and power! pulse of the continent!* Cyborg? The dictionary embedded in my MacBook Pro says: "fictional or hypothetical person whose physical abilities are extended beyond normal human limitations by mechanical elements built into the body." My hypothetical self, typically irritable. In a review of a Stephen King novel, *Duma Key*, the reviewer says, "King neatly figures the tropes of dismemberment." But it's only irritation, my response to the tropes (and to neatness); only dismemberment. We on the railroad provided a service, transportation between Bellefonte and Tyrone (or Lemont or Port Matilda or Pleasant Gap), train service; we carried or hauled instances of the body, as ticket-holders might be described or configured from afar, while, over the same route, our operating partner carried limestone and I came to understand that what was in the *back* of the train being hauled made no difference to the *vector* of the train, which is what I endeavored to become or at least merge with. We sold our service, including my labor at the throttle or my labor on the ground at trackside. A rag-tag gang of white kids stared once at Milesburg as I waited for a coal train to clear the next block before throwing the switch so we could take a full load of paying customers to a restaurant thirty miles away in Tyrone, PA, and one of them said, finally and definitively and loud enough for me to hear and not irreverently, "Candyman." Is this

C.S. GISCOMBE

disability? Undying famous black monster of filmland Tony Todd with a hook for one hand—a monster's something else. "Specifically, an animal or plant departing greatly from the usual type, as by having too many limbs." How far is it from too many limbs to not enough? And what are "normal human limitations"? And what did he *do* to white co-star Virginia Madsen? Did he dismember her with his hook? (In the movie he asked her, "Do you fear the pain or what is beyond?" "Both," she replies. "The pain, I can assure you, will be exquisite," Candyman says.) The movie, based on familiar, intersecting urban legends and set in Chicago—in storied Cabrini-Green—came out in 1992. I lost the arm in 1961—normal human limitation would have me get by with the one, and people do, but I have always had decent insurance, a middle-class shield, so come equipped with high-end metal and plastic and fabric devices to let me cook and drive and get dressed and frame doorways, suspend my weight over a lover's body, bicycle to work, and operate trains. The idea one comes across is that phantom pain is the body's attempt to *re-member* itself and I find the idea precious and tedious both. On the railroad I extended myself beyond the normal into the fictional, the synthetic, without resolution. No Garden of Eden for me, baby; no circling back.

The railroad's centerless (as Alan Gilbert has suggested) which is how it gives off beauty. And it describes the geography it traverses. We'd leave Bellefonte and creep along Spring Creek to the junction with the main at Milesburg. There we'd radio the Altoona East dispatcher in Pittsburgh for Form D clearance to occupy the track; when that came, the brakeman would get off and throw the switch. I remember how it felt to move the train onto the main line and stop so the brakeman could re-line the switch and get back on. The main was continuously welded—ribbon rail—and we'd sail down the valley at thirty miles an hour, through Unionville, Julian, Port Matilda, through the country between those places, the horn blaring as I took us over the highway crossings.

Willie McTell was known as Blind Willie McTell. From the *New Georgia Encyclopedia*: "As a person faced with a physical disability and social inequities, he expressed in his music a strong confidence in dealing with the everyday world." (On the radio as I was writing this—on March 24th, 2011—the host of the *Writer's Almanac* announced the birthday of John Wesley Powell and, not mentioning the man's missing arm, that "he and his companions were the first white people to navigate the Grand Canyon Gorge" —Mr. Powell was a promotable man.) There's an urban legend, apparently from Ohio, about a one-armed brakeman with a hook but it's not one of the famous urban legends (in spite of or perhaps because of the heightened possibility of actual brakemen losing real limbs to unforgiving equipment) and is barely a ripple in the big legend-family of hook-handed bogeymen that mostly has to do with lovers' lane jitters and "the natural dread of the handicapped"; the *Candyman* movie pushed the sex that was always there in the campfire stories and complicated it with "the instinctive dread of Negroes." Willie McTell's blindness complicates the situation of his song, his telling the listeners that they shoulda *saw* that colored fireman.

My interest in the railroad goes back to childhood—the everyday world was full of trains and references to them as instruments of travel and as places of employment; trains covered distance, trains were sexual. My railroad career was short—2002 until I left Bellefonte for a faculty job at the University of California in 2007. I saw my first black engineer in 1984 or 1985 in upstate New York and saw the second two in Illinois in the 1990s. The fourth black engineer I saw was myself in the narrow cloudy mirror in the restroom of the Bellefonte train station where I'd change into my coveralls.

No descriptive word or phrase for what I was on the train, no casual assignment. There's no tradition, aristocratic or otherwise, of one-armed brakemen—aside from the bigger one the children in Milesburg understood—or colored engineers. Nor was I a singer no matter how much I love the song; on the railroad I was something else.

C.S. GISCOMBE

from GISCOME ROAD (Northern Road, 2)

In a dream I left camp to walk to town

but the road stopped, was closed,

& I stepped off into a line of trees

coming out then into the open on a path alongside an uphill pasture
where a girl was riding a horse bareback, she

was very dark & big boned, riding barefoot w/ no stirrups through
geese & Muscovy ducks,

she rode uphill toward the crest, where the sky was deepest blue
where it touched the crest.

       By the pasture's bottom-most fence—alongside the path—
some white men in suits were following a short black man, likely her father I thought,
w/ white hair & a neat white goatee, courting him I thought:

he had one leg, the other off way high up, & got around the site
w/ a single cane, in shorts

      which showed the muscle of the one "good" leg,

which flapped empty from the other,

the white men trotting to keep up, their neckties flapping over their round shoulders.

He spotted me & called "We have some things in common" & further, leaning
across the fence to speak quietly, sd he'd been pleasuring 2 women,
one black & one white, when it happened, the blood

to the leg having "herniated" because of fucking them
at the same time, he sd,

C.S. GISCOME

making the motions of diving as though
they'd been water he was jumping down into, to go in & then to come back up in the
current:

it surfaced, he sd—meaning the *blood* did, meaning the blood *did*—, in the current.

He'd lost an eye too, he sd, in a fight
& now it was just this plastic one he had—

it had been hanging out of the socket on its own threads focusing crazily
when the doctors came he sd & they gave him something to drink that tasted like wild
strawberry, bitter & sweet at once,
       & as he was asking them what it was they'd cut the cords

"just like this" he sd, snapping his fingers to signify it all

going blank.

•

Further on up the path I lost the direction but got back just at dark
through some different paths, back to the barrier that had closed the road
I'd left camp on:

I knew now it was the countenance

of the man's woods that began at the line of trees there

that attracted me
       (my narrator's rarely-there speaking self, my traveling-on self)
to the woods of that country,

from where the road stopped, his fields too.

C.S. GISCOMBE

I saw a big animal in the trees alongside & thought it a deer or moose
but it was a horse leaping over fences in front of me & then

there were more horses leaping the fences in the moonlight.

       I tried the path past the spread of buildings & fields,
but it was frozen now because night had come, held by ice, the way

no longer to town but further in, the way frozen

into a bad initial climb on which I could get no purchase because of the ice:

so I went to the house—it was white, clapboard—& up on its big porch
& was met there at the door by a chinless white man, sweet & foppish both
my chinless Englishman was, who sd the man I was for was in the tub but that he
could use the electricity to melt the ice & threw a massive switch like in the movies
that caused crackling & popping outside & flashes at the edge of sight, at the edges
of the picture,

framing it briefly

beyond the porch,

the white man explaining that they were in competition with the H.B. Company,
which owned the horses I'd seen earlier,

that the gentlemen of that company were trying, as always, to buy them out,
which was to attempt, he sd, an impossible task:

       I made it up the slope but got lost again
in the woods up top until morning & then found myself

lost on the roads I came to on which the signs
were ambiguous & at a gas station I askt directions & they sent me

up the rocky rd that intersected the main road there

       assuring me the named road I wanted
turned off the apparent continuation of itself

the name continuing way on into the uplands even further, past
the pavement's end—

so I took it, climbing over the rocks, a jumble
of rocks until I got finally to some stairs
                (wch the rocks had become

up to a door in the side of a red wooden house perched
at the top, in the rocks at the top
of the hill.

           (first dream of the Giscome Portage)

C.S. GISCOMBE

from PRAIRIE STYLE: Two Monster Poems

Vernacular Examples

You can always say what you are. Half the time the allegory's music, how song goes
with its cornets and saxophones. Do you have something to say to me? Closure re-
gathers the shape of the original undoing, the place where memory changed or picked
up. Or it's human-looking: big-boned, about as noisy, parts missing or left out, parts
overstated. A loud brother to the divine, an admonishment; I was two men, I was
something, I was "something monstrous." Jokes just drain the spirit.

The Old Northwest

The dear old Northwest, laced up at the wrist like Frankenstein, and shambling like
him too, the old Northwest. (The name *applied* to that monster, in those movies them-
selves he was nameless and unnamed; and he never spoke, he was truly simple. What
was said later, say two big girls hulking around after you, that that was the name they
looked like. And you the singular passion—a blunt argument—that ranged around
the dear old Northwest.)

Some questions push or shove like they were magic or like they thought they were. The
monster's based on something looking enough like anybody to be a reference—you
see him when you fear yourself and give him ways to talk, what he'd say if he could
pick up a horn and have something to say; or make up stories and tell them in his voice
because voice comes to that, voice goes to that.

Amber DiPietra

from MY NOTEBOOK HAS A RIGID SPINE
OR HOW TO OPERATE THE BODY IN WRITING

Note: *This excerpt is the beginning of a talk I wrote for the* Poetics of Healing, *a series of lectures and panels curated by Eleni Stecopoulos with the support of the Poetry Center at San Francisco State University and The Creative Work Fund. The series included poets in the medical field as well as poets who were survivors of war or trauma. I was the only visibly disabled person in the series that year. While very grateful for the invitation to present at one of the events, I felt that the content of my talk had to focus on my ambivalence toward the idea of healing. My talk was complicated by certain facts: I was speaking alongside doctors from the teaching hospital that I was struggling to gain admittance to as a patient; the venue where the* Poetics of Healing *was being held was up a steep flight of stairs; and the approaching date of the talk coincided with the realization that I needed to find ways to spend less time at the computer doing my "writing" because this work exacerbates my chronic pain and physical limitations—a somatic need which, I feared, contradicted my pride at being a writer of disability poetics. At the time I wrote this talk, I was also trying too hard to figure out what kind of poet I was and what form and style I was working in.*

ALIGNMENT

It has been difficult to prepare something for this series. I had intended to write an essay on the word "healing," and specifically, the way it does not quite translate to terms such as "rehabilitation," "accommodation" and "advocacy" in the lives of persons with disabilities. I had wanted to make an investigation into why "healing" sounds so much more poetic or impactful than these terms and what can be done to infuse the language of medicine with the moving efficacy of a term like "healing." To make a new poetic pact, I had also thought to write only airy poems that contained no trace of expository physiology, but just the gestures of a kinesthetic phantom self. None of this worked out, at least not now.

A split in my process has arisen, one that is forcing my writing into a kind of fugue state. I have aligned myself with an avant-garde poetics—a realm of writing in which identity disappears, or is ejected, or is seen as aesthetically inferior or passé—at the same time, in my life, I have come to identify most strongly as a disabled person who has a set of political, professional, social and personal concerns relevant to that disability. Writing, then, becomes a pre-emptive attempt to determine my angle of incidence. I do not act, but measure the contours of a form I might take. This measurement stems from a desire to veer as far as possible from the stock characters of triumphalist media—that form which minimizes content by capsular and spectacular headlines ("Everest Climber Has No Legs!") or the sickly sweet odor (flowering trees glimpsed through hospital room window, the sugars in urine) of the old-fashioned "illness memoir."

The disabled self is always a reader of his or her own body. The disabled body is a trifold pamphlet composed of medical terms, insurance jargon, social service lingo, self-help verbiage, advocacy mottos, and more currently, ontological and epistemological rhetoric on the disabled everyman who will save us from post-modern burnout. By that last part, I mean the theory that since disability pervades all identity categories, it also dismantles them—that disability is socially constructed and, thus, everyone, in a sense, is disabled because we are all disabled by *something*. Certain disability theories formulated along these lines almost make the term "disabled" vanish and yet seem totally disconnected from the somatics of "being disabled," from what the body feels.

Being, already, a reader of my own trifold pamphlet, I do not want to author poems or essays in which I further evanesce away with my self in favor of a poetics of abstraction that de-emphasizes agency and makes thick, if not slippery, material of language. I need, instead, to write a poetics that is porous, a membrane. A text that sucks the reader through its many holes and vaporous areas while offering also a sampling of real tissues, body-systems, that another body can assimilate. To bring my body in—and yours. In my writing, I am in search of a transparent, mobile language that moves, even when it occludes. This speaks directly to the processes of the body. An elbow either unhinges or it doesn't, and yet there are all the increments between. Skin, the ulna and the humerus, the annular ligament, cartilage, cells, carbon. The more present the body, the more mutable the self. Though, also, the self is always becoming rarefied in this particulate instant of lengthening or contracting. How or how not. Anyone's arm, your arm, my arm. Here and there, where you read or hear this.

Upon observing some somatic psychology students in the halls of Naropa, Bhanu Kapil has written:

[I see] a kind of slow motion dance/traverse in the corridor, in a pod of some kind, their feet a mutual tentacle. You can't go wrong with a sloppy hybrid. Ever. Because they are the hybrid that, preanimal, hasn't carved out a spectacular niche.

So, here is my piece without niche. It exists as notes. I think of it as an artificial joint that has not been installed in a human body. Or, the exposé of an imposter. You will see that this is how I operate. In real-time, with hold music.

bunny baby fast and slow

Cortázar tells the story of a man staying in a young woman's flat while she is away. Writing to her, he confesses that he vomits live rabbits—averaging one every few days—and that they are slowly destroying her pretty European parlor things. At the end of the letter, he tells her—this Andrea—that she may come home to find them on the street, flattened on the curb—having dashed the bunnies one by one and lastly himself, out of the high window.

He is what it means to be *lovesick*. Italics are how I heart these old-timey words. I've grown so old in love now as to have learned silly things in language.

I met a man before I read this story. In earlier days, I held long conversations with him in my head. I wonder how long it's been since he's called his mother. I talked to mine yesterday and I expect her to be on the phone to me in an hour, while it's late afternoon here in California and before it's all the way dark in Florida.

it's not broken baby try to stand baby look what I
brought you bring me baby

"They're running rabbits," my grandfather used to say and all us little girls would scream—them tugging, me limping, running to the couch to fling ourselves back and throw up our sandaled feet so that we wouldn't be gnawed on by the long-eared horde that was about to rush the patio. My grandmother rolled her eyes. He said this because years ago, he misunderstood 'running rampant' and continued to use it as a threat to keep granddaughters in check. He'd click his tongue at his wife, wink and say, "It's true, baby."

baby where did you why be careful baby

My mother said never wear your good underwear when you have your period. Thirty years old, I still think of this when I select the pink sheer, the pale green thong, and the high-waisted 1940's black. It was too much for her to have said to me at fourteen—a child with swollen knees, night sweats and fevers; they carried me across parking lots and backyards. I resented any advice about a fecundity I was only tenuously guaranteed to have.

means

I just want
glom onto
small attenuated explodings
over and over again

When I first got to San Francisco, I fell in the street. A man bounded over and said, "Baby, are you hurt?" I am not a feminist or a scholar. I want sex and language only for their beauty. Doubleness—just what my weakness has won me. Come loose, bouncing from the interior of illness, between two b's.

By this he means not little girl, crooked parts—but a tensile leaning towards. Because he can see, with me there beneath him, that I can have will held hold my own.

"Can I carry you?"

don't be baby pull it tighter baby did brought you
something baby have trouble going to the bathroom baby mean to me

"I'm sorry," my mother said, "I was being a baby."

The day before, I'd come home from school to find a note slashed out from her. "You are a selfish brat, you never think of me. You knew I had time to read, but you just had to take the book to school with you."

Like warring siblings, hoarding our share of one *Watership Down*. Between her bedroom and mine, a warren whose denizens loved deeply and sometimes tore each other apart, ear from ear.

I reasoned she didn't need it; she could spend her day off with her boyfriend. And I would have the book to myself in the high school library where I ate my lunch alone.

"Fuck like bunnies," one of the girls outside the cafeteria said.

In her apology, mom admitted to be meaner in her hurt than she'd intended. I, for my part, never owned up to being just as mean as she believed. In these fights, her teeth were always sharper, but I had my dark and waiting, hiding holes.

That may have been the week the boyfriend left. That week, I lay in bed thinking of tight dens and male and female rabbits; how there was barely room in the struggle and the rush of blood. I could lie still. Damp and frenetic like that to wait.

baby wash dark with lights baby in the pan baby do you like
was I baby snoring baby please

"Unfold your arms, baby. You look like a little rabbit sitting like that."

My grandmother took my wrists and gently pulled down on them. I kept my elbows hooked up around me out of habit, so I'd be ready to shove myself to some other place, to give the high wheels of my wheelchair a little push. I hated her for saying what was true and thought, one day, she would be dead and my mother too. Who in the world would unfold me then?

Two round syllables
as several accounts
neatly fingered
and staked
to raise the hand
on any
sentence

The professor said that line about your mother is like a flashlight turned on. I understood he meant for its clarity, because I had managed to say one simple thing. I heard it as a beam shined up a hole. Bleeding from another entrance, different than mom imagined. If my nose twitches at that, it's still necessary. To say underground and hard-won. The sensation of rough confession,

[I think about how TV shows love Anne Carson for all the wrong reasons. Did *The L Word* never read those lines I did? One part bending the curve of a Sappho fragment into her own shape and the next part on hands and knees, offering a rogue academician the red tulip of her anus, one last time before he leaves forever. It's all an act, the act of curling up and thrusting out to try and catch the I. This trash about the tulip is approximation.]

the success of which comes only in the inclination.

whole days baby
can
you take them

The first time I fell asleep with him, I dreamt of buying bunnies for my mother. 3 p.m. tropical thunderstorms and cars crashing death war disaster. We stood in the middle of a Florida mall while it went black against the lime kiosk light, quietly turning a wire carousel. This one held postcards, with real, fuzzy bunny heads sprouting out of them. She took them by their ears and pulled them lightly off the rack. My body was full and thick and then when the world started to crack and it was earthquakes in San Francisco (because that was what all my family worried about—not reckless MUNI drivers or AIDS) I filled my mouth up like a pouch with all of them—my mother, my grandmother and my grandfather and the bunnies they'd picked, haunches pumping to race them out of the crumbling mall.

in your mouth
   like that

Easter Sunday, we took the man's niece to Dolores Park to watch The Sisters of Perpetual Indulgence, a band of decadent, lesbian nuns and some gay guys dressed up like bunnies. His brother's wife only spoke to the little girl in Spanish, so this is how I narrated things to her. In my halting, mangled Cuban slang. What I could remember from when my great-grandmother spoke to me this way before I was old enough to go to school. Mostly, I was trained by Mercy to demand, "Dame un besito!" and when my great-grandfather got near me, to scream and twist my head as La Meche whisked me away from his offered kiss, laughing through her cigarette smoke.

He sat me on the grass (because my knees had, after much effort, unfolded years ago, but now, did not fold up sufficiently as to allow any crouching) and put the little girl on my lap. In front of us, a man with pink hair and a big fat man were assuming their bunny heads. Just to our left, a homeless man was peeing against a bench. I glanced over, hooked my arms around the baby and pointed at the rabbits, "Mira! Mira los cajones!"

AMBER DIPIETRA

He leaned his mouth into my ear. "*Conejos*, hija. Rabbits. You just told the baby to look at that guy's balls."

I hate it when you pull staples baby out with your teeth baby OK baby don't stop do you need to spit baby?

"That's uterus!" my grandfather scoffed, and no one could stop laughing long enough to correct him.

to touch my place where the words come out

this name, a shaped space that fits

I can say this man gave me calla lilies, they keep their long throats clean, but there are story parts I shouldn't show my mother. Like holding his little rabbits and how I had to blow my nose. At the same time. Instead, I tell the part about how we both got colds soon after we started. A litter of crumpled tissues, I find them lovely white in the morning, munching dust under the bed.

everyone and rendering each
speaker as a container
brimming in the utterance

It's about peeling the paper up and putting the rabbits back in it again. And I've met another, very actual man. When he undresses for the evening, he belly flops from the heights of comedy by shrieking, "Eek, a ma-an!" A damsel a la 1950's animation, mortified by the carrot-waving rascal in her boudoir. I call my mother all the time and tell her such stories. As if she were my baby. She hears them to sleep.

baby baby	
means	*I intend*
nothing but	*to say*
made you small	*enough, everything*
in the sameness outside	*inside your name*
your name	*to carry with me*

in this instance
the soft parts
the hard parts
of speaking
bring us into

Ellen McGrath Smith

"HEARING A PEAR": THE POETRY READING
ON A NEW FREQUENCY

I've been going to the National Poetry Foundation conferences at the University of Maine for the past fifteen years. Located on the UMaine Orono campus, the conference comes along about once every three or four years. It's four days of readings, panels, discussion, debate, soft-footed walks along tall pine trails. Each conference I've attended has focused on a specific decade in poetry. The most recent one focused on poetry of the 1970s. Since I more or less came of age in the 1970s, this conference made me feel, if not as prehistoric as the Maine landscape, a lot more dated than I'd felt when I attended prior ones on the 1940s, 50s, even the 60s.

Maybe this sense of datedness had something to do with it, or maybe it's just that I face up to my hearing impairment more now than I have in the past, but this last conference in Maine, three years ago, taught me as much about my own hearing loss as it taught me about what was happening in poetry during the 1970s. The Language poet Bruce Andrews gave a reading on one of the first nights. Long a fan of his manifesto, "Poetry as Explanation, Poetry as Praxis," I looked forward to the reading, a plenary session in an auditorium with, I assumed, suitable acoustics and a more-than-adequate sound system.

But how does one define "suitable" or "more-than-adequate" when the room is sprinkled with people like me who have mild-to-moderate sensorineural hearing loss that more often than not has more to do with frequency than with volume? It's always a gamble. You go in thinking, "Will he have the kind of voice that falls inside that cookie bite on my audiology chart?" If you, as I do, have hearing aids, you might put them in and cross your fingers. But the sad truth is that if the voice falls outside of that "cookie bite" even the hearing aids are unlikely to help. Here are just a handful of consonants I'm likely to miss on the bad side of that gamble: P, H, G, K, T, F, S...or the blends: CH, SH, TH. There's a good chance I won't be able to tell "chit" from "chinola."

The humor and wordplay make it less daunting. In fact, when I spoke briefly with Andrews after the reading, explaining that I'd enjoyed what I'd been able to hear, but that much of it got away from me because of my hearing impairment, he swiftly made poetry out of the exchange: "You're hearing a pear?" he asked, in a mock-confirming voice matched by a smile. As far as I was concerned, I'd missed much of his reading but gained a bounce by the exchange. His response, in a sense, showed his understanding of what my hearing life is like: a mixture of misapprehension and generative creativity, of word-tag and wordplay. Of loss and gain.

Maia Boswell-Penc, in an essay published in *Women and Language* (2001), writes of this paradoxical relation to her own hearing impairment: "It is paradoxical that I sometimes perceive myself to be 'different'—somehow 'wrong' or 'limited'—while I also embrace my 'loss' as a 'gift,' as a mark of special awareness, a portal into an 'other' space offering 'other' perceptual encounters and insights" (p.47).

Call it maturity or just resignation, this most recent Maine conference was all about embracing. For perhaps the first time in my life, rather than fighting or denying my hearing impairment, I adapted to it. "Adapted" may not be the right word; I believe I've been adapting to it all my life—with one of the biggest adaptations, which I'll get to later, being my immersion in reading and writing, first as childhood interests, second as adult occupational pursuits. Rather, it was one of the first moments when I allowed it to enter into my experience as a positive, rather than negative, factor. This isn't to say that I didn't want to see Bruce Andrews' words on paper. I did, and when I did, it brought the same sense of recognition and relief to me that words on paper always have in the wake of a session of struggling, unsuccessfully, to process those words through air, bone and nerve.

One way in which I began, at that conference three years ago, to consciously allow my hearing loss into my creative experience emerged shortly after the Andrews reading. We'd gone on a bus from Orono to Waterville (no moose sightings) to see an exhibit at Colby College of some of the artwork of Joe Brainard. After browsing the exhibit, we gathered in a bright shiny room to hear Bernadette Mayer read. I could have told you— just by looking at the surfaces and dimensions of the room and sensing the degree of echo potential—that this was going to be another frustrating listening session...unless, by some miracle, Mayer was going to have the voice of James Earl Jones. Two minutes into it, I pulled out my notebook. "Damn it," I told myself, "I'm going to be an active listener if it kills me." The way I had through countless elementary, high school, college and grad school classes and lectures, I turned to an old friend—the page right under my nose—but with a different attitude. In those prior times, I'd doodled incessantly in my notebook as a way of working off the energy and frustration of not being able to hear.

ELLEN MCGRATH SMITH

This time, I wrote as if trying to transcribe what I thought Mayer was saying. I was listening to a poet read in a way I'd never listened before. The experience was full of stretches when I really was hearing her and writing down what I was certain she was saying...and moments when our paths divided but I went on and she went on... It was as though we were hiking in the same woods. "What is this process?" I thought to myself. Laughing, I called it "Hearing a Pear," and I've been doing it ever since: whenever I'm at a reading that matters to me but which poses the acoustical challenges that, in the past, would make me simmer with rage (Whose fault was this? Was this all because of one ear infection too many? Why wasn't something done about this when I was a child? Couldn't she just speak up?)—challenges that, on really bad days, used to make me get up and leave with a sense of failure.

These experiences and others have made me all too aware that there are likely to be people in most poetry reading audiences whose frustration due to hearing impairment is goading them, silently, to get up and leave. According to a recent survey of U.S. homes by the Better Hearing Institute, about 11 percent of the population has some degree of hearing loss, and this percentage has grown significantly over the last twenty years. Among poets and writers, there's always been a good deal of discussion about ways to make literature relevant to readers; in poetry, the notion that the genre is all-but-extinct in the culture is so commonplace now that it spawns a steady stream of essays and ideas for keeping poetry alive by finding new ways to engage audiences. Fortunately, for those who are hearing impaired, a lot of these new ways tap into the capabilities of electronic media, generally drawing on the visual capabilities of the computer. Still, in poetry especially, the reading is frequently invoked as a key vehicle for keeping the genre vital, insofar as the reading preserves its roots in orality. For instance, the critic Charles Altieri (in a 2007 issue of the litmag *No*) calls for innovations in reading styles and formats that aim to counter what he characterizes as "the alienating effect of seriatim presentation"(p.315). The cultural era in which the traditional format evolved has passed, Altieri believes. Now, that format only works well "when the performer's presence on stage affords a visible supplement to the poetry, when the work is readily comprehensible in the hearing because the institution of performance is built into its diction and syntax, and when poets are not fighting various ideologies of immediacy but embracing them"(p.314).

For the purposes of this essay, I would focus on Altieri's second condition: "when the work is readily comprehensible in the hearing because the institution of performance is built into its diction and syntax." Here, Altieri is assuming an audience without hearing loss. Even so, he argues that much of contemporary poetry, in its diction and syntax, is not "readily comprehensible in the hearing." This is all the more true when one considers that 11 percent I mentioned above.

The irony of all this is that, as I look back on my childhood struggles with hearing (we just thought it was a matter of "bad ears" from infections and swimming), I realize that it was probably the gift of my hearing loss that led me, unwittingly, to love the printed page and the written word. I couldn't wait to learn to read; seeing the phonetics of the world that so often confused me clarified and stabilized by graphic presence gave me a confidence and security that I all too often missed. It still does. I might even say with a degree of certainty that I have made a career out of writing and reading because of my hearing impairment. And, although I've not come across much that connects print literacy and hearing impairment, I suspect that many others in my position have found their comfort and competence in writing and books. This makes it all the more crucial to think about what might be done to provide more access for audiences of spoken poetry who, with or without sound systems and hearing aids, struggle to comprehend what often is, even for audience members with normal hearing, difficult to comprehend.

While Altieri's focus is not on the hearing impaired, his essay suggests various innovations to the traditional reading format that would serve listeners with hearing loss very well. For instance, he posits that:

> ...a more systematic shift might take place if poets are asked to imagine their performances as the acts of educators who carry out a distinctive mode of research...The first step is to recognize that it is fine to present poems more than once. In fact I imagine readings with only a few poems read, then discussed by the poet, then read again, or even read by audience members to see if they can catch the particular nuances the poet brings out (p.317).

Altieri's model would have a poetry reading function more as what we now call a "master workshop." This is not so feasible, though, in the large, auditorium-style readings we've come to accept as the norm. For readings such as these, accommodations could be made such as on-screen simultaneous projection of poems. Distribution of work to be read is a tricky business, given that authors want to sell their books or, for

ELLEN MCGRATH SMITH

works in progress, don't want draft versions to be in circulation. A way to address this might be to hold more book signings prior to rather than following readings, with loose copies of a few of the leading poems from the book on the book table (providing those new to the author's work with a sample that might lead to a book purchase). With the Internet, a few key poems that will be read could be posted prior to the reading date. I cannot express enough the joy I feel when I can look at a poem while an author reads it, especially when frequency and acoustics are major factors.

For much of my life, due to the lack of information on the nature of my own hearing loss, I have been silent about my struggles as a listener, primarily because I thought that they were solely my fault, my responsibility, my problem. For a long time and especially during my youth, I thought my condition was temporary (conductive rather than sensorineural) and that all my problems would just go away with lavage (irritated siblings shouting, "Just get your ears cleaned out!") or the reduction of pollens in the air. Later, as an adult working as a university teacher, when I learned that my hearing loss was sensorineural and not temporary, the blunt advice of playmates morphed into more tactful suggestions that I get a hearing aid. I now have two hearing aids, but, as anyone who uses these devices will attest, they are far from foolproof for a variety of mechanical, situational and (still) acoustic reasons.

Speakers often ask, at the beginning of a reading or lecture, whether everyone can hear them, but that often is perceived by people like me as more of a rhetorical gesture than an actual question seeking a real answer. Perhaps more important is the need to generate awareness about hearing loss, particularly the very basic fact that hearing loss is not only a question of volume but of frequency. In terms of improving hearing access to poetry, it would help if poets themselves were more honest with themselves in assessing and adapting their speaking voices to audiences. By this, I do not mean learning to project and enunciate as if all poets were hereby ordered to also become thespians! But I do think it is important to know what sort of voice you have, whether it is treble or bass heavy, and to make the necessary accommodations for that in different reading situations. I hope this doesn't sound as though I'm shifting the onus for my disability onto others. Rather, my message is more of a plea to poets (and to all who speak in public) to imagine that, within a given audience, there are people who want to and are trying to hear you, but can't, and that the number of these people appears to be increasing over time.

Afraid of the Rake

A man was raking, in white-collar clothes, raking the remnants of a year ago, taking care to make sure, once he'd raked them, they'd never come back. A woman who'd decided she wasn't a writer was writing. Needles from her Christmas tree clung to her doorstep afraid of the rake, whose shirring stirred the street. She was writing as she always did—beginning. Like Rilke, like Stein, she began and began for the sake of beginning again. For this reason, her poetry was prose. It was a cold she kept catching. The shirring was not autumn but spring. Which meant renewed hope in the sequence of the sentence. Subject verbs object. *I cupped your smooth cheek.* The man with the rake was a man with a rake, nothing more. That was the beauty—the moot declaration more likely to take root. She had chanted her way to Chicago and back, chaperoning the painful crudescence of love. Refereeing perhaps. *Om namah shivaya,* they droned, we droned, he/she/it droned, stopping only for gasgourmetcoffeetopee. Then she'd translated the Sanskrit to late-sixties pop, whereby *life would be ecstasy, you and me endlessly*—and all four wheels did their duty, and she, who dubbed herself third wheel, felt her ego downshift. All declarations would have to be kept, she decided, in the tinderbox that loss had left her. Just below the navel. She'd renounced writing, but remembered what was happening to Jack, whose poems always turned her inside-out. He was forgetting, dispersing; he was losing the left margin. Coherence was a rake, like a fence around the self (which is not given). Words like leaves blowing out beyond the property lines. There was loss, and there was joy, and there was a state in which both of them were one. But she wasn't ready to go there yet. She wrote, finally, as a way of clinging to the doorstep, afraid of the rake, whose shirring stirred the street.

ELLEN McGRATH SMITH

The Magic Word Is *Partager*

French. Infinitive. Means *to share.*
A cousin to the English, *partake,*
as in particles given to everyone, everyone
being a particle, taking part in. *Part* by itself
and in English is sad; it's so separate and final,
and *partake's* too focused on taking,
while, somehow, the French is an infinite
giving; it ends with an open vowel—Piaget
parting the shell of a mollusk to see something
still soft in its being, not to eat but to stare at it,
wondering at its mute life (like the insides of cheeks,
which take part in the structures of carapace, bone;
taking part but apart from devouring or being
devoured). *Ager* is what we're all doing—
we grow old—and we share this,
we live, we depart; it's an art.
Piaget did partake in the progress of children
—the aging of children, *his* children his subjects—
infants so like unshelled mollusks:
they sprawl in their soft, tender nudity over
the palms of whatever hands hold them.

Spelling Down

I wanted bad to advance to Washington, D.C.
I wanted bad to be anyone but me.
The nun who had trained me for the spelling bee
needed a ride, and I was so worried all the way across town
that my dad would start swearing in front of her,
I couldn't really think straight, so when
I got to the tie-breaking round with a Central Catholic boy
in an argyle sweater, I nearly tripped on the way to the mic.

"Hoo-ist," the word-distributor announced.
I couldn't hear, could never hear, so I asked him to repeat.
"Hoo-ist," he said again. I took a stab at it and spelled it
H-U-I-S-T, and the man in the toupee shook his head
and turned to Chip, who whipped out, "Whist.
W-H-I-S-T. Whist." He smiled before the judge said yes,
because of course that was the word—whist! whist!—
what on earth had I been thinking?

It was quiet as we drove over the West End Bridge.
I couldn't wait to drop off Sister Simon
so I wouldn't have to simmer in the back seat
with my mother, both of us praying he wouldn't break into
his grating vernacular. "She spells a lot better than me,"
he told Sister. "But all I write is police reports,
and spelling don't matter." She cocked her head
as if he were discoursing on John of the Cross.

Now I stand above the city. There's a murky line
where the two rivers form the Ohio, as if at first
reluctant to be mixed. And where my father's gone

ELLEN MCGRATH SMITH

might just as well be called the delta. I see him now,
in red-black light, a pen in his mouth, clipboard on his lap,
asking his partner if "domestic" is spelled with a "ck";
the guy in the back puts his face against the cage
and says, "no dickhead, P-I-G. You get that down?"

Theodore Enslin, Poet of Maine

Theodore Enslin, poet of Maine, I am closing my eyes to tune you in,
to hear your tender buttons turning inside-out toward reflections
on water, attention to stones. Yet, even though you're using a microphone,
your voice—when it follows softly on the consonantal endings—
leaks through the trough of my hearing loss. It's the same with Robert Creeley;
you and he on the same frequency that looks like a valley on my chart.
I close my eyes and try to listen with my heart to the Steinian insistence
of your long gray beard, try to soften my long-damaged ears from inoperable
shale to pale pink petals absorbing what sun this stringent coast permits.

Sometimes, this way, I get whole phrases, only to pass through other phases
where stone and skin and soul are blurred, and words fly off like startled birds,
my eyes into a soundless sky.

ELLEN MCGRATH SMITH

Denise Leto

OULIPO[1] AT THE LAUNDROMAT

I hear the stutter as a sounding of uncertainty. What is silence or not
quite silenced...a return is necessary, a way for women to go. Because
we are in the stutter. We were expelled from the garden of mythology of
the American frontier. The drama's done. We are the Wilderness.
We have come on to the stage stammering...
—Susan Howe

Into the simple pile of clothing, there must be a reach and a fold and a way to communicate that change is warranted. Many quarters are needed. Then the machine can qualify disruption and accomplishment. The clean smell in the room is now the symbol of a day during which the pretense of missing vowels and the context of exanimate movement quiets what would otherwise have become greater than the possible. The fragmented self in reality and in poetry can constitute, as Canadian poet Nicole Brossard frames, an "autobiography or the appearance of facts..." (p.29). This swampy division of poetic labor: there might be time to write. I can't make myself heard. I can't make myself. Heard. No story *there*.

In the steam is the grout. What sticks in the conversation is the void that underlies the noise: the ambient environment constraint: the whirring machine constraint. The imbricated verbal effort creates the effortless problematic. It just happens because it is both involuntary and chance, neuro-form and function. The spoken is not always reception. The disequilibrium of voice, whether on or off the page, is both subject to random, shaping forces, and the subverting and embracing of chance and intentionality. To borrow the poetics of Oulipo in the quotidian: letters and words are strategically moved about resulting in poems of limitless fixity. What results is akin to the unexpected in verbal cadence and in the cacophonous surround of daily spaces.

Speech through laryngeal dystonia is not within the speaker's, my, control. Dysfluent communication is a kind of ventriloquy. Intended words are thrown to the listener; the listener catches something else or maybe nothing at all. My disability is the listener's difference. When the world embraces only words that last the entire length of a vowel or consonant, division is exchanged.

This is how it affects my work. The poetic line becomes a callisthenic beam of the spoken. Daily life is like a concussive engagement. A continuity of spoken thought is a transient luxury mostly in transcription. Even if it isn't written well, it tricks me into praising its fluidity—its supposed "able-ness."

The desk spreads before me, monstrous and segmental. Writing abjures sitting. That kind of verbal relief = the extant physical pain. What I have causes pain. The experiment is structural, sonorous, a clamor and coronet of misdirection; it overwhelms past aesthetic strategies and is already undone as I begin. It is a confounded representation of the subject/object. Sharon L. Snyder explains, in "Infinities of Forms: Disability Figures in Artistic Traditions," "...a disability source will often anchor explanations for artistic origins even as it will seem to explain away other motives" (p.174). The keyboard clicking or the pen on paper sounds to my ear how I imagine I sound in the world, roughly enjambed, like the lines schisming across my desk.

Classification evades. Dystonia resides in my brain. It is difficult to describe except that when I try to say it, that's what it is. Uttered sound as a changeling while plunking quarters for redress, multiplied by the performance of the naked word in a nude female body.

The someone in this female body, this lesbian body, is often comforted when in no distress, or discomfited when under great duress. Here comes the gendered moment when help unneeded arrives—the way the male hero becomes a reverse swagger. For example, if her voice is "shaky" while she and her lover ask about a seat at the movies, order food or make an appointment, a desperate emotionality is assumed. This supposed emotionality becomes what is seen as articulated helplessness. Where the struggle to be heard or seen, for her a long engaged political act, is now also a disembodied acrimony. To be seen/unseen this way, to be perceived "meek," is an affront but it is also identification. "What's wrong with you?" Not by the self that is *her* self. But by subjects that are still in that story. The someone in this lesbian body picks up the bloodied words and wears them inside out.

In the public sphere, her mouth is a pod encased in a coarsely internal argument. Sprouting linguistic approximations, an odd film forms. However, in this pearly disconnect there is a listening, a past, and a forward, a feminist conversation with the spoken and written word in relation to imposed, formal constraint that manifests in my work. There is a *story* there; it follows:

DENISE LETO

The poets Juliana Spahr and Stephanie Young, in a talk entitled "Foulipo" subsequently published in the online journal *Drunken Boat*, address feminist embodiment via performance art via Oulipian procedures.[2] The result of their creative collaboration became a sound and word artifact of presence and absence in body and language:

Our writing ink was often saying I AM here-against. In the middle of a lineally it would pop up, I AM here-against. And yet it was, we had to admit, profoundly constrained when it said this. Or it was a mute lumpering, almost dumb, but dumbly asserting its presence all the same, here-against I AM, a lumpering of flesh-fly, I AM here-against. We were constrained and yet we did not expose our constricted or even really address it. We treated it as natural. We dramatized it in our poephagus. (np)

Consider their following constrained line: "So we found ourselves stutteing though laye afte lay of what we felt defined us" (Spahr and Young np).[3]

This woman in this body in this garden of quotidian mythology: riotously silent except when unlocked at the precise moment of convergence. I am on this untheoretical stage because of a blocked neuro-feedback loop. I can't make myself heard in the Laundromat. That my embodiment of strained orality masks what might be a transformative poetic exercise is a welcome conundrum, so long as this daily performance is understood as having no artifice: so long as the "poephagus" can strip layers of cultural recognition, to be heard and seen within a feminist body politic of written and performed poetics.

Plaza Series.1

Her balcony, her terrace

a chance language blankets

the rarity, the tiptoe repetition.

She is (or is not) able to travel

within the neural destruction

to a moment ago.

She watches the round of monuments.

A man passes by, many men pass by, many people with hats pass by.

The lines repeat.

She is traveling

to a measure of the order that exists

in the moment just ahead.

Quite content in the anonymous center,

the municipal surround.

She reads (without) reading.

Mimicry is a corridor.

Multiple voids present themselves.

Watching, she sees

the same people every day,

unconstrained in buttery blankness.

She thinks tangled thoughts on a bench.

Sad cranberries, pinking shears, coffee?

The lines repeat her portrait of sound.

The couple asks her to take a picture.

She tries, memorizing

what walks away.

She is not a monument.

Her fingers glitter with spit.

Many pleasing birds fly by.

DENISE LETO

She is traveling.

The color of hats.

They kick her out of celadon walls.

She gathers past activities,

the many, many women with cards.

The Lost Word Association

She had a hat full of v's.
She kept them well-hydrated and liked to pet
        their felt legs during the meetings.

He tugged absently at the hole in his throat.
      The hole in his throat, where the signifier,
expelled, riven sharp, shaves across the ear.

      She labored at the minutes,
      scribbling: erasure, erasure.
         How to report the jagged miscellanea?

(he blew on the hot coffee,
his lips remembering the shape of a "u")

they are cut up into lengths by the flexible tongue, the crafter of words, and molded
              in turn by the configuration of the lips

She kept her empty voice box
      tidy; the door shut.
 That way, what wasn't there became
less apparent, leaning into more of itself

        From A to I to "Replica"

DENISE LETO

26 Tries

Lush skull.

Reverse utter.

Vellum angel.

At the barn.

Light cubed.

Dirt apprentice.

Flour penumbra.

Moss animate.

Suffer form.

No reason.

Outside.

Hyperlink.

Time-lapse.

Mortar.

Numeracy.

Give.

Apologia.

Trespass.

The unction of sponges.

Where it began.

Nucleate drapery.

Suspense in the species.

In translation.

No mention of fish or birds.

Table of ointments.

Seams.

Crane of Angles

The earth crept, lurched upward, and took sudden hold of her shoulders. Plagued them stratospherically forward. The ground became her neck. Down the avenue the ringmaster. Though there were many tiny acrobats twisting the length of her legs making them whinny. Her proprioceptive tap dance drew spontaneous crowds, cagey looks. Flush with a string of lights beginning in the lowest quadrant of her brain, where it becomes the body. A toy helix in off beam hands careening the sidewalk. Everything that isn't Daphne. Cycles in her rapidly blinking eyes. The torque of feet and to think this is what. Closer to the movement of planets.

DENISE LETO

Jennifer Bartlett

EXIT THROUGH THE GIFT SHOP

O ften, so-called disabled poets are faced with how to address, or whether to address, their minority status as part of their poetics. This question is applicable in terms of content, form and marketing (a term I use lightly, as poetry is rarely successfully marketed). Further, what responsibility does the poet have, if any at all, to question and/or resist stereotypes? For me, the question of ethics arises, all good intentions aside, in that poets with disabilities risk the danger of consciously or unconsciously manipulating their difference to promote work in a world where there are many poets, few readers, and even fewer poetry teaching jobs.

Ethics and disability is something that has haunted my life. I want to be equal in the job market, but I want to have access to a seat on the subway too. I question certain "privileges" that come with slower movement: a half-fare subway card, teaching in classrooms near my office, and so on. Things I could do without, but make life easier. I always dwell on my own concept of "fairness." Should I be taking advantage of things that I am capable of doing without?

Poetry is something slightly more complicated than my half-fare subway fare. The marketing of my work as an identity poet has never been something with which I'm comfortable. It strikes me as disingenuous. (I'm not even comfortable with po-biz in general, and like to think of poetry as a vocation: a spiritual blessing and/or curse.)

Do we need more poets with disabilities? A resounding yes! However, I want my work to be strong enough to exist on a level playing field. I want to be, like Larry Eigner, a good poet who happens to be disabled. This does not mean that I won't even address disability in my poems. Nor does it mean that I will stop questioning the exclusion of people with disabilities. But, it means that I've given a lot of thought on how I want it to happen. I don't believe art is merely to entertain. When I read a poem, I want to work, to feel, to be challenged, to learn something about language or something about life. If I want to be entertained, I would watch *Law and Order*. For me, entertainment is about *checking out*: poetry is about *checking in*. I think, perhaps naively, that poetry is meant to change the world.

So, when I do address disability in my work, I want to present my vision of what it means to have cerebral palsy. I feel that, as a poet with a disability, I have an ethical responsibility to challenge the norm of how society perceives disability: that it has been the most difficult thing in my life [hardly]! That I would prefer to be able-bodied [not really]. That I do not love my body or am *less than*. Nor would I want reviewers to use the typical words that are markers for disability disempowerment: afflicted, invalid, diseased and so on. As a poet, I cannot always control who criticizes my work, but I can have some control over who publishes the poems and how they are presented. That may require decisions that others might deem sacrifices. But, most of all, my work needs to reflect the integrity of my struggle for civil rights, along with maintaining the integrity of the poems themselves, which *always comes first*. This is not to say that I have always followed my own ethics. Yes, I have noted that I have a disability on my NEA application, when submitting poems to mainstream journals, applying for jobs and so on. The irony is that it has rarely, if ever, helped.

At first, I avoided writing about/mentioning disability at all. Throughout my twenties, denial was my attempt at finding equality. In my thirties, I changed. I wanted equality not in spite of who I was, but because of who I was. In short, I didn't have to "pretend" that I wasn't disabled anymore because I realized there is nothing wrong with my disability, only others' perceptions of it.

As I delve into my next project, which is directly about disability, I am back to the question of ethics. Typically, disability is viewed as a tragedy. In my experience, even many people with disabilities want to cling to the negative aspects of disability. My new work challenges those stereotypes and asks society to look at the misnomers they have applied to disability.

This is *not* to dispel the real pain, physical and emotional, that derives from being disabled—although I would argue that most, if not all, of the *abled* people I know are in chronic physical and/or emotional pain of some form. People with disabilities do have any host of difficulties, but these difficulties are constantly exacerbated by a society that gears itself toward ableness—in architecture, the media, the job market, the housing market, and, yes, even academia. (How many first-year writing programs include disability as part of their multicultural curriculum?) I would argue that *all* of my "pain" surrounding disability has derived from prejudice. Still, for me, there is also a happiness in having cerebral palsy. Yes, my life has been really hard in terms of aversion. But, it has also created what David Byrne calls special*ness* and who doesn't want that?

5 poems from AUTOBIOGRAPHY

to walk means to fall
to thrust forward

    to fall and catch

the seemingly random
is its own system of gestures

based on a series of neat errors
    falling and catching

to thrust forward

sometimes the body misses
then collapses

sometimes
it shatters

with this particular knowledge

a movement spastic
    and unwieldy

is its own lyric and
the able-bodied are

tone-deaf to this singing

some

      falling

            is of its own grace

some

      falling

            rather occurs

out of laziness or distraction

here, the entire frame is shaken

these are the falls

where I tell myself

            you shouldn't have fallen

I mean to inflict

while the critic of the world watches

o stupid, stupid world

to be crippled means to have a window
into the insanity of the able-bodied

to be crippled means to
see the world slowly and manically

> *to translate*

to record

> *to adapt*

to be crippled means to have
access to people's fear

of their own eroding

main part

primary figure

the opposite of the soul

      opening

mere container

the thing that transitions

shelter me

flawed shelter

      unwieldly

spastic soldier

invalid of no legal force

composed primarily
of water and light

this is my body
I am its light

a mere shadow remains
so that, the body is erased

excepting movement

I am all motion and
this motion is neither weak nor hideous

this motion is simply my own

Cynthia Hogue

THE CREATURE WITHIN: ON POETRY AND DIS/ABILITY

Well, nothing is predictable with pain
Did the old poets write of this?
—ADRIENNE RICH

I'm writing about poetry and what I have come to think of as the dis/abling illness I have, and suddenly feel as blank as the blank page of the unwritten volume of the new. I can't write myself except through reading others' words. Will try again later.

Later, I take up the delicate Paris Press edition (2002) of Virginia Woolf's essay, *On Being Ill*. It's too beautiful to read more than a sentence or two. "Considering how common illness is, how tremendous the spiritual change that it brings, how astonishing, when the lights of health go down, the undiscovered countries that are then disclosed...what ancient and obdurate oaks are uprooted in us by the act of sickness," Woolf wonders why illness is not, like "love and battle and jealousy," among the great literary themes. In this description, Woolf captures the sense of how it feels to get a serious and debilitating and finally disabling illness, that it's like arriving in a country one never thought to visit. When I landed there, I wanted to book a flight right back out. All planes grounded for life.

As for why few write about illness, I reason that everyone falls in and out of love, is jealous and gets over it (or doesn't), fights or is fought for, but not everyone gets a disabling illness. And there's the rub. Why would anyone write about illness except the ill? And at first, too, the experience is too close for the ill person to be a reliable witness. The mind doesn't want to write *about* the body's condition but to change it, for in dreams the body can still dance!

Trying to dance around the question of my poetry's relation to my illness, I read Woolf's inimitable prose, which I register viscerally, because my nerves are on the outside of my skin now. I experience the words as *excruciatingly* truthful. They make me squirm, not dance: "The creature within" the ill body, Woolf writes, "can only gaze through the pane [or pain]—smudged or rosy; it cannot separate off from the body like the sheath of a knife or the pod of a pea for *a single instance*" (emphasis added). I think, "I" became that "creature within," that "it" when I became ill. Why in the world would I want to write about *that*?

Reading Woolf's essay, like being ill, is an odd—and ethical—experience of having the self mirrored back as *other*, of being unsettled by the otherness of the ill body of which she writes so movingly and so coldly. When I got ill, I began to feel an empathy for this othered self with which I could not yet identify, which was suffering, and which *I* was being forced to suffer. I also felt empathy for *others* who, I began to notice, were imperiled by circumstances (in that way the unconscious ruptures language with truth, I first wrote imper-*illed*). Woolf writes that a statement like "I am in bed with influenza" cannot convey the depth or clamor or distortion of perception of this insistently embodied experience: "How the world has changed its shape," she exclaims. What one learns about human nature! Friends change toward the ill person, some revealed in their strange and beautiful kindness and some exposed in their utter, ugly selfishness. A friend cannot perform "friendship" to an ill person, because she will see right through it. The ill have no time or energy for anything other than the raw and startled truth of another's soul. To an ill person, subterfuge is transparent, and though she may not blurt out what she sees (to which, when healthy, she was blithely blind), she will eventually write about it. Both poetic and existential excess is scraped away. The decorative and the distractive are dropped like old habits one has outgrown.

I have been moved by poetry that conveys the essential. I live with, contemplate Adrienne Rich's poems and essays about having rheumatoid arthritis (as it happens, the very disease I have). I never took in the details until I was myself living them. Rich reported news I had no way to understand, because it was about a body's experience I did not share, and described the indescribable (pain). Then, her words became my guides to an expanded, although unasked-for, awareness.

Sometimes, I try to write about the phenomenology of ill health by describing it tangentially. The alienation I have felt from my old life and from the world of the healthy resembles culture shock, another phenomenon I have experienced, because I have lived and traveled abroad a good deal. What interests me about both these conditions is the sensation of the self's erasure: the disappearance of the signs by which one knows one's self. In the poetic series I worked on during the first decade of my illness, I collaged in medical descriptions, quoted specialists, discovered a visual and symbolic text within a poem, words within words leaping out at me as I struggled to find poetic language in the face of cognitive impairment. I found myself using the second person pronoun, on occasion, the "I" becoming an addressee, a "you," and the poem an apostrophe designed to conjure "me" back to the world. "The whole landscape of life lies remote and fair,"

Woolf writes. I watched myself turn into a stranger who lived inside a bell glass, far away from all I'd known. All of it was gone—poof!—as if "it" or "I" had never been.

Writing connects what had been to what is. I write from inside a slowly disabling illness to avert extinction, not to understand the mystery. I don't want to translate this experience into something that is neat or simply meaningful. I want to open the mind to the majesty of perspective—all that dis/ability proffers—which sounds a dissonant but resilient note. I want the poems to resonate with this tone. Call it an aspiration. On the blank page, I see the poems hover in the air like charms, potent and poisonous, magical and medicinal, instructive of a spiritual journey no one chooses, and onto which one stumbles clumsily, trying to catch one's balance, looking at times wistfully back at the road one missed before looking ahead again, carrying on.

CYNTHIA HOGUE

Green surrounds the mind of summer

Taking time, patience
This new body a new land
The doctor said, "Let's say
that people with green haIr
are more likely to cOntract
this disease, so for our purposes
it's as if you have green haIr."
He wOn't kill
but he cannot

                    cure you

There is nO cure
Now there's nO there

        your mind left
        without your body
        Where did "you"
        gO?

> The study of individual illness, with the notion
> of **social illness**, is a window for us to look at the
> characteristics of social experience in our society,
> as well as the development, maintenance and
> treatment of disease.

This happens dAILy
This unspecified this, a waking
and thinking This Is It this!
Take it, beLIEve this is
not in your control

You do not read about this

                       "isn't news"

If nothing means anything

the medical report

a construction of meaning

to mean something

> The paradigm of the **healthy social world of normal people** sees social support therapy as a rite of passage. The person with chronic illness is cast into a permanent liminal state.

then *disease-free*

is a state of being

you can claim

to emBODY, saying if

you do, you do, and you dO

(it's a lie)

In a Mute Season

Questions rail along the field
where winter wheat lies hidden
in snow. (We lie to justify
indefensible behavior, to protect
unprotectable innocence, inhaling
and exhaling with an evenness
of spirit to which we aspire.)
Who calls the sky gray?
or the seasons from hell?

I visit doctors because
my body drives me to them,
beyond my dictates. Ailing,
I am healing before
my mind understands
that the phenomenology of pain
harbors words which refuse
syntax and order, predictable,
eventual inevitability,

until I grasp that order
eludes us, dispersing,
a wall of fog we drive through,
so frugal of speed, spendthrifts
of time. To feel alone is merely
the mind's last defense—
a physiological white-out—
from the spirit's largesse.

Radical Optimism

I held the cup, which emptied.
Possibly I watched. I balanced
on a bench. The room chattered,

a party. I dashed notes:
Can you be with not knowing,
living the separation, cult.

of grief (culture or cultivation)?
A broken heart is a whole (I'd torn
it away). Grasped a filled cup.

Around me swirled laughter
as if the glimmering sprawl
of the Milky Way emerged

when wisps of clouds scuttled past
in the night's wind. I couldn't look
up. If outside, I'd not have

noticed. This lasted hours,
then morning came. The words
were clouds swept away

by laughter. I scribbled,
trying to preserve the invisible
ink of memory, and that breaking.

Danielle Pafunda

MEAT LIFE

In 1980, I was hospitalized with a plummeting white cell count. Blood samples, marrow samples, gothic looking x-ray machines. Beyond naked, I was split, spread, flayed, spun, separated. I shrieked and kicked and bartered. Bolt upright on the surgical table, I hissed, "Doctor, what did I ever do to you?" But I soon learned that there is no stick sharp enough to make that eye blink.

Like the male gaze, the medical gaze doesn't exist discreetly in the human eye, but as a sort of collective eye. A cultural peeper. The medical gaze, leering ever pointedly since the end of the nineteenth century (see Foucault), works two ways: 1.) it reveals things about you that you yourself did not know, and 2.) if it cannot see your illness, your symptoms don't exist.

Frustrated with recalcitrant doctors, my father brought the results of my blood tests to our veterinarian (true story), who diagnosed me with chronic severe neutropenia. Neutrophils normally make up 50-70 percent of the white blood cells. In my case, zero. In my case, an idiopathic neutropenia, out of the idiot blue. With hindsight, we can wager environmental toxins, overuse of antibiotics, wrong time, wrong place, bad karma, coal mine canary. My very kind hematologist never discovered its source, couldn't predict its future. He kept me alive, and helped return me to more or less normal—I got out of isolation, could be touched by human hands and attend school with other children. How could I ask for more?

Today, my autoimmune disorder manifests most notably as fibromyalgia. While its symptoms have been observed for centuries, we didn't define it as such until the late twentieth century. Between the early 1980s and late 1990s, there was no medical reason for my pain. Now MRIs prove its neurological components! Medications abound! Television commercials for medications abound! Serotonin! Substance P!

I have fibromyalgia, I say, and now the look I receive is sympathetic.

We know that pain is inarticulable (Elaine Scarry is particularly articulate on that point).

We know that we must speak in metaphor about what we are feeling.

In medicine, the body is an object with mechanical properties, and under the medical gaze, its feelings must always be secondary, may not be valid. The (female) body is an object, and under the male gaze its feelings may not exist.

As a woman, I'm subject to the male gaze, but I was sick before I was a woman, and so am profoundly, perhaps equally, subject to the medical gaze. They often work in collusion. They constitute me. And yet the male gaze also reminds me that my illness is largely invisible.

I know there is an immense difference between my largely private experience of illness and limitation and the very public ways in which people with visible disabilities must confront the gaze. Baroque staring (see Rosemarie Garland-Thomson), public insult, desexualization, forced sterilizations and other socio-physical nightmares—our culture has been, and remains, intensely invested in the able body.

My body can pass for able. The question: should I allow it to do so? Am I a dilettante in the realm of disability, dabbling in limitations? Or, if I allow the male gaze to categorize me as normal, am I in league with the ableist agenda? I don't know. I do know I have always had to, and will always have to, live consciously within the meat of the body, and this meat life influences every fiber of my politics/poetics.

In poetry, I try to do at least this one thing consistently: to attract the gaze, to pin it or fix it in place, and then show it those sights which will brutalize, horrify, repulse or shame it. It's the legacy of Plath, whose speakers find strength, dignity and satisfaction in their own debasement. It's a perversion of Kristeva, wherein the speaker experiences abjection, but instead of sacrificing a portion of the self to rid herself of the abject material, the speaker uses the abject material as a gateway out of the normative structure in which she has been imprisoned, broken or otherwise subjugated.

DANIELLE PAFUNDA

In this Plate My Illness is Visible

I wear a bag of hammers. I alter
my gait through the knife house.
My face pigs and expels symmetry.

What will you ask me to do,
my *tunica intima* thick with teeth
and my neck herky-jerky
with an ethanol samba?

My illness is visible. For the first time
in centuries. A technician
can wheel me into the sick meat tube
and my meat will register.

In this Plate My Illness is a Wire
that Can Easily Cut Meat and Bone

Lately, my illness agitates
just beneath the skin layer.
In the dark, it will dumb you. It will twitch
over the border and take your hand.

My muscles flare, bullish. Contracted,
I accompany them above the bed. I lapse
just a ml. of fluid, I lap you.

I did not want a bridle infection,
but now I am mad with injustice.
I string you, a fucked instrument,
a wire riddled perma-slaughter.

I shard and glisten. What sludge
for a bridegroom.

DANIELLE PAFUNDA

In this Plate I Receive My First Diagnosis

Because the veterinarian solved me,
I am now his dog.

And a girl, and I go to school
where everyone
jumps my dog bones.

I dress for everything that might kill me.
In kitty ears
and a pair of my brother's plaid boxer shorts.

I drink Windex.

My mother serves it to me.

I eat apocalypse steak.

I have a bitch seizure.

Of course my rhinestone collar
keeps me from swallowing my tongue.

I swallow my boyfriend's tongue.

He's not my boyfriend. He's a dog.
He's a man and he hates me.
He's molding his loose ham into my friends in front of me.
Or he's calling me long distance
because it's years ago and he's plagiarizing
someone he just met, and he wants
to describe her kustom built pelvis.

He's a girl, actually. I put my hand

in her pants and grab something.

For all these years, no one says anything
about the long trail of worms
weeping out of my britches.

DANIELLE PAFUNDA

In this Plate My Traumadome
Has Come Unzipped

I had a special linen woven out of my
voluntary tissue. I had it wrapped tightly
to a depth of twenty layers.

It was a traumadome and also a mummy cage.

I hooked electrodes to the linen, and these,

they frothed and burned me.

I became beautiful

where pretty nippers fingered my outlet.

But far too soon thereafter
fat with suet, my seams split.
And out seeped all the jolly worms
I'd been hoarding.

In this Plate My Illness Splits Time

I'll never manage a big enough hole. I mean,
I'll never tack down this hole. This hole
is in fact expanding, and I call it future hole.

I put money into its velvet clutch, and wait
for the hole to tremble.

I look a man, Grandmother, a folk singer,
I look something squirrel and vomit.

Hungry.

Something is wrong with the buildings, here.
The audio is off, and explosions
come hours after collapse.

I need a shave, or maybe I'm sitting in shadow.
I walk like Princess Scab Bitch,
who just happens to be performing
in the gutted gymnasium.

I have heard that blood expires, but I'm keeping
this sack close by. It's tied to a body
holler in the bedroom, and I will use it
to scuttle my way back in.

DANIELLE PAFUNDA

Rusty Morrison

TO SATURATE THE MATTER OF THE PRESENT

I am walking in Manhattan on a warm afternoon, looking at the glass and chrome and polished marble of skyscrapers, at micro-mini skirts worn with cargo boots or high-tops on beautiful bare legs, at children who are the only New Yorkers who return my stare, and who do so with pure interest. I'm looking everywhere, but at my feet, when I trip on a concrete lip of uneven sidewalk and hurt my knee so badly that making it back to the hotel room seems laughable. I remember seeing the edge of up-risen pavement just as it catches my foot unprepared, though this seems logically impossible. How could I see it, since the instant it would have been in my vision is already passed, once I realize that I am falling. But the distinct sharpness of its edge and the gray density of its concrete are embedded in my memory nonetheless.

I am lying on the hotel bed, before dawn, the day after my incident, icing my knee, staring back into memory, into what seems the cellular grain of that gray edge of concrete, at its absolute clarity. I don't feel a sharp-edged density in the pain when I am icing my knee, only a vague, almost incorporeal, slowness, like the slowness of the sidewalk opening a crack in its pavement: it might take decades for such a crack to form, but only an instant for me to find it.

I am re-translating my understanding of pain. What I thought was a distinct and immediate sharpness when I hurt my knee, I realize now was only a surface sharpness: beneath that is a more potent expanse, an expanse that is continuing to widen. And in the pain I realize that the idea of "immediacy" too is false: pain's provenance is more porously languid than immediate, more akin to the drift or mis-direction of my attention, which brought it on.

Somehow, both the pain and this failure of attention are as old and as continuously forming as the crack in the pavement, which I seem to recall so vividly, though this isn't logically possible, given the circumstance of my falling.

"While we perceive something, we simultaneously remember and forget it," says Giorgio Agamben. Maybe it's also true that while I perceive something, I am simultaneously perceiving more and less than I understand can logically exist within the limits of my perception. Maybe every act of particularly fraught or shocked perception is partly a shock because it is accessing a new aperture through which perception might focus. Maybe a shock is a kind of creation, if only because it opens the opportunity to de-create at least some of my relationship to perception. I might say to Agamben that the color and texture of a crack in the pavement I didn't see have been working on me; interestingly, the crack has grown very large, larger to me now than it was during the incident in which it may or may not have existed, at least as I qualify existence.

"Memory does not follow perception, but rather is contemporaneous with it...and can produce a 'false recognition'... 'a memory of the present'... Such a memory, [Bergson] writes, 'is of the past in its form and of the present in its matter'" (Agamben, quoting Henri Bergson). I can imagine that a shock can thoroughly and continuously saturate the matter of the present, seeping right through its formal container, made of time, drawing perception with it into an emptiness outside of time and sense, or into an experience of what is beyond or outside the idea of physical containment, where all is encompassed, or all is un-encompass-able, though I might, from my limited experience, simply call this senselessness.

I have hepatitis C. It's a disease that steadily consumes my liver, but it seems that its symptoms can be slowed or heightened by how well I am caring for my body's needs, which do not remain steady, and to which I must apply a diligence of attention unparalleled in my past experience. Of course, the disease proceeds as it will, not by my will, so there's both hubris and naïveté in proposing that I have control over its periods of onrush. Still, I have seen that when I overindulge in sugar or salt, or overwork, or put myself into a stressful situation, then the next day is usually not a good one. And so it feels increasingly important that I must not walk into a day without attending devotedly to how I will choose to take each step. Yet sometimes the pull of my old expectations regarding what I should be able to have, or to accomplish, can thrust me forward, compromising my intention, and I'll miss seeing some critical rupture that I'm entering, some dangerous crack, and I will fall—I'll fail myself. The shock and the shame, the confusion of falling into illness—of failing myself—seems sharply concrete and immediate; yet it too is a false concreteness and immediacy. Like the pain in my knee, the feelings that I sum up as failure are porous and larger than the immediate moment.

RUSTY MORRISON

Whenever my symptoms flare up, I spend a few days outside of what I think of as my usual clarity and intellectual acuity. I drift; the direction and dimensions of that drift are difficult for me to locate in my usual repertoire of mental states. I say to myself that I am not fully alive to my senses, but I've come to realize that this is a traditional, and possibly limited, understanding of what senses can perceive.

"It is above all the unexperienced [event], rather than just the experienced [event], that gives shape and consistency to...personality and historical tradition," writes Giorgio Agamben. It's curious that the Latin root of the Middle English word for tradition, *tradere*, means not only to "impart" and "give over," but also to "betray." What of my old understandings, my historic traditions—those that are so innately a part of me as to be impossible to observe—is my illness giving me the freedom to see as a betrayal? What has illness begun to alter within the traditions in which I act, or that act upon me and upon my awareness?

I've begun to imagine that such an opening of awareness might have a shape or a latent structure, and that it might be reproducible, in the way that a grammar is reproducible, and that I might be able to shape myself to hear and to speak such an opening. I've begun to think of my chronic illness as a new language that my body is acquiring. I don't mean to suggest that my mind, when under the sway of illness, is speaking in words that are foreign to me. Rather, I believe that the way my body incorporates the information offered to me by experience is altered by illness. This alteration, which is a different form of communication between myself and my world, I am calling a language. Learning to hear it and to speak it with increasing fluency will allow me access to certain departures from understanding, departures from acuity as I have known it—departures that, at least initially, can be spoken in, or through, this new or altered language, which the fluencies of illness are offering to me.

Last week, I read a *New York Times* article about the ways that language influences how we perceive and understand our world. One of the simplest examples the author offers is that "the colors that our language routinely obliges us to treat as distinct can refine our purely visual sensitivity to certain color differences in reality, so that our brains are trained to exaggerate the distance between shades of color if these have different names in our language. As strange as it may sound, our experience of a Chagall painting actually depends to some extent on whether our language has a word for blue."

Nothing I've said in this essay changes the fact that I also perceive my illness as a terrifying constraint: physically limiting, but also psychically limiting when fear of the future takes hold of me. But by thinking of chronic illness as a language, I can become engaged in an observation of what fluency might mean, the fluency to speak in a language entirely different from my body's language of health. I can then try to use words to communicate this fluency, recounting my experience of body, of this opening to what is the altered or increased or dispersed perspective that illness provides or simply stimulates. But words are the second order of speaking in my body, through my body, and I have to be sensitive to the histories that each word calls forth, the traditions, which will reflect meaning in a different way than a healthy body would recall them, or understand them. I've discovered that the body is a surprisingly "elastic" medium for appreciating, for translating the languages at its disposal. Perhaps there are more than these two—the body's language of health and of illness—but these two are where I begin.

So, it seems essential that I stay attentive to their difference, and that I do not fall back upon the language of health, the syntax of my relation to body and world that health has given me, when I attempt to give words to this translation, which my body is already the active record of. "Bodies are always re-converging around the elasticity of their becoming" (Erin Manning). But to translate my body's changes, my voice must allow itself to become foreign to itself. And I must allow myself to examine, even to give up, my previous understanding of "translator," if I am to become one.

> The basic error of the translator is that he preserves the state in which his
> own language happens to be instead of allowing his language to be powerfully
> affected by the foreign tongue. Particularly when translating from a language
> very remote from his own he must go back to the primal elements of language
> itself and penetrate to the point where work, image, and tone converge. He
> must expand and deepen his language by means of the foreign language
> (Walter Benjamin quoting Rudolf Pannwitz, from Benjamin's "The Task of
> the Translator").

Interestingly, the more I think of this work as a translation that I find and follow within my body, the more I feel that words are a formal limitation to what I can communicate about it. But, of course, as a poet, I have experienced directly the ways that a formal constraint can hone the clarity, intensity and inspired power of a writing project. In

RUSTY MORRISON

similar ways, a physical constraint, such as illness, can engender surprising perceptual attunement in the body. With hepatitis C, the physical limitations that I suffer always come seemingly "ill-timed," and exhaust my powers of thought. Yet there is a different form of "time," and "power," and even "thought," involved in the language that I want to learn to translate.

I don't say this to minimize or conceal the anger that I have when facing the physical effects that this illness has had on my body, or the sadness, fear and frustration that also accompany those effects. It is, in fact, the ways that these especially debilitating emotions and sensations shift as I attempt to clarify them that will offer me glimpses of a deeper grammar of relation in life than I previously have understood. Interestingly, once I become aware of this alteration, I can begin to listen for it in the most subtle of experiences, those that I have not always taken the time, or had the fluency, to translate into understanding.

Of course, I am not surprised by either the volatility or the subtle variability of my emotions or my experience of physical sensations. "Breathe into the feeling, label it," the Buddhist practitioner will tell you, "and watch how the feeling shifts." What has surprised me is a deeper coherence beneath these shifting emotions and sensations—a coherence I hadn't seen before. Or maybe it's simply that I hadn't needed to look beneath them when my darker, more disruptive, feelings were not as overwhelming or as common, when they were more balanced by those of a healthy body that was more able to right itself, to maintain its equilibrium, even buoyancy.

I am tempted to use the word "gravity" to describe the pull that draws me to sense a deeper coherence, to label that coherence, since it seems to be a force of motion common to all my experiences when I am deeply engaged with the illness. But to use a word like "gravity" will create just the kind of falseness, the kind of limitation to meaning, which keeps it constrained in my old understandings, and that is what I want to avoid, what this illness has taught me not to trust.

Instead, I will say that there is a focus to even my most enervated lack of focus; I'd almost call it a "yearning toward," but toward what? The sense of "yearning toward" seems both diffuse and expanding, as though its presence were enlarging the stillness in what may be the empty, non-individuated core of every moment.

I find myself wanting to say I'm drawn into the inexplicability of focus itself, to its undifferentiated core where there is a force of emptiness or fullness, rather than be limited by the old architectures of meanings I would ascribe to the word "gravity" or "focus," meanings which are barriers that my yearning, when I let it exist outside of logic's parameters, neither legitimizes, nor recognizes. But this kind of talk is circular and returns to concepts that my language of health can understand. Instead, the writing I am doing in order to attend to this new fluency wants to move in the force of experience itself, and let those experiences work out their own language.

I am icing my knee. I am looking out our Brooklyn hotel window as the light on the building outside, which is the light of just-coming dawn, reaches a white stain on the red brick wall across the street; the stain surrounds what might be a deserted window, with a fire escape ladder. I could say that the light is a language in which the red brick and white stain on the brick and the fire escape ladder all gain meaning as morning comes on. But I could also say that the dark out the window, before dawn, the dark I hadn't been paying attention to, was a language communicating my inability to perceive the stain, the window, the bricks.

We are leaving New York today, so I won't be in this hotel room again tonight to look out the window. I am tired, my knee isn't much improved and my hepatitis C is flaring up. I can feel it coming. I could compare it to the inevitable return each morning of dawn, or of the loss of light that is night. But such comparisons are heavy with the language and symbolism that health has taught me to speak. Illness is less sure, less accurate, more hazy; its seeming intangibility, its dizziness frightens me. But dizziness can be the opposite of a loss of stability, of acuity—instead, though sometimes for only an instant, it seems as though I'm feeling too many points of stable contact, of acuity, at once.

The hotel window has become very bright with morning, too bright for my eyes to tolerate. I know better than to force them. It will be another very warm day in New York. Already, the automatic air conditioner, just below the sill, is blowing the sheer cotton curtain up at such a gravity-defying angle of stillness that my interest in anything else in the room pales. Its motion's life cycle, of course, has its own grammar, which I have not the skill to translate. But I am learning to give over to observing what I fail to understand, and let that "giving over" have a space in my translator's diary.

Rusty Morrison

Ill-timed (24.1)

Outside my window, construction workers use an electric compounder to compact the sand that will support the bricks of our new driveway.

My drifts of thought

                between actual thoughts

are similarly condensed by any happenstance of sudden sound—

the pounding, a ringing phone, my husband's voice from the other room—

      condensed within the entire accumulation

                of now inaccessible meanings that are my

unremembered past,

      which I feel this morning as light

                through my window, arriving from an

incomprehensible distance.

Ill-timed (24.2)

A slight texture to the book's first pages,

                discernible to fingertips alone. Blank pages,

which I thought were meaningless, are now adding texture

                    to my attention.

      A slight book, readable in one morning. This morning.

Which had seemed, at first, a slight morning.

                Which my habit of 'simply thinking'

      would have otherwise

unaccountably absorbed.

A space within thought that the texture of illness, too, unaccountably amplifies.

Ill-timed (24.3)

I close the toilet lid and sit down to listen

to what you are telling me from the shower,

an easy thing, about our day's plan, but the easy

choice I make to listen

splits in two,

and what I follow

is the other thought. Its face in profile

could be anyone, since the street it travels is growing dark,

I see only how its pale cheek has caught the darkness,

and all the parts of my day's plan—my pack of acupuncture needles

still in my hand, your voice beside me, coffee

waiting in the kitchen—all

the privilege of inventing future

as a thought

moving ahead of me to hold

whatever I ask of it, simply splits in two

any meaning I could make of a face, now entirely in shadow,

already having turned a corner on the street

in the story I was reading last night, Aschenbach

and his boy—

lean, aristocratic,

pale with illness, or made pale

by the eye of illness

that splits in two any purpose I might

make of following wherever illness draws the eye

to see how everything pales,

delicate, almost unearthly—

RUSTY MORRISON

tiles on the bathroom wall, these celibate cups of coffee

before the coffee is poured,

which I want to string one beside another

to secure my usual passage from object to object

through a day,

all of their surfaces curiously similar,

as illness sees them—

like beads

polished nearly to transparence,

so as to mirror back to me whatever surrounds them,

even shadow,

which can turn from inquisitive, a fawn's gray,

to inquisitional, the hoarder's black,

changes that split along what I sense are a moment's

natural fault lines,

moment within moment, as I follow the feel of the 'splitting' itself,

its sharpness, which is everywhere this morning,

arising now as coffee too hot on my tongue, or the sun, too bright from behind

the curtain, or the acupuncture needle

I've learned to guide into my skin, into the thickness,

so as to feel the shock

of piercing through—

as though, under the skin, an emptiness

might be reached,

where a boy-feeling is turning a corner

within a shadow, within

the illness, within this sharpness most of all.

This morning, a slight shine
along a ridge of my hand, yesterday's needle marks
beginning to scar,

which I stare at too long. The dizziness,
its prickly wounds, might be a menagerie of sharpnesses,
or might be one sharpness
that the rest are only mirroring, and sharpness itself
another bead to string

along the formlessness of deep pursuit, which is more painful
today than usual,
as though the core of something
were wanting to be exposed, to have its mirrored surface scratched,

too easy
to call it emptiness.
I had a blue stuffed rabbit, given to me when I was three
that I carried everywhere for years.
I don't know what happened to it, but I do remember
looking into its eyes and no longer feeling it
look back.

Something always looking back
in everything I've forgotten—in the origins
of this illness,
or now, years later,
in the origins of its healing—
another city
always sealed within the walls of this city,
seemingly unreachable,

RUSTY MORRISON

where the intuition that follows
sharpness
naturally is drawn

where the needle goes, which won't
be hurried.

Aschenbach decides he will go on a journey; this is what he tells himself. "Not far—not all the way to the tigers." (Thomas Mann)

Ill-timed (24.4)

In the middle of the night, in the kitchen, I find the loaf of cranberry nut
bread in the refrigerator, and I eat a slice. It isn't the worst thing in the kitchen for
me to eat. It will do my liver the least damage, of the possible damages I could
choose. It is grainy and sweet with the flavor of failed discipline,

which tastes like staring at a mirror into my own eyes
long enough to see nothing but surface
evaporating into shape drenched with sky, its dark blue skirt swirling
within all the surfaces that
surface
denies to sight.

Licking the last bread crumb from my finger, I sense
a whorled crevice of warm shadows within the crumb's flavor, a home
to slip inside of,
where I want to stay
but can't,
though it surrounds me,
being both sides of memory at once—
    behind me, as what I can't ever return to
        and before me, as what I still can't wake up to.

RUSTY MORRISON

Ill-timed (24.5)

Lifting a necklace—
      a polished piece of oddly-shaped ivory on a thin leather strap, which I

haven't worn in years—
from its hook on my bedroom wall, next to the window,

and another bedroom wall lifting itself from out of my forgetfulness
        where there had been a necklace of thought I'd draped daily

around the hope
of moving on from that room,

though I was mostly just looking out the window at an evergreen,
        probably a pine, taller each year,

but, in any given moment,
its absolute stillness seeming entirely beyond the life I was living,

or beyond what I understood life to mean,
        a lifelessness

in such stillness, shot through with green, would sometimes
fill the window,

until looking itself was
      a lifelessness

that, years later, could coincide with whatever self
I hadn't understood I'd been becoming.

David Wolach

BODY MAPS AND DISTRACTION ZONES

just as certain building types remain missing
because their functions are yet unknown,
certain functions are unknown because their
behaviors are still untried.
—ROBERT KOCIK, from *overcoming fitness*

from poem to (or as?) a poetics of action

The writing of *occultations* and a smaller "companion" book, as yet unpublished, *hospitalogy*, began as a subtle loss of motor function, which followed a sudden loss of balance. in late 2004, while it was becoming clear that the iraq occupation was going to last a long time (along with the bush regime), questions of domestic surveillance (just how are we being watched?) began to more publicly meld into questions of outsourcing law enforcement and the suppression of information (just who is watching us? and how are we watching one another? in what capacity/to what end?). nearly at the same time, while working as a labor organizer and as performing artist, this so-called body began to underline its own becoming, showing itself to be as degenerative (or as on-the-move) as our supposed "rights." this head would fall to the side. these arms wouldn't move as quickly or as accurately as before. widespread pain took up residence without paying rent. what strange processes were at work *here*? what i could *not* see or feel was what was *really* happening, said doctors. and what was really happening was programmed before i was born, they said.

the body as occulted and occulting metaphor, that evidentiary "social becoming," which both makes perceptible and hides (at once) its histories, identities and vulnerabilities— this is more than "merely metaphorical." finding myself increasingly closed off from what, in the early part of a lifelong illness, i called "primary" information sources, i.e., being *part* of an alt. news story, being *involved* (in the case of labor activism, lgbt rights campaigning or anti-war activism) rather than getting information online or in the newspaper, and "closed off" from particular activities i had taken as primary to at least

DAVID WOLACH

one identity, i asked not: what is this situation of accelerated becoming good for? but: in what ways has this so-called body *always* been a site of occultation, a deluded witness, where my understanding of agency has been predicated on layers of mediations much thinner than anything *here* should allow for? to frame things this way is to think of the body, or poem, as shorn predicament, where its languages, this predicament's public utterances, are not only muted and constricted and shaped by the catastrophes of late capitalism (including the medical industrial complex), but are also in some ways necessarily complicit in the making (narrating) of catastrophe. as constantly shifting locus of where the felt and yet to be felt touch, a body becomes associated with the *wound*, its constant chatter the reaction to, and evidence of, its violation or deletion, such that the mythos of body-as-enclosure is either reinforced or, at least temporarily, obliterated. to choose to speak or to say under such conditions is supposedly to choose to act in this way instead of that, but choice here becomes part of the predicament: there's an open question as to whether under constant surveillance, constricted, this degraded motor of constant utterance, the becoming subject, can meet kocik's ideal of taking its-self *as* -selves, a desiring multiple, capable moving outside of its (their) usual environs, habit (at)s, *poetic quarters*, and make new (and salubriously new) behaviors.

and yet i take it as imperative that the question of capability, hence one formulation of agency, be temporarily suspended, that we lay bare, as poet rob halpern writes, to the possibilities that suspending a "proprietary relation to one's own enclosed individuality" might afford us (brolaski, kaufman, and grinnell, 77). or in any case that we must act under the assumption that we *can* make new behaviors however confined or vulnerable our situation becomes. when poet and activist allison cobb reads from *the poems of guantanamo* at public gatherings, i am viscerally reminded that if the tortured prisoner of occupation can assume the responsibility of putting voice to occulted atrocity, then so might any of us *act*. and so a couple years into the writing, after doing the first few corporeal procedures/performances for the books (and sometimes of necessity), various connected urgent questions, many of them informed by nonsite collective's discussions on agency and somatic practices, began to emerge. i mention again one of these: what is this situation of accelerated becoming good for? where by "good" i mean this body's (bodies') potential as site(s) of resistance and re-narration. as i got deeper into *occultations*, i felt a growing sense that what this body-poetic might be good for is a blanket unknown, and should be, cannot help but be: as kocik notes, to *conceive* of new functions entails *active construction* of new behaviors.

in conversation with somatic practices found in dance, in body work, and lately in the work of several contemporary poets, *occultations* and *hospitalogy* begin as site-specific corporeal procedures, or "live arts performances," the output of which is the written, the oft-called "poem." i think of both "projects" as forming non-enclosed investigatory aesthetic ecosystems, where the poem is (as can be argued to be always the case) more than or beyond what occurs at the site of the page. *hospitalogy*, at one point part of *occultations* the book, is an ongoing series of poems, many of them epistolary, written in hospitals and medical clinics, and reciprocally performed or shared in hospitals and medical clinics. i'm interested in "queering" these landscape, registering affectively the systemic reductionism that is the medical industrial complex, exploring the "sick society" contra the "sick" or "disabled" human animal (to paraphrase writer susan parenti). *occultations* likewise (but written away from hospitals and clinics) makes use of (four) different corporeal practices, one per section, ranging from collaborative ritual (thanks to performance artist and poet kythe heller) to staging "distraction zones in miniature," which, as i note at end of the book, involve writing poems that:

> ...are transcriptions...the object was to create an environment, a "**distraction zone in miniature**," part of which would be the "subject-body" attempting to "voice" thru signing, thru lyric, thru direct address, its struggle to "enunciate" or "speak" or "articulate" its fractures, multiples, constrictions, and, it turns out under such circumstances, its univocality, under staged duress, not to compile or to shape what has been compiled...these poems struggle to (un)map and (de)articulate the body's position within a zone of pre-established discomfort, distraction, "noise," indicative of the **surveillance-industrial complex**, allegorizing and modeling larger or more systemic zones of distraction which, in often hidden ways, mediate experience and construct the subject, in which necessarily, more thorough apprehension, re-narration, or articulation of that zone and its effects is precluded by the establishment of the zone itself: the increasing difficulty of *voicing anything* as distress presses down. how might one see, or hear, for instance, the logic of privatized militarism, not through a poem

DAVID WOLACH

but through a degraded poem-attempt, and in what ways does that logic construct (constrict) how we see or hear? in what ways can the distraction zone in miniature make legible such occulted phenomena, or at least make visible the traces or imprints of such phenomena on the poem (body)? such a "staging" hopes to, in some small way, radicalize the participant...

perhaps as someone marked as "disabled," or as gendered by heteronormative discourses, i've become acutely interested in a militancy or radicalism of vulnerability, leading me, in collaboration often, to draw out the unacknowledged redundancy of everyday alienation, that the subject becomes so alienated ("super-alienated") that merely staging in domestic space crude recapitulations of the partitioning violence that is already pervasive, simply framing it, shakes us up, produces rather new feelings and behaviors, not least of which, the affective, somatic, kinesthetic, and not merely cognitive acknowledgment that we've been enduring such repressive conditions for a long time without giving such endurance that much affective attention—the resulting behavior that of relating to one-another (as collaborators) after the fact as if experiencing alienation or violation for the first time. such a project is, in a sense, a sort of abject erotics but also a sort of mediation, and owes much to the **investigatory-somatic** work performed by david buuck and ca conrad, among others, and to poet's theater generally. examples of distraction zones performed (usually in groups of 4, where solitary actions are performed in rotation over hours, days or months) are:

- *writing while being fed my writing—one hour of handwritten "confessional poetry"—as exploration of appendix m of cia memorandum on use of food as tool for interrogation.*

- *writing while watching 1) online homemade pornography (no audio), and 2) surgical imaging stills of the inside of my urinary tract. oscillating between viewing (1) and (2), 30 second intervals.*

- *writing in rain 34f, just after running for one hour on treadmill at midnight with neuromuscular disease— exploration of appendix m of cia interrogations manual: stress holds.*

- *writing in silence after sitting in a chair and being watched by collaborator for 9 hours. trading positions afterwards.*

- *writing a poem after staying in one room of a house alone for 4 weeks ("home-bound"). followed by recorded sounds of sex as collaborative poem.*

so, in thinking about the ways our aesthetic practices both hide and make perceptible occulted phenomena (including our utterances/practices themselves), i began tracing out what i kept calling (to myself) *body maps* and *distraction zones*, a set of site-specific and corporeal procedures that would interrogate "this body," what "the body" can do as both metaphor and metaphor-maker. i was and still am interested in mapping social hot zones through bodily response and sensorial archeology, doing so through various language games. in *occultations* i focused on *this* shorn predicament in relation to the larger sociopolitical frame as a problem regarding how to imagine mapping (undermining the notion of the map brought to us by colonization) a so-called body's invisible alleyways, its (*their*, as after all, "the body," again, should not presuppose locational or temporal unity) hidden, often invisible "marks" left by social forces not benign. i started with the body-as-map, and the body-map as abstracted constellation of sensed differences, gaps, causal movements, traced wounds, home-bound presuppositions, contradictions and mediations, where tracing this body's symptoms in relation to an ableist neoliberal world, a world in which the hospital industrial complex makes "obsolete" different bodies, becomes one that resists, at the same time, referentiality and the sort of identity politics that potentially makes of "the body" or "a body" a visible commodity, a "bland fetish," as halpern once called such sedimenting discourses, an abstraction lacking the contradictions and stakes of real bodies, the boundaries of which are, contrary to normative ascriptions, unknown, perhaps nonexistent. in both *occultations* and *hospitalogy* the poem hopes to be both affective and a data-like (lyric as data, as score?) form of care, a place that lays bare, and in so doing, hopes to be that derridean "gift of death," or as i've been thinking of it since, an *abstracted commons*, where, crucially, this commons *becomes* habitable, a shared space for nourishment, through submitting itself as document and investigation to further use, further action.

both of these frames, or lenses, that of the body as shorn predicament and as potential commons, i brought to the writing in very different ways in both recent books. this is by no means to suggest that the books in any way succeed in offering a kind of care, or help us towards forming a common or aggregate space/body of non-enclosure, or

DAVID WOLACH

do trace out relationships between the political and the personal body. nor is it to imply that i think "success," or poetry simpliciter, would come from a sort of legibility. rather, care-taking, performance of reclamation of our lived and affective environments, a sort of radicalization and attempted trigger for action, are, for me, among just a few ways i've been thinking of lately viz. how poetry, and here, a poetry emerging from post-ableist disability, could be potentially useful—beyond, of course, as sensuousness mode of production, as simply useful in and for itself.

3 poems from OCCULTATIONS
(muted domestic pornography)

DISTRACTION ZONE STAGING: *written while watching 1) online homemade pornography (no audio), and 2) surgical imaging stills of the inside of my urinary tract. Oscillating between viewing (1) and (2), 30 second intervals.*

1.

Never so held in held
Suspense : the long

Disease is pornographic
Graphic despite I knowing

What will come of this
This narrative as usual

As so much underpaid
Hunger there is *some* I

Tensing with a perverting *here*
Here the sheen of a slowly open

Curve a depth I've seen this before
Before I roamed corporate clinics

My holes are a constant testing
Ground perpetual breaks of strata

In continuity becomes continuity : I
I here cannot see is a here with yet no

Name his delivery system holds I up
Up by its penis a story halos above

It : degraded lyric as convergence of aporias
The strange tremor the unusual poverties

Of not knowing what will come of this

DAVID WOLACH

2.

I huddles in that middle zone between distraction and con
traction—
"that is my job," said an old woman, my grandmother
were she still alive, then later with so
many *strings* attached, hazard
lights marionetting her sagging refills, "how do you work
this thing?"
pressing prosthetic buttons furious & impatient—
the bed's not a coffin it's a video game! & only because
my job is to thread that *somewhere*, where *here* is,
impossibly, what I
can do, it's the lack part of it
that allows "I" to appear where it does, & "my"
possessed to push thru this
night,
tell you a story from yr past,
where rehearsal will have taken the shape of
sheets, its body's impression made,
seen only after—& in its dissipative, changing telling

DISTRACTION ZONE STAGING: *written in rain 34F, just after running for one hour on treadmill at midnight with neuromuscular disease—exploration of Appendix M of CIA Interrogations Manual: stress holds.*

3. (corporeal ~~self~~ punishment)

this poem wants 1:17 to perform sexual acts
on whatever grammar trick counts as its pleasure
center, pop up thru what it did to it-
selves 1:22 ~~declaration~~ desecration ~~calls~~
crawls from in side, can *feel* it this basic 1:25
training

> (*pop up* was the first phrase that came
> ~~to mind!. to minded!!.~~ what does
> that say about *this* mind? what does it say
> about *this mined* that a post-facto 1:27
> deep read in our dark parking lot ass-
> umes ~~eupham eupham~~
> euthanistic thinking on my
> other part?)

got a phrase stuck in my mindless
phytness jaunt, EXTREME POETRY
up in shiny red lights, above a strip
mall's not-yet-empty storefront, & like
all poetry ideas 1:31, this one non-
profit too but w/ low flying over
head we would sell only ~~hardcover~~ 1:33 hard-
core poetry booklets & shakes & protein
by the bulk up more, a place where all
the *manlee* conceptual poets could go to rest
to test their *endurance* for the *reading*

(digging thru land

fill to find this corpse)

1:34 knotted urethra song a song not
to be written, knot now & ~~the radiate. the~~
~~radiate.~~ the irradiated, why we don't
run, & is ex-ercise ~~proof~~ 1:37 left
side burns feels punched 1:38 is ex-
ercise poof of self hood?

poem all by its self-
help the lone foodstuff on
that night conveyer belt
of self-evident un-
civil obedience, neck in
spasm pen a loose nail 1:41
it stoops a chance
of witness if it asks 1:42 whose
running who

DISTRACTION ZONE STAGING: *written while being fed my writing—one hour of handwritten "confessional poetry"—as exploration of Appendix M of CIA Memorandum on use of food as tool for interrogation.*

(forced feeding 1)

my at home ex

perience @ kitchen ~~skin~~ sink

—ing

thru w/ the teleo-vision he says

open wide

we need *an enhanced sit*

-uational under-

standing

      blood-

      sugar poeman ~~introverted~~ inverted milgram

ex-peri-mint

"Eat Up" "Eat Shit" "Shut Up" "Stand

Down"

wears a hogtied ~~sauce~~

rouge, mouth the entire apparatus

a protrusion dug into, some bodys

looking for some things

a chocolate de clares: yr thru w/ And Now We Shall Fast-

-er engine work

      —ing on come

      —ing

      a rhyth mea culpa *Is*

morsel code, my drums tap says-cant-think what-

      ever comes, leeks

      out

DAVID WOLACH

(the un

    willing mute)

  whyle he

stuffs gas-o-

    line

  rag In ~~whole~~ hole

& says talk all ready, tell us what

  You Want to Know

    (charitable giving surveys

      the eyes for signs of death's witness this

        intelligent gathering)

  unfettered by intel over

site my personal MP calls

this *inter-*

course

a tasting of power

~~play~~ plated, public shame

    —ing

dines out-ed, can feel the hand

wipe

    —ing the lips, so i refluxively bend

over

Kara Dorris

BENIGN BONE TUMOR CITY

For years I avoided writing about my disability. How did one avoid sounding melo-dramatic and self-pitying? My own poetics lean towards erasing, running and eventually disassembling illusions. But I couldn't help being a critical reader of my body. Have I always considered myself disabled? Short answer: *yes* and, of course, *no*.

My mother, brother and I suffer, perhaps I should say we *have*, we *own* osteocon-dromas (bone tumor growths). Excess calcium pools or dams at the joints. As we grew, so did the bone spurs, interfering with normal growth patterns. So yes, my right leg is shorter, my right arm is several inches longer, and I have strange knobs of bone sticking out. All that said, I walk, jog if I must, dance and hopscotch (although not well or grace-fully), but mostly I read, sink into fairytales through Angela Carter's eyes.

What does all this mean? It means that I never knew my body was supposed to act differently, that the body often compensates without conscious effort (*that I should be ashamed of my body, that I shouldn't?*). Can you miss something you've never had?

So I write. I write to merge the gap between who I think I should be (*want to be*) and who I am. I strap on poems, masquerade, murderess-dress because I am not dangerous or wild or carefree and sometimes I want to be. I want to be Cindy Sherman or Buffy the Vampire Slayer or Anna Karenina, to write past fact and role-play, become a catalyst, a poem, a temporary, pseudo-escape from the body and personality (and as T.S. Eliot said, only people with emotions and personalities want to escape from them). A silent mode of transportation. And yes, I know, I never really become her; I never escape myself.

So I write more. I believe part of what I struggle to do is to write the female body, to write the female body as choice and art, to write the female body as deformed/choice/art. I could say, I do this, to paraphrase Adrienne Rich, to "place me nakedly face to face with both terror and anger"...the breakdown of the world as I have always known it, the end of safety...the end of hiding, but not entirely of wanting to. I'm still rebelling.

Sometimes the notion of calling myself disabled makes me want to disappear, but the baseball-sized tumor on my ankle is indestructible. I cover myself in leg warmers and sweaters. In sixth grade the school nurse diagnosed me with scoliosis; all day I thought I was deformed; I was ill. She was wrong, but until then, I'd never considered how my body might be different. I want my body to have purpose. Not me, you see, it's a common mistake, I mean, my *body*, this vessel. How to show you? The most damaging tumors are deep within tissue and ligament, and you can only see the beauty and mass destruction, the clusters shaped like Marilyn Monroe in X-rays.

In order to make sense of it, I need to chart my way to the reasons within my body, which, in turn, shape the reasons of me. Why I, rare genetic bone disorder, benign tumor cavity, am a city. Why cities like mine aren't beauty. In pictures I can't help but see the stunted growth, and when I stretch I feel the tendons scraping, tearing over tumors. How can that be beauty?

I can't live in my city for long with ankles that tremble under my weight as if I'm always one second from buckling. I need to create new towns and cattle-guard the city limits. I've had tumors removed, but the inflammation and ripping still occurs. For every one tumor removed, a hundred remain because the tumors aren't invaders, they are my body, entwined with muscles, tendons and veins. So I wear strategic clothes and walk slow, let others step me into their version of existence.

In "A Season in Hell," Rimbaud says: "À chaque être, plusieurs autres vies me semblaient dues" [To me it seemed that to every being several other lives were owed]. I believe this because I've spent a lifetime reading about those who live, living those other lives as doctors told me *be careful, don't play sports or roughhouse because an already broken body shouldn't be broken again.*

So I carry other writers inside me—Barthes' and Jenny Boully's discourses of the body and identity, Keats' ideas of beauty and negative capability, Tim O'Brien's search for the human heart and mind—and I write and I walk a line between wanting (What? Another body, a better body, a sense of self-rightness, plastic surgery?) and wanting to the point of deformity.

I believe, as James Branch Cabel wrote, "poetry is man's rebellion against being what he is." Through poetry, the poet is trying to define herself and her perceptions of the world. Through my writing, I am seeking to trace and retrace myself, my strange and estranged body and learn how to live best within it. I can't name each tumor yet, although I realize each unseen cluster is its own city limits. You see, I have a lifetime to map them out, but I still can't fully accept this reality, imagine this tumor-ridden body when I imagine myself. Does my body make me disabled or do my perceptions of my body? Rich says, "Until we can understand the assumptions in which we are drenched we can never know ourselves."

Self-Portrait with Framing Effect

Sitting behind a screen
underneath blankets of leopards
& running stitches,

I almost forget I am a frame job:

It's delinquent, an inamorata butcher
& cracked fang of things I've collected:

diamond cut vignettes
panoramic Venus hips
chase soundtracks.

Like potassium or plums
our bones produce, contract, read—

how I sponge-curl my hair
or knife an apple.

Swirl
my 2 umbrellas, the one above
my drink & the one in my head.

Try through leather straps & steel pins
to mash limbs together

(I say again, to mash together again,
but the idea that I was ever
whole

is a fable, a myth my mother told
when I couldn't sleep).

Flags,
my flush face in the crowd,
the smokestacks.

KARA DORRIS

A crow necklace is just the black
feathers of operation,
another anesthesiologist saying,
she's under.

It took less than a crash to take me apart,
but Greyhound
is what I remember.
All those dead babies & smooth limbs
I couldn't feel
that might have been my own.

Red beads mean something.
That birds love when I wear my hair down?
But is it my hair or a monkey's hand?

In my first surgery, I flipped
everyone off, handed out the bird,
kept the pulse light up in faces, bright.

After, I tried to sit up by myself
secretly in front of surgeons
& the maize behind,
yes, the maze you gimp through.
(One gimp knows another.)

Chlorine hands—
Nowhere else but here.
Don't you see?
Our swimming pool doesn't use chlorine.

A girl who stands in doorways.
I've never come this far before.

Never drown.
Momma, isn't that all I've ever done?

KARA DORRIS   349

Breton's Song of the Lark

At the end of wheat,
where gold-dust stalks lean, sway
away & are pulled back,
is the moment you know what calls to you.

Scythe in hand, barefoot halo, you
dress in a ruby-pinked sun as if to kill.

Your strawflower sack skirt suspended
like the step forward you were taking
before your feet heated in want.

& now you know. Tightness
so stretched you're unable to move.

Why you turned from
the timbered cottage burned, simmered
by the sun
you clothed yourself in.
Fist clinched. Mouth sighed open.

Unable to embody dusk-dark rapture,
the wanton need to be—
teacup overflowing.

To feel the wisps of wheat on your feet
that foretell seasons. A halo of egg whites.

You, a dandelion blown, a backlit quarry, a bonfire.

How that husk grain should have been
a deeper shell,   shelf,   shelter.

KARA DORRIS

Fairytale: How Spring Comes to the Land of Snow and Icicles/(Dream Map)

The body burns & smells like fake,
like ammonia & blood & guts.

Barbie leg arrows,
black & white bust sizes,
swords as houses, & you swing it all.

Say, all you want to do is fuck.
Because between it &—

a place we invent to need
even as we know not this skin.

Why else this plastic design,

our bodies:
jello or scar?

I say, save the grotesque & it saves you.

I say, wish us open, cupped, surgeon knots
in the form of girly stuff:

gothic lipstick,
sedimentary mascara,
arabesque eyelashes.

Yes, a circle, a light, an allow.

Wanting to Be a Girl

When I close my octopus eyes, I see 4 arms, 4 legs lift. I want only 2 of each. The sky said stay, meant to be, this parasitic twin, a bleed to what a girl should be. But I ache for what my body is—fused spines, one heart dissolved in another, doubled ribs protecting lotus flower lungs. For what it could be—knee socks & Mary Janes. To stake flags marking the scatter pattern of debris: an arm, a metacarpal, an earring, a virginity. Who does a goddess pray to?

I asked the sea, help me lose this extra being. I swam through skins, churning placentas, breathed wide open, pulled oxygen through 4 eyes, exposed my vertebrae, double-edged knobs. Cast back. Even a sea wants to worship something.

KARA DORRIS

Gretchen E. Henderson

POETICS / "EXHIBITS"

For over a decade, I've carried around the word "disabled" with an agitated ambivalence that has slowly (in)formed a generous and generative aesthetic of deformity. Jim Ferris has written intricately about "The Enjambed Body," drawing upon A.R Ammons' description ("A poem is a walk"), adding of himself: "when I walk, I aim to get somewhere. If my meters are sprung, if my feet are uneven, if my path is irregular, that's just how I walk. And how I write."[1] The prose poem, boxed as it is, for me seems to embody a want for movement—physical, aural and otherwise—made apparent by limitations and liminality of its boxed-in body. My poetics arise from a curiosity and hope for whatever movements occur within this boxed-in body: at times dueling with, but fueling, shifting perceptions within the sentence of each sentence.

To some degree, the question involves architecture. As Tobin Siebers writes:

> When a disabled body moves into a social space, the lack of fit exposes the shape of the normative body for which the space was originally designed...While people with disabilities have little power in the social world, their identities possess great theoretical power because they reflect perspectives capable of illuminating the ideological blueprints used to construct social reality.[2]

Genre classification matters less to me than the ability to engage these "perspectives capable of illuminating," as Siebers describes, to enter concretely here: a compressed stanza (in the sense of "room" or "dwelling")—to hear its acoustic potential, implied lineation, sonic logic.

By calling my poetics "Exhibits," I evade a specific genre label and enter the gallery (as my collection is titled: *Galerie de Difformité*), where exhibits A, B, C, etc., aggregate among other genres like a curated collection and thus involve narrative(s), even when seemingly otherwise. Generally in a gallery, there's not a determined path, since each vectored variation suggests alternate paths and, thus, requires choice. Guided by some curator and bound by a traditional entrance and exit, displacement is engaged: to draw awareness to where we are, where we've come from, where we might yet go.

In the context of *Galerie de Difformité*, dismembered from a larger body (that is, the book), "Exhibits" exist through-and-with other *mani*-pulations (since "exhibit" involves the hand, literally, meaning "to hold out") and carry political implications: allied with exhibits, as in a legal trial. By re-imaging old tropes (disability as dysfunctional, partial, ugly, freakish, monstrous, etc.), my poetics of deformity attempts to tap the "theoretical power" to which Tobin Siebers refers. To make this process manifest, I am inviting people to materially deform my deformity-filled book before and after its publication, to collaboratively redefine *deformity* (directly or indirectly articulated: as beautiful, useful, desirable, engaged, worthwhile, complicated, confounded, _____ [*fill in the blank*]). In addition to the online display (http://difformite.wordpress.com), selected deformations will join an actual exhibition, to travel in the tradition of antiquated freak shows.

Since poetics is not platitude, but rather hinged to perception, this collaborative gallery of material deformations evokes questions rather than answers, within and outside the body of any "Exhibit." With deference to da Vinci too: "If the sound is in 'm' and the listener in 'n,' the sound will be believed to be in 's' if the court is enclosed at least on 3 sides against the listener."[3] Analogy may be made with *Galerie de Difformité*: if a sound is made in one Exhibit while Gentle Reader resides in another, (s)he may seek out additional Exhibits to coordinate the orchestrations.

What can we learn about sociocultural beliefs about deformity by engaging in material acts of deformation? The verdict is still out, and will be, if ever decided: always deforming (or said another way: evolving). Beyond that, deformation sounds a bit like defamation: not to be confused. By asking readers to metamorphose the physical object of the book, I am asking them to participate in a creative act that might be viewed, from one cultural stance, as an act of defamation, in contrast to what otherwise might be considered spiritual, communal, and/or healing (in the vein of Navajo or Tibetan sand-paintings), not to mention a number of other connotations. As *Galerie de Difformité* looks forward and back like the two-headed Janus, it masquerades as a funhouse of mirrors, reflecting distortions (less of bodies than of perceptions) of whoever enters.

In participating in this masquerade, I cloak my experiences in language rather than wear it as a badge. Life has taught me some ironies of this fraught word: "disabled." The better I am at maintaining my physically adaptive lifestyle, the more "normal" I appear, even if never achieving that level of function. Nor can I shirk being "disabled" in order to participate: in education, in employment, etc. Caught between these two wor(l)ds—

GRETCHEN E. HENDERSON

"normal" and "disabled"—I wonder: is there a way for poetics to pave ways for new states of being?

Just as the narrator of my "Exhibits" (a deformed reincarnation of Dante's Beatrice) is recontextualized throughout *Galerie de Difformité*, her beauty and deformity are left to the eye of each beholder. As I write in an apologia for the collection: "The many faces of Bea, taken together, suggest what's missing. The seeking of Bea becomes the seeking of 'we,' ever changing. More than trying to decipher *her*, then, her *ability to change* may serve as a better guide."[4]

In following Bea—less her persona than the questions she embodies—I am interested in our ability to change perceptions of ourselves, our expectations for and explanations of our bodies, our definitions of deformity and disability, our physical and psychological and sensory capacities for metamorphosis—and how this is embodied in the voice. Physiology underscores language; bodies are tethered to voices (vocal, gestural, what have you): living and breathing. Like John Cage famously went into an anechoic chamber ("a room without echoes") to hear absolute silence: hearing two sounds, one high and one low (which the sound engineer identified as his nervous system and blood circulation), Cage realized that true silence doesn't exist. Although silence in my "Exhibits" may be less visually apparent than in lineated poems (in terms of white space, as described by Mallarmé), it exists as pulses of nerves and blood, coursing within its boxed-in body, as Cage discovered in his echo-proof chamber. Only here, outside such a chamber: echoes reverberate.

2 Exhibits from GALERIE DE DIFFORMITÉ
Exhibit "H"

Finger painting. Prints on walls in the Lascaux caves. Veronica's veil, an act of *acheiropoietos* ("not made by the hand of man"), seated near the right Hand of God. Relics of St. Ninnidh in Ireland, St. Stephen I in Hungary. Guidonian hands were solemnized, marked with syllables joint by joint for sight-singing, illuminated in manuscripts. *Manu*-factured. *Manu*-mitted. Mudras. Hypocrites and Galen practiced palmistry, reading between lines and mountains—of Venus, Jupiter, Saturn, Mercury, Mars, Luna, the Sun—the veritable cosmos, held in hands. Wrapped in papyrus or gloves, cut into wood by Vesalius, cast and sculpted by Rodin, photographed by Lange, burned in Dresden, painted with henna, holding a stylus or spoon, living hand-to-mouth. Skin and sinew conceal phalanges, metacarpals, knuckles. On the other hand, get all hands on deck, in order not to be short-handed or reduced to shorthand, studied by graphologists, or perhaps, too heavy-handed to be written, held in hand, kept on hand, growing out of hand—

This is a language of clasping; hence, to lose hands denotes loss of possession, custody, charge, authority, power, disposal, agency, instrumentality—putting into other hands what wants to be held in your own: "terminal part of the arm beyond the wrist, consisting of the palm and five digits, forming the organ of prehension characteristic of man." (And woman—albeit by Roman law, that four-letter word conveyed the power of husband over wife.) Left-handed, I have already joined hands with another (here we are) to change one definition that seems to rest in my hands, as I want a hand in something else, nothing underhanded, preferring the archaic meaning, "breath," as articulated in *A devoute medytacyon,* in which Hampole wrote in 1340, "His nese oft droppes, his hand stynkes."[1] Nothing like the sun, roses, snow, those eyes and cheeks and breasts; what of her hands? That four-letter word, like a curse. Unless substituted, striated, with meaning: a hand, a breath. (*Breathe.*)

In printing, a conventionally extended forefinger drew attention to what came next, like a lion's gaze in Luxor, or a colon prompting an actress in a play: Antigone, who dies by her own hand, or Medea, who cries: "Let no one deem me a poor weak woman who sits with folded hands, but of another mould."[2] Made by lost wax, four-armed Shiva has another pair of hands waiting in the wings—unlike *A. afarensis*, *A. africanus*, *H. sapiens*—me.

Thus, Into Thy Hands I commend my Spirit, amid this flourishing chorus of voices, and submit:

My hands. Crippled, as they are. As exhibit A, B, C, and the rest. This is my Gallery, what I will display, cued by the hand that rocked the cradle too hard, breaking rules and a body, making it deformed, having to learn to breathe all over again. To remobilize the spine, the neck, the arms and, last but not least, the hands. And so I stand before you, trying to raise a conventionally extended forefinger to draw attention to what comes next:

Exhibit "U"

Here comes the unclasping—there is no way to hold onto this. It's a matter of resistance, then release. Hands stroke strings, press keys, pull stops, as scores direct fingers forward through bars, movements, cadences, and cadenzas. Musicians learn about touch through painstaking practice, sensing every inch of an instrument, to elicit its tonal center. (True of a vocalist, too, whose instrument is the body, prone to the dissonance of disease, and warbles of woe.) A cellist learns "through mastering movements like vibrato...the rocking motion of the left hand on a string which colours a note around its precise pitch; waves of sound spread out...like ripples from a pool into which one has thrown a stone."[1] The arm is an orchestra, then, with fingers as instruments among instruments (thumb, palm, wrist, elbow, shoulder, the body)— "miracle of form and function," capable of the greatest delicacy and danger.[2]

With abilities to play violins, pianos, guitars, flutes, and harps comes the capacity to pull triggers, throw punches, and detonate bombs. Aristotle wrote: "A man can have many defences [*sic*] and always change them, and can have any weapon he pleases on any occasion. For the hand is a claw and a hoof and a horn, and a spear and a sword, and any other instrument whatever."[3] Avowing danger and debilitation, this thesis (deforming as you read) does not follow like *Clockwork* but re-views paleoanthropology and the evolution of *Homo erectus*, through which "this new hand reflected a modification...and brought with it the opportunity for a new class of situational knowledge based on as yet unexplored and undefined use of the hand. This change by itself was nothing but a mutation until its utility gave it the status of an adaptation."[4] Both instinctive and learned, manual manipulations have taught the mind through movements—faster, lighter, longer—to apprehend new thoughts.

To learn to play an instrument, then to lose the ability to play, is like dying.

Lying *apprehensio* (at the root of grasping and cognizance), we are what we feel—touch & play—like *What's Bred in the Bone*: "the hand speaks to the brain as surely as the brain speaks to the hand."[5] "Put your finger into every bottle," Swift

GRETCHEN E. HENDERSON

advises, "to feel whether it be full, which is the surest way, for feeling hath no fellow."[6] Diderot wrote that Chardin "use[d] his thumb as much as his brush," and a long history reveals communicative hands: holding a stylus, quill or pen, reckoning or gesturing through three-dimensional signs.[7] *Ars memorativa* involves metonymy and mnemonics, embodied by "the first instrument," "the framer," "the most noble and perfect organ" by (and about) which Helkiah Crooke wrote in 1615: "we promise, we call, we dismisse, we threaten, we intreate, we abhorre, we feare, yea and by our hands we can aske a question."[8]

What was the question?

By which we call another name: to learn and make music, language, love. Rendering fingers and joints to measure melodic intervals, or to memorize: it's an ancient art. Not physiognomic. From West to East; played and sung. Reverential, improvised, referential. Stylized on paper. Conducted or cheironomic. Watch closely—hands may yet grace the air like birds. Taking flight. Imagine the fluttering: that singing.

Whatever the subject, memory often teaches with a dis-membered hand, drawn (or re-articulated: *deformed*) by an artist, as if that appendage (peripheral, yet central) could live apart from the body. Like a bone, with a heart-shaped hole. Illustrated & reproduced & re-rendered. Regenerating when split in two, like a planarian. Or imagine: a rebellion of Hands or Bones seceding from the Body, forming their own Kingdom. To be, or not to be:

...a quandary, between beheading and begetting. Like M.C. Escher drew a hand coming out of paper to draw another hand that drew the original hand. Round and round. Back where we started: Which came first, as currently conceived—hand or brain, heart or bone—or are they too innately tied to be unbound?

Nodding to Crooke, will my hands stay tied? "This progresse and insertion of these [flexor] muscles is an admirable and strange worke of Nature: for they are so severed, that the fingers in their motion might orderly follow one another, and each of

GRETCHEN E. HENDERSON

them bend inward." With fingers figuratively severed, taking on a life of their own, I ask again: Nothing like the sun, roses, snow, those eyes and cheeks and breasts; what of her hands? *Manu*-mitting—master or slave, part of (yet apart from) the core of a body, closer than my shadow, as bound as busy. Wings, no longer. Rubbing eyes, itching skin, brushing teeth, holding hands, clasping pens, hefting loads, touching hearts: I have lost and found my flesh. Traversed with lines of fate, and laced by nerves and flexors, hands work wonders within and without, enabling *mani*-pulations of meaning from matter. *Manu*-ally, they point the way like Virgil (or me, Bea) to litigious and lofty layers of our lives, to buried scenes and senses too essential to ignore.

GRETCHEN E. HENDERSON

Bernadette Mayer

STATEMENT ON POETICS

I had a cerebral hemorrhage in 1994. Since then I've relearned how to walk but still can't run or hand write. Like the poets who could never write their poems down, my memory's improved. I memorize license plates when I'm bored. I'd never have done this kind of writing unless I had to. I can't do exquisite corpses or take notes. I haven't been able to afford the voice-recognition computer software and I don't remember my dreams as often. My right hand is just for show.

Sonnet Edmund Leites

I had a dream that
you showed sensuality
by showing your penis
this is what's wrong
with the language school
they didn't go far enough
there was a very scary guy
who threatened us with pain
you see? the guy who died
by firing squad chose that
method over lethal injection

you can't be a Marxist-
Leninist if you have a car

BERNADETTE MAYER

4th of July Demon Moped

for Dave Brinks

fireworks look like jelly fish
but jellyfish don't resemble fireworks
gee, logical causal reasoning
must be inaccurate. I was hoping
you'd ask me what those birds are
I'd say, "they're swallows,"
then you'd say, "What are they doing?"
& I'd say, "they're swallowing mosquitoes"
not many jokes are as bad on paper
as they are in person but this is sure one
except of course it's not even a joke
it's just a lame thought like omigod
I found the pudgy pie pan & the slotted spoon
I also found the spatula; the colander
never got lost; did you ever list
all the diseases you don't have?
best to a doctor who's nice
now that is the end of that

Chosca Mass Tinek

I live through the creek
I do not live the way
you'd want me to, who
ever you are, mister!
or miss peachy keenness
half the time, it's as if
I took a drug you never heard of
or ingested a substance that made me
lower-case green as a field in june
hello sir I can make you turn to stone
with my wit alone, thank you for blooming
those that did, the others
you missed your appointment
and now you will pay, life
will be unruly, you must eat
all your meals at kay's pizza
sacrifice someone who looks
just like you & be buried alive
till the season of nuclear winter
when you will rise from the dead
& die for all our peccadilloes, ok?
then you will start a pointless
civilization & be driven from the verdant
fields of your startling anonymous days
till the dark time, then you will return
home for a scone & unexpectedly you'll have
a grilled cheese & a cup of the tea
of your liking & a fine dessert of
asparagus ice cream with organic foam
accompanied by a breath mint or two

BERNADETTE MAYER

EYJAFJALLAJOKULL

I am the volcano
& every volcano
you've ever met
not metaphorically
but really, I disrupt
my job title is
Disrupter In Chief
rest assured you
will be disrupted by me
gently but firmly
now & forever amen
backwards I am
LLUKOJALLAJFAYE
okay?
p.s. though I'm
retiring, I'll continue
to disrupt full-time

NOTES

A Short History of Disability Poetry: Michael Northen

1. The capitalization of "Deaf" here is used to indicate a cultural identification. Writers in this anthology like John Lee Clark and Raymond Luczak make a distinction between "deaf" and "Deaf." Bascially, deaf (lower case d) refers to the physical impairment and describes a specific individual. Deaf (captial D) refers to Deaf culture and identity with other D/deaf people. When a poet like Luczak or Clark says, "I am deaf" he is referring to the physical fact of his inability to hear. When he says, "I am Deaf" he is identifying with a whole culture or, at the very least, with other D/deaf people. There are still many people who consider themselves deaf, but not Deaf, and may even deny the existence of a Deaf culture.

Missing Larry: The Poetics of Disability in Larry Eigner: Michael Davidson

1. George Hart has written an excellent article on Eigner as a nature poet, "Reading under the Sign of Nature" and Benjamin Friedlander has written a useful encyclopedia entry on him in the *Gale Dictionary of Literary Biography* series. The latter is the best introduction to Eigner's life and work.

2. Eigner's reticence in foregrounding his cerebral palsy aligns him with another Berkeley poet, Josephine Miles, who lived with rheumatoid arthritis from an early age but who did not identify as disabled or with the disability rights movement. Susan Schweik has made the case that despite her reticence, Miles' early work often anticipates "conditions for the emergence of a new contemporary social group—but only if that group is understood in both broad and complex terms" (p.489). If we understand "disability rights" in the contemporary, post-civil-rights sense, then Miles does not accept the label "disabled." Schweik locates Miles' acknowledgment of disability in a discursive resistance to the language of reason and rationality. See Schweik's essay "The Voice of 'Reason'" in this anthology.

3. Benjamin Friedlander notes that in 1962 Eigner underwent cryosurgery to freeze part of his brain in order to control his spastic movements (p.121). The successful operation is described in a letter to Douglas Blazek:

> Sept. 62 cryosurgery, frostbite in the thalamus (awakened to see if i was numbed, test whether they had right spot, felt much like killing of a tooth nerve!), tamed (and numbed some) my wild left side, since when I can sit still without effort, and have more capacity for anger etc. Before, I had to be extrovert, or anyway hold the self off on a side, in this very concrete, perpetual sense. A puzzlement of the will. (qtd. in Friedlander: p.121)

Friedlander notes that prior to the surgery, "Typing, of all activities, provided relief from the wildness, from the distraction of the flailing, and from the effort of holding the body still, or trying to" (p.121).

4. The four-volume set of *The Collected Poems of Larry Eigner* edited by Bob Grenier and Curtis Faville honored his page size by printing all three volumes in an 8½" by 11" format and in a font

that approximates his typewriter font. Congratulations to Stanford University Press and the editors for making this wise, yet costly, decision.

5. In his letters, some of which have been published, Eigner tends to fill the page, writing even in the margins and blank spaces of the page:

> Well letters get crowded just from attempt to save time, i.e., cover less space, avoid
> putting another sheet in the typewriter for a few more words as I at least hope there
> will only be. There've always been so many things to do. For instance with only my
> right index finger to type with I never could write very fastto say what I want to when
> I think of it, before I forget it or how to say it; I sometimes say 2 things at about the
> same time, in two columns. It'll be from not deciding or being unable to decide quickly
> anyway what to say first, or next. Or an after thought might as well be an insert, and
> thus go in the margin, especially when otherwise you'd need one or more extra words to
> refer to a topic again (*areas*: p.149).

Here is a good instance of how a textual parataxis that one associates with the Pound/ Olson tradition can be read differently by a poet for whom the act of changing a sheet of paper or typing a few more words is a considerably more difficult task. The desire to render the phenomenological moment remains the same for Eigner and Olson, and certainly the look of the page is similar, but the physical circumstance of writing must be factored in as well.

THE VOICE OF REASON: SUSAN SCHWEIK

1. A note on what I mean by "disability." For two very useful summaries of the history and politics of the definition of the term, see Johnstone 1998: pp.5–13 and Epstein 1995: pp.13–17. Epstein reprints and analyzes a 1993 U.S. National Institute of Health chart illustrating some crucial distinctions between the terms *impairment*, *disability* and *handicap* as they have been defined in the contemporary literature of physical health and rehabilitation. The watershed definition is that of the World Health Organization in 1980, with its three-part distinction between impairment (defined as "any loss or abnormality of psychological, physical, or anatomical structure or function"), disability (difficulty with tasks) and handicap (social disadvantage resulting from impairment or disability). Epstein compares this with the later revisions suggested by the U.S. National Advisory Board on Medical Rehabilitation Research in 1993, in which "functional limitation" takes the place of disability, and disability comes to describe what the WHO had called handicap: the range of social, cultural and environmental arrangements that stigmatize, isolate and oppress people whose bodies deviate from a supposed norm in form or function. This 1993 revision is in line with the use of the term *disability* in much of the work of contemporary disability activists and theorists, and in general I will follow its model. I proceed here with the sense, informed by much recent work in disability studies, that, as Thomson (1997: p.15) puts it, disability "is an overarching and in some ways artificial category...The physical impairments that render someone 'disabled' are almost never absolute or static." Rather, they are "dynamic, contingent conditions."

2. The "social model of disability" was formulated in English by members of the Union of the Physically Impaired in the United Kingdom in the 1970s and then sharpened and refined across the next two decades by an international group of scholar-activists. The model is described succinctly by Paul K. Longmore and David Goldberger (2000: p.3). Disability is no longer to be seen, they write, as "the exclusive and inevitable consequence of physiological impairment," or as "a series of objectively determinable, pathological clinical entities located in...bodies." Rather, disability is to be understood as a process, "the result of a relationship between individuals with impairments and socially created barriers," and as a role, "a culturally constructed identity, an elastic social category shaped and reshaped by public policy, societal arrangements, and cultural values." Some important recent work in disability studies has found the basic binary distinction between (physiological) impairment and (socially constructed) disability far too blunt a tool. "The relatively pragmatic character of the classification," Henri-Jacques Stiker wrote presciently in 1982, "conceals a deeper analysis, in sociological or anthropological terms, of the collective figuring of disability and of what the issues are in this domain" (Stiker 1999: p.204). Recent work that problematizes the distinction between supposedly objective, material "impairment" and the realm of the social includes Hughes and Paterson 1997 and Barnes, Mercer and Shakespeare 1999. Still, the initial sharp edge of the distinction between impairment and disability allowed for the creation of a powerfully productive "social model" in disability studies, one that can attend to how someone like Miles was "disabled" not by rheumatoid arthritis per se but by a society that sometimes denied her access to schooling, saw her as desexualized, tokenized her, infantilized her and medicalized her.

3. On the "poetics of presence," see Morris 1995. As a literary figure, Miles preserved her privacy, relying on what Timothy Morris (1995: p.105) calls "the larger social institutions of reticence" to maintain a critical decorum that muted, if not entirely suppressed, allusion to her physical impairments. Morris is referring to Elizabeth Bishop's identity as a closeted lesbian; critical queer theories of the closet resonate here for disability poetry as well. His argument reminds us that the best approach to "closet poetry" is not simply through recuperative reading (bringing Miles "out" as a "poet of disability") or condemnatory reading (criticizing her for denial) but by reading the poems as "existing...in their own irrecoverable, but identifiable, historical moment" (Morris 1995: p.125)—a moment made no less irrecoverable for me by the fact that late in her life Miles and I were colleagues.

4. A brief note here on what I mean by "I am nondisabled." Of course, there is no firm binary divide between "disability" and "ability." "The longer we become theoretically absorbed in the question of who is disabled and who is not," writes Deborah Marks (1999: p.18), "the more an answer seems elusive." In the late 1980s, some activists began to employ the tongue-in-cheek term "temporarily able-bodied" to describe someone like me and to challenge the security of the "able-bodied" position. I prefer the equally tongue-in-cheek term suggested by Marks (1999: p.18), "contingently able-bodied," which implies the possibility, rather than the inevitability, of a shift in status and which also calls into question "the fantasy of 'ability' and the denial of the universality of impairment." Eli Clare (1999: p.67) offers another suggestive term: "But if I call myself disabled in order to describe how the ableist world treats me as a person with cerebral

palsy, then shouldn't I call nondisabled people enabled? That word locates the condition of being nondisabled, not in the nondisabled body, but in the world's reaction to that body. This is not a semantic game."

5. For discussions of the figure of FDR in the context of disability criticism, see Gallagher 1985 and Poore 2000. On the tropes of the cripple and the overcomer, see Longmore and Goldberger 2000. The critique of the narrative of individual "overcoming" is everywhere, and fundamental, in disability studies. For one forceful summary of this line of analysis, see Linton 1998: pp.17–22.

6. I take the concept of affability from Gerber 1993.

7. The association of woman with machine, not as driver or freely mobile passenger, is atypical of how vehicles (and their "tenors") work in Miles' poetry overall. In her insightful review of Miles' work, Nell Althizer (1994: p.144) notes:

> There may be more internal combustion machines in her poems than in those of male poets more commonly associated with auto mechanics... We are on the road as we read and going somewhere with the poem as vehicle, and for detour directors the voices Miles creates as ragged with region as those we hear, rumbling from state to state, on the car radio. Much of Miles' work might be said to explore, sometimes uncritically and sometimes critically, what Celeste Langan calls "the ideology of freedom as automobility"... In Miles' first small gathering of poems in *Trial Balances*, for example, we find the famous exploration, in "On Inhabiting an Orange," of how the most "erect and sure" world traveler "mak[es] down the roads of Earth" only "endless detour," for "All our roads go nowhere" (Winslow 1935: pp.21-22). Against this critique of automobility we can place the remarkable figure, in "Portrait of the Artist," of the self as paper blown into the street, at once deprived of agency, inadvertently moved, torn, already imprinted and read, and at the same time delighted in its state of rest, "stirring" in response, and ready—curious, nerved: "I have a body to be caught by the wind" (Winslow 1935: pp.22-23).

8. On gender and disability, see "Feminist Theory, the Body, and the Disabled Figure" in Thomson 1997, Fine and Asch 1988, and Wendell 1996: pp.57–84.

9. Robert McRuer's work on how compulsory heterosexuality is intertwined with "compulsory able-bodiedness" is pertinent here and has influenced my thinking. See McRuer 2001 and McRuer n.d. The most interesting account of Miles and gender is developed by Eve Kosofsky Sedgwick (1982).

10. For instance: a review in *Choice* in March 1984 comments that "despite the adversity in Miles' own life, the poems are notable for their consistent focus on happiness rather than on disappointment" (cited in Liang 1986: p.304). The biographical blurb in the first edition of the *Norton Anthology of Literature by Women* also uses a "despite" clause: "Despite a lifelong struggle with rheumatoid arthritis..." (Gilbert and Gubar 1985: p.1759). There are two significant exceptions that I know of in the literary criticism on Miles: Sedgwick's essay and Smith 1993—the one important piece that addresses Miles' disability at some length in the context of a theory of aging.

11. On the therapeutic theme, see Whyte and Ingstad 1995: p.4. The poem can also be read within the context of the mind/body split in lyric tradition.

12. See Larney 1995: pp.32–34 for Miles' account of her father's "battle" for "compensation from his insurance companies." I have as yet found no independent corroboration of Miles' narrative. Whatever it had to do with the facts of what happened between her father and his insurers, her family story tells us much about the importance to the poet of making sense of her father's death and his relation to a social category of disability.

13. See, for instance, Miles' (1983: p.216) Vietnam-era poem "Officers," in which a campus police officer who smashes "his billy club down on the elbow of my student driver" stays his hand when he recognizes the disabled woman he ordinarily assists.

14. Compare Sally Stein's (1994: pp.58–59) argument about the connections between "the experience of illness, the effects of disability, and the making of the woman and the artist" in the case of Dorothea Lange, who said of herself, "I was physically disabled, and no one who hasn't lived the life of a semi-cripple knows how much that means." Stein offers an excellent model of the nonreductive, politicized study of the kind of incorporation I explore here. Her epigraph from the French philosopher Maurice Merleau-Ponty—"It is by lending his body to the world that the artist changes the world...To understand these transubstantiations we must go back to the actual, working body—not the body as a chunk of space or a bundle of functions but that body which is an intertwining of vision and movement"—links her work on Lange to the recent phenomenological turn in disability studies, exemplified by texts as varied as Georgina Kleege's *Sight Unseen* (New Haven, Conn.: Yale University Press, 1999), Gelya Frank's *Venus on Wheels* (Berkeley: University of California Press, 2000) and the work of Russell Shuttleworth.

15. Compare recent work in disability theater in plays by Susan Nussbaum and Judith Wolffe, in which the relation between assistant and client is more fully explored. Several examples are described and quoted in Lewis 2000.

16. Note, however, that Miles provisionally praised poets with axes to grind: "She believed that madmen move the world forward, even as they move poetry. 'They have some axe to grind,' she wrote, 'and they are better at the grinding than at the poetry.' But often too they have more to teach than 'major' poets, who 'tend to use most fully the emphases already accepted and available to them in the poetry of their time'" (Miles 1985: p.10).

17. David Gerber (1993: p.8) writes of the actor/veteran Harold Russell and others who commonly maintain "an affable public presentation of self that is, in effect, acting, the purpose of which is to put able-bodied people at ease during their first encounters. But this affability is not an end in itself. For it is accompanied by 'display and avowal,' a presentation of the body that openly challenges the ablebodied stranger to confront visible physical differences and move beyond them—or, failing that, to move away."

18. Carolyn Smith (1993: p.275) points to an early Miles poem, "Dec. 7, 1941," written on the day of the Japanese attack on Pearl Harbor, which contrasts the "little wars" of civilians—including the fight of "crutch with stair"—with the wars of soldiers.

19. The citations given in the *Oxford English Dictionary* for "—— is my middle name" all come from sources like Agatha Christie novels, as John Shoptaw has pointed out to me.

OULIPO AT THE LAUNDROMAT: DENISE LETO

1. Oulipo—the *Ouvroir de Litterature Potentielle* or "Workshop for Potential Literature"—was co-founded in Paris in the early 1960s by mathematician and writer Raymond Queneau and Francois Le Lionnais. Oulipian writers impose constraints such as "slenderizing," for example, removing the letter "r" or "N + 7," in which a writer takes an existing poem, and substitutes each of the substantive nouns with a noun appearing seven nouns away in the dictionary.

2. "Foulipo" (Feminist Oulipo), combined feminist body art and the formal procedures of Oulipo. Spahr and Young stripped nude three times during the performance of their text. Noulipo Conference, October 2005.

3. As described by the poet and scholar Jennifer Scappettone: "The two cycles of oulipian procedures to which Spahr and Young's reflections are subjected highlight both the materiality of the text itself and its reinflection by the body or machine rehearsing it. The two poets took turns speaking the 'slenderized' tracts, forced to sound foreign, maimed, or abject in the process; 'slenderizing,' also known as 'asphyxiation' or 'lipossible,' feeds semantically off of a reduction of flesh routinely tethered to the social injunctions of femininity. The 'N + 7' sections of the text were prerecorded and broadcast, disembodied, for contrast, as the two women blandly undressed and redressed themselves...The bodies-becoming naked that bear mute witness to these passages are not unwitting fonts of womanhood but act on the contrary as screens for social truth...Caroline Bergvall proposed that the women's apparent speech impediment was corrected only when they were seen and not heard, stripped bare, as culture continues to demand them to be seen" (pp.182).

POETICS/ "EXHIBITS" GRETCHEN E. HENDERSON

1. Ferris, Jim. "The Enjambed Body: A Step Toward a Crippled Poetics." *The Georgia Review* 58:2 (Summer 2004): pp.219-233.

2. Siebers, Tobin. "Disability as Masquerade," *Literature and Medicine* 23:1 (Spring 2004): p.8.

3. Winternitz, Emanuel, ed. *Leonardo da Vinci as a Musician*. New Haven: Yale University Press, 1982. p.119.

4. Henderson, Gretchen. "The Many Faces of Bea." *The Kenyon Review* 32:3 (Summer 2010): p.199.

EXHIBIT H

1. *Oxford English Dictionary*, 2nd ed., s.v. "hand" and "breath."

2. Euripides. *Medea, Hecuba, Hippolytus, The Trojan Women and The Bacchantes*. Whitefish, MT: Kessinger, 2004. p.32.

EXHIBIT U

1. Sennett, Richard. *Resistance: The Auditory Culture Reader*. Eds. Michael Bull and Les Back. Oxford: Berg, 2003. pp.481-84.

2. As Aristotle wrote in *De Anima*: "...the soul is like the hand; for the hand is the instrument of instruments." Qtd. in Sherman, Claire Richter. *Writing on Hands: Memory and Knowledge in Early Modern Europe*. Seattle: University of Washington Press, 2000. p.7. "Miracle of form and function" refers to Leonardo da Vinci's anatomical studies of hands. Qtd. on p.105.

3. Ibid., p.23.

4. Wilson, Frank. *The Hand.* New York: Vintage, 1998. p.59.

5. Davies, Robertson. *What's Bred in the Bone.* New York: Penguin, 1986.

6. Swift, Jonathan. "Directions to Servants." *The Works of Dr. Jonathan Swift, Dean of St. Patrick's Dublin: Accurately Corrected by the Best Editions, with the Author's Life and Character, Notes Historical, Critical and Explanatory, Tables of Contents and Indexes; More Complete Than Any Preceding Edition; in Eight Volumes.* Edinburgh: G. Hamilton, 1757. p.363.

7. Qtd. in Josipovici, Gabriel. *Touch.* New Haven: Yale University Press, 1996. p.137.

8. Crooke, Helkiah. *Mikrokosmographia. A Description of the Body of Man...Collected...Out of All the Best Authors of Anatomy.* London: Cotes and Sparke, 1615. Qtd. in Sherman, Claire Richter. *Writing on Hands*, p.25.

CONTRIBUTORS

TOM ANDREWS (1961-2001) grew up in West Virginia and taught writing at Ohio University. His first full-length collection of poems, *The Brother's Country*, was selected for the National Poetry series by Charles Wright. His second book, *The Hemophiliac's Motorcycle*, received the 1993 Iowa Poetry Prize. His collected poems, *Random Symmetries*, were published posthumously in 2002 by Orelin Press. Andrews was also the editor of a collection of essays on William Stafford: *The Worth of Local Things*. Andrews had hemophilia.

JENNIFER BARTLETT was a 2005 New York Foundation for the Arts Fellow. Her collections include *Derivative of the Moving Image* (UNM Press 2007), *Anti-Autobiography: A Chapbook Designed by Andrea Baker* (Saint Elizabeth Street/Youth-in-Asia Press 2010) and *(a) lullaby without any music* (Chax 2011). Bartlett has had cerebral palsy since birth.

SHEILA BLACK was the 2000 U.S. co-winner of the Frost-Pellicer Frontera Prize, given annually to one American and one Mexican poet living along the U.S./Mexico border. Her collections include *Love/Iraq* (CW Press 2009), *House of Bone* (CW Press 2007), and a chapbook, *How to be a Maquiladora* (Main Street Rag Publishers 2007). Black has X-Linked Hypophosphotemia (XLH), a failure to absorb phosphorus that results in symptoms that mimic nutritional rickets.

JOHN LEE CLARK was born deaf to an all-deaf family and became blind in adolescence. Clark is author of the chapbook *Suddenly Slow* (Handtype Press 2008) and editor of *Deaf American Poetry* (Gallaudet University Press 2009). He is married to the deaf cartoonist, Adrean Clark, with whom he runs Clerc Scar, a small press for the signing community.

NORMA COLE'S most recent books of poetry are *Where Shadows Will: Selected Poems 1988—2008* and *Natural Light*. A book of essays and talks, *To Be at Music*, just appeared from Omnidawn Press. Cole has received awards from the Gerbode Foundation, Gertrude Stein Awards, Fund for Poetry and Foundation for Contemporary Arts. She teaches at the University of San Francisco. In December 2002 she had a stroke, compromising her speech and her right side.

MICHAEL DAVIDSON, Distinguished Professor of Literature at the University of California, San Diego, is author of five books of poetry. He has written extensively on disability issues, most recently, *Concerto for the Left Hand: Disability and the Defamiliar Body* (University of Michigan, 2008). His forthcoming book, *Outskirts of Form: Practicing Cultural Poetics*, will be published in November 2011 by Wesleyan University Press.

AMBER DiPIETRA is arthritically a living fossil. Originally from Tampa, Florida, she works in San Francisco as a disability advocate. Her newest project is Write To Connect—life-writing workshops for radical and everyday embodiments (www.writetoconnect.blogspot.com). Poems and prose pieces by DiPietra have appeared in *Make, A Chicago Literary Magazine, Mirage Period (ical), Tarpaulin Sky, Mrs. Maybe, Monday Night* and *Try!*

KARA DORRIS is a doctoral candidate at the University of North Texas. Her chapbook, *Elective Affinities* was published by Dancing Girl Press in 2011. Dorris is the editor of *Lingerpost*, an online journal. Dorris was born with a genetic disorder which causes calcium to form benign tumors on the joints of the bones interfering with normal growth patterns.

LARRY EIGNER (1927-1996), the author of over seventy-five books and broadsides, was born "palsied from hard birth" (as he phrased it) in Lynn, Massachusetts. With the exception of two teenage years in residence at the Massachusetts Hospital School in Canton, Massachusetts (and summer camp and later two brief airplane trips to St. Louis and San Francisco), Eigner spent his first fifty years at home in his parents' house at 23 Bates Road, Swampscott, Massachusetts (two blocks from the Atlantic Ocean), where he was cared for by his mother, Bessie, and his father, Israel, and where he came to do his writing (on his 1940 Royal manual typewriter, with right index finger and thumb) in a space prepared for him on the glassed-in front porch (where he could observe and contemplate everything that was going on, within the range of his seeing and hearing and imagining), basically every day.

JILL ALEXANDER ESSBAUM is the author of several collections of poetry including *Harlot* (No Tell Books, 2007) and *Necropolis* (NeoNuma Arts, 2008). She teaches in the University of California, Riverside, Palm Desert Low Residency M.F.A. program.

ROBERT FAGAN (1935 -2009) received his Ph.D. in English Literature from Columbia University. His poetry and fiction have been published in many literary journals. His publications include a collection of his poetry—*Stepping Out* (Red Moon Press, 2007)— from which the selections in this anthology were taken and several books of poetry, fiction and literary criticism. He contracted chronic Guillian-Barre syndrome as a young man.

JIM FERRIS is author of *Facts of Life* and *The Hospital Poems*, which Edward Hirsch selected as winner of the Main Street Rag Book Award in 2004. His book *Slouching Towards Guantanamo* was published by Main Street Rag in 2011. Past president of the Society for Disability Studies, Ferris currently holds the Ability Center Endowed Chair in Disability Studies at the University of Toledo.

KENNY FRIES is the author of *The History of My Shoes and the Evolution of Darwin's Theory*; *Body, Remember: A Memoir* and two books of poems: *Anesthesia* and *Desert Walking*. He is also the editor of *Staring Back: The Disability Experience from the Inside Out*. Fries received a grant in innovative literature from Creative Capital for his new book *Genkan: Entries into Japan*. He teaches in the MFA creative writing program at Goddard College.

LISA GILL is the author of five books of poetry. Her most recent collection, *Caput Nili: How I Won the War And Lost My Taste for Oranges*, recounts how Gill fought to get her diagnosis of multiple sclerosis in 2003. Gill is the recipient of a National Endowment for the Arts Fellowship, the New Mexico Literary Arts Gratitude Award, an Achievement Award from the University of New Mexico, and the Red Shoes Award. She serves as artistic director for Local Poets Guild in Albuquerque, New Mexico.

C. S. Giscombe's poetry books are *Prairie Style, Two Sections from Practical Geography, Giscome Road, Here, At Large* and *Postcards*; his prose book—about Canada—is *Into and Out of Dislocation*. C. S. Giscombe was the 2010 recipient of the Stephen Henderson Award in poetry, given by the African-American Literature and Culture Society. He has worked as a taxi driver, a hospital orderly, a railroad brakeman and edits *Epoch* at Cornell University. He teaches poetry at the University of California, Berkeley.

Ona Gritz is a poet, columnist and the author of two children's books. In 2007, she won the Inglis House poetry contest and the Late Blooms Poetry Postcard competition. Her poetry chapbook, *Left Standing*, was published by Finishing Line Press in 2005. Gritz's essays have appeared recently in *The Utne Reader, More* and *The Bellingham Review*. Her monthly column on mothering and disability can be found online at www.literarymama.com. Gritz has cerebral palsy.

Gretchen E. Henderson received the 2010 Madeleine P. Plonsker Emerging Writer's Prize for her *Galerie de Difformité*, forthcoming from &NOW Books. Henderson recently was awarded a two-year Mellon Postdoctoral Fellowship at MIT and invites participation in the collaborative deformation of her *Galerie de Difformité* at difformite.wordpress.com. She has lived with dystonia for over a decade.

Laura Hershey (1962-2010) was a Colorado-based poet and writer, activist and mother with spinal muscular atrophy. Her poems recently appeared in *Gertrude, Shakespeare's Monkey Review, Trillium Literary Journal,* and in the anthologies *Fire in the Soul: 100 Poems for Human Rights* and *Their Buoyant Bodies Respond.* She held an M.F.A. in Creative Writing from Antioch University Los Angeles. *Spark Before Dark*, her most recent poetry chapbook, is published by Finishing Line Press. Her website is www.laurahershey.com.

Cynthia Hogue's most recent collections are *The Incognito Body* (2006), which includes the title sequence about contracting rheumatoid arthritis that is excerpted in this anthology, *Or Consequence* (2010) and *When the Water Came: Evacuees of Hurricane Katrina, interview-poems and photographs* (2010, with Rebecca Ross). In 2003, she joined the Department of English at Arizona State University as the Maxine and Jonathan Marshall Chair in Modern and Contemporary Poetry. Currently, she is working on a collection of essays entitled *Wayward Thinking: Notes on Poetry and Poetics*.

Anne Kaier's recent work appears in *The Gettysburg Review, Kenyon Review, Bellingham Review, Under the Sun, Philadelphia Poets, American Writing* and other venues. Her chapbook, *In Fire*, was published in 2005. Holding a Ph.D. from Harvard University, she teaches literature and creative writing at Arcadia University and Rosemont College. She has lamellar ichthyosis, a rare skin disorder caused by a genetic mutation which causes her body to make too many skin cells that do not shed normally.

Petra Kuppers is Artistic Director of the Olimpias Performance Research Series and Associate Professor of English at the University of Michigan. Her academic publications include *The Scar of Visibility: Medical Performances and Contemporary Art* (2007), *Community Performance: An Introduction* (2007) and *Disability Culture and Community Performance: Find a Strange and Twisted*

Shape (2011). A poetry/cross-genre book, *Cripple Poetics: A Love Story*, with Neil Marcus and Lisa Stickman, appeared with Homofactus Press in 2008. Kuppers is a wheelchair user, and lives with pain and fatigue.

STEPHEN KUUSISTO is director of the Renee Crown Honors Program at Syracuse University. He is the author of the award-winning memoirs *Planet of the Blind* and *Eavesdropping: A Memoir of Blindness and Listening*. His first collection of poems, *Only Bread, Only Light* is available from Copper Canyon Press, which will soon publish a collection of political poems about disability, *Letters to Borges*.

LAURIE CLEMENTS LAMBETH's debut collection of poems, *Veil and Burn*, won the 2006 National Poetry Series. A poet who has lived with multiple sclerosis since she was a teenager, Lambeth holds Ph.D. and M.F.A. degrees from the University of Houston's Creative Writing Program, where she was awarded Michener and Barthelme fellowships. She is currently working on a memoir and her second collection of poems, *Bright Pane*. She teaches at the University of Houston and at Inprint Houston.

ALEX LEMON is the author of *Happy: A Memoir* and three collections of poetry: *Mosquito, Hallelujah Blackout* and *Fancy Beasts*. His writing has appeared in *Esquire, The Believer, The Huffington Post, Dallas Morning News* and numerous other publications. A recipient of a 2005 literature fellowship from the NEA, he lives in Ft. Worth, Texas, where he teaches at Texas Christian University.

DENISE LETO is a poet and senior editor at the University of California, Berkeley. Her work has appeared in *Puerto del Sol; Wolf Magazine*; Arts Council of England; *Aufgabe*; and *Xantippe*. She was guest editor for *Sinister Wisdom*, artist in residence at Djerassi, a reader/sound artist at "Breaking Ranks, Human Nature," Headlands Center for the Arts, and a fellow for the University of Michigan's Symposium, "Movement, Somatics and Writing." A collaborative chapbook, *Waveform*, is forthcoming from Kenning Editions. She moves through the world with dystonia.

RAYMOND LUCZAK is the author and editor of more than ten books, including *Assembly Required: Notes from a Deaf Gay Life* (RID Press). His four collections of poetry include *St. Michael's Fall* (Deaf Life Press), *This Way to the Acorns* (Clerc Scar), *Mute* (A Midsummer Night's Press) and *Road Work Ahead* (Sibling Rivalry Press). His novel *Men with Their Hands* (Queer Mojo) won first place in the Project: QueerLit 2006 Contest. A playwright and filmmaker, he lives in Minneapolis, Minnesota. His web site is www.raymondluczak.com.

BERNADETTE MAYER was born in 1945 in Brooklyn, New York. She received her B.A. from the New School for Social Research in 1967. From 1972 to 1974, Mayer and conceptual artist Vito Acconci edited the journal *O TO 9*. With Lewis Warsh, she edited United Artists Press. She has taught writing workshops at The Poetry Project at St. Mark's Church in New York City for many years and she served as the Poetry Project's director during the 1980s.

JOSEPHINE MILES (1911-1985) received her B.A. in English from the University of California at Berkeley and went on to continue her academic career there, becoming a professor of English and the first woman to be tenured there. Miles' poetry spanned over forty years from the publication of *Lines at Intersection* (1939) to *Coming to Terms* (1979). Her work was nominated for a Pulitzer Prize. In addition to poetry Miles was a scholar of grammar and rhetoric as well as working in the field of literary criticism. Miles lived with rheumatoid arthritis from the age of two.

VASSAR MILLER (1924-1998) received B.S. and M.S. degrees from the University of Houston. Miller's first book of poetry, *Adam's Footprint*, appeared in 1956, and in 1961 she was nominated for a Pulitzer Prize. In 1985, Miller edited and published *Despite This Flesh*, the first anthology of poetry about disability, intended for use by teachers. Her work culminated in the publication of her collected poems *If I Had Wheels Or Love* (SMU Press 1991). The Vassar Miller Prize for poetry is awarded each year by the University of North Texas Press. Miller had cerebral palsy.

RUSTY MORRISON'S *After Urgency* won the 2010 Tupelo Dorset Prize. *the true keeps calm biding its story* (Ahsahta 2008) won the 2008 James Laughlin Award from the Academy of American Poets; and The Ahsahta Press 2007 Sawtooth Poetry Prize, selected by Peter Gizzi; the 2007 Poetry Society of America's Alice Fay Di Castagnola Award, selected by Susan Howe; and the 2009 Northern California Book Award for Poetry. Her first poetry collection, *Whethering*, won the Colorado Prize for Poetry (Center for Literary Publishing 2004), selected by Forrest Gander. She is co-publisher of Omnidawn Publishing.

MICHAEL NORTHEN is the facilitator of the Inglis House Poetry Workshop, editor of the annual Inglis House poetry contest chapbook series and editor of *Wordgathering: A Journal of Disability and Poetry*. An educator for over forty years, in addition to adults with physical disabilities, he has taught women who are on public assistance, prisoners, and rural and inner-city children. Much of the material in his essay in this anthology is taken from his doctoral dissertation, *Disability Literature: Its Origin, Current State and Potential Application to School Curriculum.*

DANIELLE PAFUNDA is the author of *Iatrogenic: Their Testimonies* (Noemi Press), *My Zorba* (Bloof Books), *Pretty Young Thing* (Soft Skull Press) and the forthcoming *Manhater* (Dusie Press Books). She is a member of the board of directors of VIDA: Women in Literary Arts, and an assistant professor of gender and women's studies and English at the University of Wyoming.

SUSAN SCHWEIK is professor of English and associate dean of arts and humanities at University of California at Berkeley. Her book *The Ugly Laws: Disability in Public* is out in paperback in 2011 from New York University Press.

DANIEL SIMPSON currently provides technical support for the Library of Congress' digital talking book download service for the blind and serves as access technology consultant to the Free Library of Philadelphia. His work has appeared in *Prairie Schooner, The Cortland Review, Hampden-Sydney Poetry Review, The Atlanta Review, The Louisville Review* and *Margie*, among others. His recently completed poetry manuscript is entitled *Inside the Invisible*. He has been blind since birth.

HAL SIROWITZ is the author of four collections of poetry: *Mother Said; My Therapist Said; Before, During and After;* and *Father Said* (Soft Skull Press). A prose piece on living with Parkinson's appeared in a 2010 issue of the *Manhattan Review*. He is in many anthologies, including Billy

Collin's *Poetry 180*, Garrison Keillor's *Good Poems* and *Poetry in Motion from Coast to Coast*. Sirowitz is former poet laureate of Queens and is married to the writer Minter Krotzer.

ELLEN MCGRATH SMITH teaches literature and writing at the University of Pittsburgh and in Carlow University's Madwomen in the Attic program for women writers. Her critical work has appeared in the *Denver Quarterly, American Book Review*, and *Pittsburgh Quarterly*. Smith's poems have appeared or are forthcoming in: *Cerise, Weave, The Same, The Best of the Prose Poem, Southern Poetry Review, Pittsburgh Quarterly* and others. Smith is also the reviews editor for *Sentence: A Journal of Prose Poetics*. She has dealt with neurological hearing impairment since childhood.

BRIAN TEARE is the author of *The Room Where I Was Born, Sight Map* and *Pleasure*, as well as the chapbooks *Pilgrim* and *Transcendental Grammar Crown*. His most recent writing concerns embodied and medicalized consciousness and addresses both the symptoms of and treatments for gouty rheumatoid arthritis, celiac disease and multiple food sensitivities. An assistant professor at Temple University, he lives in Philadelphia, where he makes books by hand for his micropress, Albion Books.

JILLIAN WEISE is the author of the poetry collection *The Amputee's Guide to Sex* and the novel *The Colony*. Her work has appeared in *The Atlantic Monthly, The New York Times* and *Tin House*, among others. She was a poetry fellow at the Fine Arts Work Center in Provincetown and a Fulbright fellow in Tierra del Fuego, Argentina, before joining the faculty at Clemson University. Weise is a cyborg.

DAVID WOLACH is editor of *Wheelhouse Magazine & Press* and an active participant in Nonsite Collective. Wolach's first full-length collection is *Occultations* (Black Radish Books 2011). Other books include the multi-media transliteration plus chapbook, *Prefab Eulogies Volume 1: Nothings Houses* (BlazeVox [books], 2010), the full-length *Hospitalogy* (chapbook forthcoming from Scantily Clad Press, 2012), and *book alter(ed)* (Ungovernable Press, 2009). Wolach is professor of text arts, poetics and aesthetics at The Evergreen State College, co-curating the PRESS Text Arts and Radical Politics Series there, and is visiting professor in Bard College's Workshop In Language and Thinking.

KATHI WOLFE was a finalist in the 2007 Pudding House Chapbook competition and her chapbook, *Helen Takes The Stage: The Helen Keller Poems*, was subsequently published by Pudding House. Wolfe has received a Puffin Foundation Grant and was a winner of the 2010 Moving Words Poetry Competition, a competition conducted by the Arlington County (Virginia) Office of Cultural Affairs and Metro, the Washington, D.C. area transit authority. Wolfe is legally blind.

ACKNOWLEDGEMENTS

All work is reprinted with the permission of the authors unless otherwise noted.

Tom Andrews' poems—"The Hemophiliac's Motorcycle" and the excerpts from "Codeine Diary"—are both from his collection *The Hemophiliac's Motorcycle* (University of Iowa Press, 1994). All work is reprinted with the permission of the University of Iowa Press.

Jennifer Bartlett's essay "Exit Through the Gift Shop" originally published in a slightly different form as "Ethics, Poetry and the Identity of the Disabled Body" in *Wordgathering* (July 2010).

Sheila Black's poem "What You Mourn" first appeared in *Dancing with Cecil* (Inglis House Poetry, 2004) and "Reconstruction" in *Mediphors*. Both of these and the poems "Objects Waiting to be Dangerous," and "Playing Dead" all appeared in *House of Bone* (CW Press, 2007). An earlier version of her essay "Waiting to be Dangerous" appeared in *Prime Number Magazine*, No. 7 (July 2011).

John Lee Clark's poem "Long Goodbyes" from *Suddenly Slow* (Handtype Press, 2008). "Deaf Blind: Three Squared Cinquain" originally appeared in *She Asks for Slippers While Pointing at the Salt* (Inglis House Poetry, 2009). "Beach Basketball" and "Clamor" originally appeared in *Two Reviews* (2111). His previous version of his essay, "Translating and Reading ASL Poetry" was published in *Their Buoyant Bodies Respond* (Inglis House Poetry, 2011).

Norma Cole's poem "Speech Production: Themes & Variations" from *Collective Memory* (Omnidawn, 2006). Her essay "Why I Am Not A Translator" previously published in *To Be At Music: Selected Essays and Talks* (Granary Press, 2010).

Michael Davidson's essay excerpted from "Missing Larry: The Poetics of Disability in the Work of Larry Eigner." Originally published in *Sagetrieb*, 18 (1) 5-27, 1999. Reprinted in *Concerto for My Left Hand* (University of Michigan Press, 2008).

Amber DiPietra's poem, "bunny baby fast and slow" originally appeared in *Tarpaulin Sky* (Summer 2008), and "scars, a thread" in *Monday Night* (2010). *My Notebook Has a Rigid Spine or How to Operate the Body in Writing* was part of The Poetics of Healing Symposium, 2010.

Kara Dorris' poem "Fairytale: How Spring Comes to the Land of Snow and Icicles/ (Dream Map)" has been published in a radically different form in *Thirteen Myna Birds* (2009).

Robert Fagan's poems "Proem" and "Siege" originally appeared in *Stepping Out* (Red Moon Press, 2007). His essay is from *Pieces* (Red Moon Press, 2009).

Jim Ferris' poem "Poet of Cripples" from *The Hospital Poems* (Main Stret Rag Publishing, 2004). "Lost Hyoid" from *Slouching Towards Guantanamo* (Main Street Rag Publishing, 2011). "Poems with Disabilities" originally appeared in *Ragged Edge* 21.2 (March/April 2000). "From the Surgeons: Drs. Sofield, Louis, Hark, Alfini, Millar, Baehr, Bevan-Thomas, Tsatsos, Ericson, and Bennan" originally appeared in *Ragged Edge* (March/April 1998).

Kenny Fries' poems "Excavation," "Body Language," and "Beauty and Variations" from *Anesthesia: Poems* (1996, The Advocado Press). His essay is adapted from the introduction to *Staring Back: The Disability Experience from the Inside Out* (Plume, 1997).

Lisa Gill's poem "Wicker-work: A Sestina for Zukofsky" originally appeared *1913: A Journal of Forms* (2009). The excerpt is from *The Relenting: A Play of Sorts* (New Rivers Press, 2010).

C.S. Giscombe's poem "Northern Road, 2" was originally published in *Giscome Road* (Dalkay Archive Press, 1998.) "Vernacular Examples," and "The Old Northwest" are from *Prairie Style* (Dalkay Archive Press, 2008). Reprinted by permission of Dalkay Archive Press.

Ona Gritz' poems "No" and "Prologue" originally appeared in *Wordgathering* (July 2010). "Hemiplegia" first appeared in *Bellevue Literary Review* (Spring 2009). Her essay "A Conscious Decision," is constructed from several of her columns in *Literary Mama*.

Gretchen E. Henderson's poem "Exhibit U" originally published in *Double Room* (2009).

Laura Hershey's poem "Thousand Island" originally published in *Wordgathering* (March 2011). Reprinted by permission. "Working Together," "Morning," and "Telling" are all from her book *Spark Before Dark* (Finishing Line Press, 2011). Reprinted by permission of Finishing Line Press.

Cynthia Hogue's poems "Green surrounds the mind of summer," "In a Mute Season," "Radical Optimism" from *The Incognito Body* by Cynthia Hogue. Copyright © 2006 by Cynthia Hogue. Reprinted by permission of the author and Red Hen Press. Her essay "The Creature Within: On Poetry and Dis/Ability," originally appeared as a guest blog on writing practice in *Her Circle Ezine* on 29 September (2010).

Petra Kuppers' poem "The Origin of My Wheelchair" originally appeared in *Wordgathering* (June, 2007). "Crip Music" is from *Cripple Poetics: A Love Story* (Homofactus Press, 2008). *Spherical Song Cycles*: performance *script, fragments* published in *Disability Studies Quarterly*, *Poets for Living Waters* website, *Humanities Epistemologies Journal*, and performed as part of *Bare Bones Butoh* (SF) and various Olimpias actions. A version of her essay "Sound of the Bones" was published in *Disability Studies Quarterly* (26.4).

Stephen Kuusisto's poem "Only Bread, Only Light" from *Only Bread, Only Light* (Copper Canyon Press, 2000). Reprinted by permission of Copper Canyon Press. His poems "Borges, they are kicking the wind out of me in Iowa City" and "Letter to Borges from Houston, Texas" both originally appeared in *The Red Wheelbarrow* (Spring 2010).

Laurie Clements Lambeth's poem "Seizure, or Seduction of Persephone" from *Veil and Burn* (University of Illinois Press, 2008).

Alex Lemon's poems "Mosquito," "Other Good," and "Cocoon" all from *Mosquito* (Tin House Books, 2006). "And No More May I Be" from *Hallelujah Blackout* (Milkweed Editions, 2008).

Raymond Luczak's poem "Hummingbirds" from *St. Michael's Fall* (Deaf Life Press, 1995). "Instructions to Hearing Persons Desiring a Deaf Man" first appeared in the journal *Van Gogh's Ear* (2004).

Josephine Miles' poems "Doll," "Album," "Before," "Intensives," and "Payment" are from *Collected Poems, 1930-83* (University of Illinois Press, 1984). Copyright 1983 by Josephine Miles. Used with permission of the poet and the University of Illinois Press.

Vassar Miller's poem "The Common Core" from *Wage War on Silence* (Weslyean Press, 1960) and "Subterfuge" from *Selected and New Poems 1950-1980* (Latitude Press, 1981). Those and "If I had Wheels or Love" and "Dramatic Monologue in the Speaker's Own Voice" are included in *If I had Wheels or Love* (Southern Methodist University Press, 1991). Reprinted by permission of Southern Methodist University Press.

Michael Northen's essay "A Short History of American Disability Poetry" appeared in a somewhat different version in *Wordgathering* (March 2008).

Danielle Pafunda's "In This Plate My Illness is Visible" and "In This Plate My Illness is a Wire That Can Easily Cut Meat and Bone" first appeared in *Bone Bouquet* (2009). "In This Plate I Receive My First Diagnosis" first appeared in *Court Green* (2010).

Susan Schweik's essay "The Voice of 'Reason'" first appeared in *Public Culture*. (*13* (3), pp.485-505). Reprinted by permission of Duke University Press.

Daniel Simpson's poem "A Few Things" originally published in *Cortland Review* (November 2001), "Broken Reverie" in *Disabilities Studies Quarterly* (Fall 2008), and "School for the Blind" in *Wordgathering* (September 2009). His essay "Line Breaks the Way I See Them" appeared in slightly different form in *On the Outskirts* (Inglis House, 2006). "About Chester Kowalski I Don't Know Much" is from his *Audio Chapbook* (2008).

Ellen McGrath Smith's poem "Theodore Eslin: Poet of Maine" first appeared in *Wordgathering* (June 2010). Her essay "'Hearing a Pear': The Poetry Reading on a New Frequency" is from a paper presented at the 2010 Associated Writers Convention and first printed in *Wordgathering* (June 2007).

Hal Sirowitz's poem "A Step Above Cows" first appeared in *Apple Valley Review: A Journal of Contemporary Literature* (Spring 2010) and "Avoiding Rigidity" was published in *Bellevue Literary Review: A Journal of Humanity and Human Experience* (Fall 2009) "A Famous Ball Player" first appeared in *Hanging Loose 95* (2009).

Jillian Weise presented her essay "The Disability Rights Movement and the Legacy of Poets with Disabilities" as a lecture at The Poetry of the 1970s Conference in 2008. It was also published that same year in National Poetry Foundation's online *Mesh*. Her poems "The Amputee's Guide to Sex," "The Body in Pain" and "The Old Questions" are from *The Amputee's Guide To Sex* (Soft Skull Press, 2007).

David Wolach's poem "corporeal self-punishment" originally appeared in *Cannot Exist*, (Issue No. 6) and is from the full-length *Occultations* (Black Radish Books, 2010). "Costuming/Marked in Holiday Complex" first appeared in *Elective Affinities* (2009). Parts of his essay "Body Maps & Distraction Zones," stem from the process note for *Occultations*, and from his talk, "The Common Body," for The Nonsite Collective's Summer Suite: Curriculum on the Commons (2010).

Kathi Wolfe's poems "On the Subway," "Ashes: Rome, 1946," "She Loved Hot Dogs So Much" and "The Sun is Warm: Nagasaki 1948" are from *Helen Keller Takes the Stage: The Helen Keller Poems* (Pudding House Press, 2008). "Helen Keller: Obsession and Muse" was published in a slightly different form in *Wordgathering* (June 2007).

OTHER GREAT BOOKS FROM CINCO PUNTOS PRESS

Incantations: Songs, Spells and Images by Mayan Women
by Ambar Past, Xalik Guzmán Bakbolom and Xpetra Ernandes

Out of Their Minds: The Incredible and (Sometimes) Sad Story of Ramon and Cornelio
A novel by Luis Humberto Crosthwaite
translated by John William Byrd

The Resurrection of Bert Ringold
A book of poems by Harvey Goldner

White Panties, Dead Friends, and Other Bits & Pieces of Love
A book of poems by Bobby Byrd

Questions & Swords: Folktales of the Zapatista Revolution
by Subcomandante Marcos
illustrated by Domitila Domínquez & Antonio Ramírez

Elegies in Blue
A book of poems by Benjamin Alire Saenz

The Shadow of the Shadow
A novel by Paco Ignacio Taibo II

Frontera Dreams: A Héctor Belascoarán Shayne Detective Novel
A novel by Paco Ignacio Taibo II
translated by Bill Verner

Just Passing Through
A novel by Paco Ignacio Taibo II
translated by Martin Roberts

Six Kinds of Sky: A Collection of Short Stories
by Luis Alberto Urrea

www.cincopuntos.com